THE GLOBAL

EDITED BY JOHN TURNBULL

GAME Writers on Soccer

THOM SATTERLEE & ALON RAAB

UNIVERSITY OF NEBRASKA PRESS | LINCOLN AND LONDON

Acknowledgments for the use of
previously published material appear
on pages 285–91, which constitute an
extension of the copyright page.
© 2008 by the Board of Regents
of the University of Nebraska. All
rights reserved. Manufactured in the
United States of America
∞

The publisher has no control over and
does not assume any responsibility
for author or third-party Web sites or
their content.

Library of Congress
Cataloging-in-Publication Data
The global game: writers on soccer /
edited by John Turnbull, Thom
Satterlee, and Alon Raab.
p.   cm.
Includes bibliographical references.
ISBN 978-0-8032-1078-3
(pbk.: alk. paper)
1. Soccer.   2. Soccer—Cross-cultural
studies.   I. Turnbull, John, 1963–
II. Satterlee, Thom.   III. Raab, Alon.
GV943.G57   2008
796.334—dc22
2008018138

Set in Scala by Bob Reitz.
Designed by A. Shahan.

Preface

Compilers of previous English-language anthologies of soccer literature often apologize for the quality of writing from which they have
had to choose. Ian Hamilton, editor of the most recent anthology of
soccer writing to appear in the United States, *The Faber Book of Soccer*
(1992), characterizes the game as "a sport without much literature."
"Unlike cricket or rugby," he continues, "it has few links with higher
education." Although assembling a more comprehensive collection
mainly for American readers, the late George Plimpton in *The Norton
Book of Sports* (1992) takes the trouble to say:

> Soccer has no important literature at all that I can find, though it
> is such a universal activity that surely I am at fault here—I must
> have missed a South American novel, or a Yugoslav's essay on
> the bicycle kick, or an appreciation by a Frenchman on the ex-
> istential qualities of the game. Albert Camus once played goal
> for the Oran Football Club of Algiers but did not seem moved
> to write about it. The best I've come across is Pelé's *My Life and
> the Great Game* [*sic*]. The evident lack may have something to do
> with the practitioners of the game, who tend to be more agile
> with their feet than with articulation. A well-known definition
> is that soccer is a gentleman's game played by thugs, whereas
> rugby is a thug's game played by gentlemen.

Plimpton's interest lay in lifting up literary traditions related to the
games more popular in the United States, especially baseball, boxing,
golf, tennis, thoroughbred racing, and so on. Perhaps Plimpton was,
to some degree, trying to make the task of selection easier. But it is
curious that the worldly editor of the *Paris Review* would appear so
dismissive of literature of non-American origins—"a South American

novel . . . a Yugoslav's essay"—and not know that Albert Camus, in the same year that he won the Nobel Prize in Literature (1957), had written a widely quoted article about his time as goalkeeper at Racing Universitaire Algérois. (And to take Plimpton up on a factual point, Camus played for l'Association Sportive de Montpensier in Oran.)

Low regard in other parts of the world toward soccer's literary canon perhaps stems from the game's dominance and from the elitist's assumption that such a popular sport—a game played by "thugs," no less—could not produce fine art. In part to challenge the view that cricket has literature but football does not, Peter J. Seddon amassed his *Football Compendium* for the British Library (1999). At more than eight hundred pages, the volume has the heft of an exhaustive biblical concordance. Further, Seddon only included works published in the United Kingdom or Ireland. Meanwhile, books about soccer have continued to proliferate, from pulpy, ghostwritten player biographies and hooligan confessionals to academic and literary treatments of the sport's cultural importance.

One important realization concerning soccer around the world, especially for those to whom the game still seems "foreign," is its everyday quality. Reverend Ellen Harris Dozier, who helps direct a Presbyterian mission for women in and around San Felipe, Guatemala, writes that women with whom she works typically give prominence to the soccer field when asked to draw maps of their villages. The game and the space in which it is played are central, both geographically and in offering cultural identity in a broader sense. Soccer as a featured element on holy days can also give cause for theological reflection, as Dozier writes in 2000 in an online Presbyterian Church (USA) mission diary:

> On the morning of Christmas Day . . . I watched as pickup trucks full of people . . . pulled into the seminary and people piled out. Then families began to arrive, again by the truckload. I had been told that there would be a soccer game, but it looked like much more than one soccer game! As it turned out, there was a soccer tournament on Christmas Day, beginning at 8 a.m. and concluding at 5:30 p.m. . . . I spent most of the day watching the

games, enjoying the warm sun and the visits with neighbors and friends. I am still trying to understand what it means to play a soccer tournament on Christmas Day. Perhaps you have to be Guatemalan to really understand.

In choosing entries for this anthology, the capacity of selections to evoke places and emotions associated with soccer weighed more heavily than treatment of big matches and players. Iconic names—Pelé, Cruyff, Maradona, Zidane—do flit across the pages, along with names of clubs of international reputation, such as Real Madrid, Barcelona, Internazionale of Milan, Juventus, Ajax, Liverpool, and River Plate. Yet even entries from celebrated writers such as Günter Grass, Ted Hughes, Charles Simic, Gay Talese, and Mario Vargas Llosa tend to emphasize associations apart from the moneyed fields of "big soccer": men in "bunting colours" struggling to head the ball in a gale (Hughes); an unreliable radio that offers a child's only tether to the World Cup, thousands of miles distant (Simic); a run-down *hutong* (alleyway) in Beijing along which a famous player's family lives, with the player's cleats and other mundane effects in evidence (Talese).

Given soccer's place as not only the most popular ball game worldwide but as a cultural expression in itself, the best method of organizing this book seemed to be through concepts native to the game and everyday life. Thus, while striving for diversity of selection by genre and region, we did not adhere to groupings by date or predetermined topics, such as history, players, World Cups, and so on. As one argues over the greatest matches and goals, the reader can judge whether the editors chose well when selecting writings that address some of the qualities inherent in both soccer and the human experience: space, improvisation, challenge, loss, belief. Some of our selections could fit under more than one heading, or they might strike themes different from the section in which they landed. No doubt we did not always succeed in our creative choices.

We relate such decisions to the existential quandaries facing the midfielder, who continually must negotiate competing urges of hanging back or going forward.

Acknowledgments

All the editors thank Robert Taylor and the University of Nebraska Press for confidence in us and this idea. We also thank the talented individuals who prepared new translations for this volume—Kirk Anderson, Albert G. Bork, Geoffrey Brock, Erica Johnson Debeljak, Christopher Finney, Toshiya Kamei, Sandra Kingery, Anna Kushner, John Penuel, and Miranda Stramel—many of whom offered their work gratis. Thanks to their gifts we have new insight into the worlds of football.

John Turnbull thanks Yigit Akin; Jens Sejer Andersen and Play the Game in Copenhagen; Vladimir Borkovic and streetfootballworld in Berlin; Sara Brady; The British Library, London; Lawrence and Rob Cann and the Urban Ministry Center, Charlotte, North Carolina; Ellis Cashmore; Jayne Caudwell; Ellen Harris Dozier; Elise Edwards; Álvaro Enrigue; Brian Farenell; Katja Fischer; Franklin Foer; Richard Giulianotti; David Goldblatt; Serge Guillas; Katherine Hite; Buddy Hughes; Billy Kay; Simon Kuper; Nicholas Laughlin; Colin MacDonald; the Manuscript, Archives, and Rare Books Library, Emory University, Atlanta; Carlos Marañón; Andrew Marshall; Thomas Möhlmann; Pallab Muhury; Mark Nuttall; Paul Olchváry; Ian Plenderleith; Georgia Popplewell; Cathy Quiñones; John Barrett Reed; María Graciela Rodríguez; Rami Saari; Martha Saavedra; Nicole Selmer; Charles Simic; Jennifer Stanton; Uli Steinheimer; Beatriz Vélez; Bea Vidacs; David Wangerin; Dave Wasser; Markus Wegner; all participants in the Metropolitan Atlanta Casual Soccer League; and especially Keri and our Shetland sheepdog, Zoie, for their loving kindness.

Thom Satterlee thanks the American Literary Translators Association; Kirk Anderson; Sarah Barr; Erik, Inge, Niels, and Mette Carlsen;

Toby Charles; Jo Ann Cosgrove and the Taylor University Zondervan Library; John DuVal and the MFA in Literary Translation Program at the University of Arkansas; Andrei S. Markovits; Steve and Betty Messer; Douglas, Virginia, Danny, Dea, Mike, and Susie Satterlee; Ed, Betsy, Troy, and Chris Sipes; Don Snell; Ken Staples; members of the Taylor University Department of English; Alan Tomlinson; and, of course, my soccer-watching buddy and lifelong love, Kathy.

Alon Raab thanks the following friends and kind souls for their generosity: Amir Ben-Porat, Jack and Pat Boas, Simona Bortis, Andrew Branch, Colleen Brazil, Eckhard Breitinger, Sungwook Choi, Paul Darby, Julian D'Arcy, Victor S. Dugga, Robert Edelman, Goudarz Eghtedari, Amin Eslami, Morad N. Fareed, Grant Farred, Paul Goodrich, Seth Goradietsky, Gabriella Györe, Martha A. Jones, Cheick Oumar Kante, Ray Keenoy, Stacey Knecht, Jena Knudsen, Onno Kosters, Laila Lalami, Zoe Ludlow-Raab, Jeff Magoto, Alexander Mathäs, Tamara Neuman, Hadassah Raab, Joli Sandoz, Aviva Raab-Shohat and family, David Short, Mary Sillman, Smokey, Tamir Sorek, Nelson Soza, Ezra Tishman, Maxim Tarnawsky, David Wood, Colin Wright, Mona Zubair, and the students in The Sociology of Soccer classes at Portland State University. This book is dedicated with boundless love to Rachel Hibbard and to the memory of Israel Tzvi Raab Z"L, who played soccer with me every day throughout childhood and youth and nourished my love of *kadooregel*, the Hebrew term for football.

Note to Readers

Entries in this anthology as well as supporting editorial material meander between use of the words *soccer* and *football*. The same game, with the full name of *association football*, is always in view. Authors, editors, and translators have used the term with which they felt most comfortable, without an attempt to standardize.

In general *soccer* is the preferred term in North America, South Africa, Australia, New Zealand, and the Republic of Ireland where rival football codes—rugby union and rugby league as well as football using American, Canadian, Australian, or Gaelic rules—are active. Linguists believe that *soccer* gained usage early in the sport's development in Britain as a diminutive of *association football* in the way that *rugger* became a shortened form for *rugby football*. Variants included *socca'* (appearing as early as 1889, according to the *Oxford English Dictionary*) and *socker*.

The word *soccer* is used freely around the world and does not, contrary to some thinking, represent an American corruption of the name for the world's game.

Other linguistic skirmishes—such as the differences between *field* and *pitch, forward* and *striker, bleacher* and *terrace*—have been resolved according to the author's, translator's, or editor's preference.

THE GLOBAL GAME

Part 1. Space

I just go where there is
space to express myself.
— THIERRY HENRY,
FC Barcelona and France

Introduction

The broadcaster at the 2004 European Championships was almost beside himself watching the Portuguese winger maneuver into his favored territory along the right-hand touchline: "Luis Figo finds space . . . and Luis Figo loves space!" The attacking player's goal is to find space, the defender's is to close it down.

More broadly, however, the concept relates to the soccer field as a floating green zone of fantasy—one that shuts out worldly concern but meshes with life such that it seems a marker of the species, an inheritance from the ancients. Both Eduardo Galeano and Nalinaksha Bhattacharya in selections to follow reach for primeval origins to explain the lure that football spaces offer women and men.

An intriguing aspect of the modern game is that despite—or perhaps because of—relatively fixed rules and codes of behavior ("Has football . . . become a universal constant?" asks Erik Eggers) a myriad of cultural expressions find a place on the field and among spectators. In Cameroon the confines of the capital, Yaoundé, permit children to join impromptu games, even a small girl who pops into a side street while still wielding a long kitchen knife. In Peru the stadium serves as auxiliary living space, "a huge public dining room or picnic area spread out over the bleachers," writes Julio Ramón Ribeyro, where spectators feel comfortable enough to perform bodily functions and from which stories are born and evolve. In Mexico pieces of personal history become so wedded to the *fútbol* grounds and the players associated with them that they are "readymade," according to Álvaro Enrigue, akin to found objects in art. Even in the unlikely setting of America's Great Plains, Bridget Carson finds that a soccer field produces site-specific memories for "the strikers/searching for a way through air."

That soccer provides such a range of meaning and memory should not obscure that the space in which it is played is always contested. Rival fans hurl vile insults. Women search for their place in a male bastion. For scholar María Graciela Rodríguez, her first football match adds new insight to "the other," that foundational concept in the study of philosophy, social relations, and gender: "If the other didn't exist, who would you yell 'asshole' at?"

1. The Orb

Klaus Rifbjerg
Translated from the Danish by Thom Satterlee

A game of football begins with a ball, and the ball might be an orange or a grapefruit, it might be rags or plastic bags tied together, or it might be the most recent innovation found at a sporting-goods store in an urban mall or on the Internet. In the ancient place and time that FIFA, the world governing body of football, recognizes as having developed one of the earliest forms of football—China, some two thousand years ago—the word for the game already incorporated the key object: *cuju* translates literally as "kicking a ball with the foot." By the sixteenth century references to air-filled leather balls appear in English schoolbooks, but it is not until the end of the nineteenth century that the modern football emerges. Credit goes to Great Britain for patenting the rubber bladder and the valve for air pumps we associate with today's balls. The Germans came up with the alternating black-and-white hexagonal pattern in the 1970s. Improvements (depending on whether one is a striker or a goalkeeper) continued in the shooter-friendly design of the official 2006 World Cup game ball.

Still, as Danish writer Klaus Rifbjerg demonstrates, a group of young players intent on playing a game of football can make do with almost any "orb," even a beat-up ball whose bladder sticks out of the sides and is stretched nearly to the point of popping.

> It wasn't round
> I don't know what it was
> But it wasn't round.
> Even so, we called it "the orb."
>
> It was a friend
> Who had it
> And as soon as the ice and snow melted
> Out it came.

We walked beside a hedge of whitethorns
And Herman carried the orb under his arm.
It rested safely inside the crook
Lopsided and bulging as it was.

The goal stood in the raw wind.
It was March and there was war.
Spring. Football. Boys.
And so the ball got its first kick

Sailed seasick up into the gray
Came down and was chased.
Here! Here! we all shouted
And hoped for the next kick.

Hoped to get it in
To score a goal to be with others
To be simultaneously oneself and every boy
To be best!

Then the sore broke open
The ball the orb
A blister, pink, protruded
from between the stitches

And our spirits sank
Because if it burst everything was over
The last hope a patch
Alongside sixteen other.

A penalty kick was called, and it went in
But the piece of crap held together
And there are plenty of old tubes
And thousands of patches

And thousands of knees and thousands of boys
Who play football
Kicking whatever they can
Like that time long, long ago.

2. The Origins

Eduardo Galeano

Translated from the Spanish by Mark Fried

Born in 1940, Eduardo Galeano is a Uruguayan writer, journalist, and political activist. Forced to leave his homeland and then later Argentina for opposing their military regimes, he lived in exile for a decade until his return to Montevideo.

A staunch enemy of economic systems that impoverish the many while enriching the few and of structures imposing universal values that center on consumption and violence, Galeano has embraced contrasting impulses, including—at its best moments—soccer. His 1995 book, *El futbol a sol y sombra* (*Soccer in Sun and Shadow*), had its genesis in the love he developed for the game as a child. "Like all Uruguayan children I wanted to be a soccer player," Galeano writes. "I played quite well. In fact I was terrific, but only at night when I was asleep. . . . Irredeemable klutz, disgrace of the playing fields, I had no choice but to ask of words what the ball so desired denied me. From that challenge, and from that need for expiation, this book was born."

As is typical of his works, the book is composed of short chapters, each a page or two in length. Galeano below writes about the ball games of China, Egypt, and Japan; football's ties to sacred ceremonies of the sun in Central America; intense followers; and the game as a type of sublimated war.

Galeano rescues the game from the clutches of money and power by celebrating its beauty, magicians, and sense of comradeship. Along with the Italian Marxist Antonio Gramsci, who called soccer "the open-air kingdom of human loyalty," Galeano feels that the game "unravels the mysteries of the human soul."

In soccer, as in almost everything else, the Chinese were first. Five thousand years ago, Chinese jugglers had balls dancing on their feet, and it wasn't long before they organized the first games. The net was in the center of the field, and the players had to keep the ball from touching the ground without using their hands. The sport continued from dynasty to dynasty, as can be seen on certain bas-relief monuments from long before Christ, and in later Ming Dynasty engravings which show people playing with a ball that could have been made by Adidas.

We know that in ancient times the Egyptians and the Japanese had fun kicking a ball around. On the marble surface of a Greek tomb from five centuries before Christ a man is kneeing a ball. The comedies of Antiphanes contain telling expressions like *long ball, short pass, forward pass*. . . . They say that Emperor Julius Caesar was quick with his feet and that Nero couldn't score at all. In any case, there is no doubt that while Jesus lay dying on the cross the Romans were playing something fairly similar to soccer.

Roman legionaries kicked the ball all the way to the British Isles. Centuries later, in 1314, King Edward II stamped his seal on a royal decree condemning the game as plebeian and riotous: "Forasmuch as there is a great noise in the city caused by hustling over large balls, from which many evils may arise, which God forbid." Football, as it was already being called, left a slew of victims. Matches were fought by gangs, and there were no limits on the number of players, the length of the game, or anything else. An entire town would play against another town, advancing with kicks and punches toward the goal, which at that time was a far-off windmill. The games extended over several leagues and several days at the cost of several lives. Kings repeatedly outlawed these bloody events: in 1349 Edward III included soccer among games that were "stupid and utterly useless," and there were edicts against the game signed by Henry IV in 1410 and Henry VI in 1447. These only confirmed that prohibition whets the appetite, because the more it was banned, the more it was played.

In 1592 in *The Comedy of Errors*, Shakespeare turned to soccer to formulate a character's complaint: "Am I so round with you as you with me, / that like a football you do spurn me thus? / You spurn me hence, and he will spurn me hither. / If I last in this service you must case me in leather." And a few years later in *King Lear*, the Earl of Kent taunted: "Nor tripped neither, you base football player!"

In Florence soccer was called *calcio*, as it still is throughout Italy today. Leonardo da Vinci was a fervent fan and Machiavelli loved to play. It was played in sides of twenty-seven men split into three lines, and they were allowed to use their hands and feet to hit the ball and gouge the bellies of their adversaries. Throngs of people attended the matches, which were held in the largest plazas and on the frozen waters of the Arno. Far from Florence, in the gardens of the Vatican, Popes Clement VII, Leo IX, and Urban VIII used to roll up their vestments to play *calcio*.

In Mexico and Central America a rubber ball filled in for the sun in a sacred ceremony performed as far back as 1500 BC. But we don't know when soccer began in many parts of the Americas. The Indians of the Bolivian Amazon say they have been kicking a hefty rubber ball between two posts since time immemorial. In the eighteenth century, a Spanish priest from the Jesuit missions of the Upper Paraná described an ancient custom of the Guaraníes: "They do not throw the ball with their hands like us, rather they propel it with the upper part of their bare foot." Among the Indians of Mexico and Central America, the ball was generally hit with the hip or the forearm, although paintings at Teotihuacán and Chichén-Itzá show the ball being kicked with the foot and the knee. A mural created over a thousand years ago in Tepantitla has a grandfather of Hugo Sánchez manoeuvering the ball with his left. The game would end when the ball approached its destination: the sun arrived at dawn after travelling through the region of death. Then, for the sun to rise, blood would flow. According to some in the know, the Aztecs had the habit of sacrificing the winners. Before cutting off their heads, they painted red stripes on their bodies. The chosen of the gods would offer their blood, so the earth would be fertile and the heavens generous.

3. Hem and Football

Nalinaksha Bhattacharya

Women's soccer has become a popular sport worldwide, although one would not know about this popularity to judge from the nearly nonexistent representations in mainstream media. In India its development has followed that of the men's game, with pockets of strong support in West Bengal, in the eastern part of the country; in states such as Manipur along the border with Burma; and in Goa, the former Portuguese colony on the western coast. From 1992–2006 either Manipur or West Bengal had won every senior women's national football championship. Yet, according to researchers Boria Majumdar and Kausik Bandyopadhyay in *Soccer and Society* (June–September 2005), women's soccer is still taboo in many middle-class homes in India.

The attraction of the sport, spurred to some extent by the prominence of the London-based Sikh footballer Jesminder Bhamra (portrayed by Parminder Nagra in the film *Bend It Like Beckham* [2002]), was captured presciently by Bhattacharya in his two-book series on a Bengali girl, Hemprova Mitra (or Hem), and her passion for soccer. In the author's note preceding the first of the two volumes, *Hem and Football* (1992; the second, published in 1995, is *Hem and Maxine*), Bhattacharya writes that characters and situations are "entirely imaginary." But he adds that "the consistent good performance of Bengal's women footballers and their bleak prospects . . . are, however, real." He later marks the point again through Hem's school coach, Mrs. Bhowmik, who warns the players that they will receive little recognition for their efforts: "Here in Bengal all you get for bringing in those shining trophies year after year is a cheap garland of marigolds and a pat on the back from a minor official at the railway station when you get down from your second-class compartment, and if you are lucky enough, a four-line report on the back page of a Bengali daily with your name invariably misspelt."

Bhattacharya's imaginings concerning a scriptural basis for football, which can be found in this selection, have a rough parallel in the Popul Vuh, the foundation myth of the Quiché Mayan culture in Mesoamerica. The second part of the Popul Vuh concerns the origins of "divine ball players" who contest the gods of the underworld, writes David Goldblatt in his monumental history, *The Ball Is Round: A Global History of Football* (Viking, 2006). The ball game, Goldblatt writes, "provided the physical and symbolic fulcrum of an entire continental culture."

It was Uncle's powerful influence over Mother that gave me the idea to harness him in the cause of football. I explained my plan to my sisters and approached Uncle one noon as he stretched out on the four-poster, belching, for a longish nap after his lavish five-course meal. Bula pressed his feet, Maya gently ran her fingers through his hair and I combed his beard. Uncle grunted appreciatively and soon started snoring. We waited till Mother locked up the kitchen and went out on her daily round in the colony to ascertain the impact of Uncle's last discourse and then, as planned, Maya pinched him hard on his arm. Uncle woke with a start and blinked. "Now girls, what are you up to?"

I told him about my problem and affected a sob.

"You must do something for our didi," pleaded Maya. "Or she will take poison."

"Cast a spell on Mother," implored Bula from the foot of the bed. Uncle frowned and shook his head. "I quite sympathise with your problem, dear, but what can a holy man do about these mundane little problems? In fact, there is really nothing in the scriptures to support football."

"But surely you can invent something," we suggested.

"Never. How dare you suggest that I misuse my religious powers to meet your personal whims? Impossible."

"Bring Supreme Being, Om Tat Sat, or something powerful and restore football," said Bula, her nose already dilated in distress.

"Nonsense!" cried Uncle, "It seems you girls are bent on dragging my kundalini downwards to the navel. No wonder the scriptures advise enlightened souls to stay away from women."

We threatened to withdraw our services at once if Uncle didn't relent and Bula gave a dark hint that she would pinch one or two important items from Uncle's rucksack.

"Leave me alone, you vicious little women," cried Uncle and sat bolt upright. "Let me see if my guru permits me to meddle in your earthly business." He drew up his legs in lotus posture, closed his eyes and established a telepathic link with his guru a thousand miles away in the Himalayas. After five minutes, he opened his eyes and said, "You girls be present at my evening discourse on Sunday. That will be my last."

I counted fifty heads on Sunday evening. The veranda could only accommodate the women, so the men had to stand in the courtyard. A petromax lamp was placed on a stool and two kilos of sugar wafers were brought from the grocer's for distribution of prosad. After the Ram-Shiva-Ram chant Uncle closed his eyes and recited a Sanskrit sloka in a resounding voice: "Om Akhandamandalakaram vyaptam jena characharam—Praise the Supreme Being who pervades the undivided, round universe." Sandwiched between Kali Ghosh's obese wife and an old woman who had the habit of making faces at unruly children, I listened to Uncle's discourse with rapt attention.

"Brothers and sisters, on my last evening with you I propose to take up a light entertaining subject. As usual I start my discourse with a simple question: which game do you like most?"

"Football . . . cricket . . . volleyball . . . cards . . . carrom," responded the men from the courtyard.

"Ludo . . . cards," mumbled a few women.

"There is a popular notion that all these games evolved in the West and white men introduced them in our land. It's a big lie. From atom to aeroplane, all the great inventions, be it in science or sports, were made by the wise people of our motherland, Bharatvarsha."

"But Swamiji, isn't it a fact that the Wright brothers invented the flying machine?" asked Prodip, a bright bespectacled lad of our colony who had won several inter-college quiz contests and was considered a fountain of knowledge by his juniors.

"No Right or Wrong brothers had anything to do with the invention of the flying machine," said Uncle emphatically. "I am astounded by your ignorance, young man. Go home and read the Ramayana. Pushpak raths, the flying chariots, were ferrying our gods and goddesses across the horizon from the beginning of time. Even favoured mortals like Ram had an occasional ride in them at a time when the predecessors of your Right brothers lived in caves, ate raw uncured meat and, as my American disciple so succinctly puts it, had a limited vocabulary of two words—'wa' and 'wu.' The first meant eating and the second stood for defecating. So much for the advancement of Western civilisation."

There was a loud applause for the superiority of Indian civilisation. "Keep your trap shut, you idiot," the old woman on my side shrieked and made a face at Prodip. "Swami Gajanand has enough erudition to sniff you in like a pinch of snuff through one nostril and sneeze you out like snot through the other."

"No more digression, please," Swami Gajanand raised his hand for quiet. "Today I shall talk about the origin of just one game, say football; how it was introduced on Earth as written in our scriptures."

"Harpastrum was its original name," piped up the incorrigible Prodip. "Later it took the name of feetballe. It was played in its various crude forms in Sparta, Greece, Rome and later in Ireland and England and it was an Englishman, Mr J. C. Thring, who first drew up the rules."

"Shut up you devil!" thundered Kali Ghosh's wife, waving her massive arm menacingly.

"Shameless licker of white man's boots," shouted a male voice. "Throw him out."

"Give me your broom, didi," called out Monu Master's wife to my mother. "I will swipe out that irreverent beetle." There was a scuffle in the courtyard as some men pounced on Prodip who shouted even as he was thrown out: "Imposter! Liar! I'll bring *Encyclopaedia Britannica* . . . *Pears General Knowledge compendium* . . ."

"Shraddhaban lavate gyanam," observed Swami Gajanand. "The respectful learneth. Sorry for the interruption. Aatha charma goloka katha, the story of leather ball. The scriptures tell us that the first football match was held between the gods and the asuras, the demons, in heaven. The bet was that the winner would get Lakshmi, the goddess of wealth and prosperity. As you can understand, the stakes were very high and the preparations on both sides naturally became rather frenzied. I won't go into the details as to how Kartikeya and Britrasur, the captains of the gods and asuras, trained their players. You can find out the details from Khelpuran which mainly deals with the competitions and recreational activities of gods. The important point to remember is that the asuras were a better team because they had been playing the game secretly for a few millennia before the gods even came to know about it.

"The game started and, as feared, from the very beginning the asuras dominated. Ganesh, the elephant-headed god, had earned some reputation as a goalie but Maghasur, the asura striker, defeated him again and again. Unable to cope with the asuras, the gods finally invoked the power of the elements. Storms rose, the ground was flooded and the wind carried each shot of the gods straight into the goal. But the asuras were still winning. Then there was an earthquake; the ground shook and great chasms appeared, sucking in a couple of asuras, and yet they could not be contained.

"During the recess Kartikeya said to Narad, the trouble-shooter among the gods, 'O wise Narad, tell me if there is still any hope for us.'

"'There is only one solution I can think of,' said Narad. 'In the kingdom of Vidisha there is an earthling called Pundarik, a cobbler by profession, and his wife Bhamini who are incorrigible football players and have popularised the game among the lower ranks. They have incurred the king's wrath by drawing away a huge crowd from his annual archery competitions and are now counting their days in a dark dungeon. I think we should bring them to play for us. The couple have mastered some novel techniques like reverse kicks and back headers which the asuras haven't yet heard about. We can easily camouflage these mortals as gods.'

"To cut a long story short, the gods won the match with the help of the two mortals and Lakshmi was retained by the gods.

"'Ask three boons,' said Lord Naryan, the consort of goddess Lakshmi, to the cobbler couple.

"'My lord, may we be allowed to introduce football on Earth?' said Pundarik.

"'Granted. With my blessings football will be the most popular game on Earth.'

"'But my lord, unless you protect the football players from the wrath of kings and their armies, how can we introduce the game on Earth?'

"'From today,' assured Lord Naryan, 'he or she who persecutes a footballer will be thrown in Raurab, the most frightening of all hells. But Bhamini, your husband has asked two boons. Now it's your turn.'

"'If you are so bountiful, my lord,' said Bhamini, 'bless the woman who takes to football with early marriage, abundant male offspring and long life.'

"'Granted,' said Lord Naryan."

"Did you like my discourse, darling?" whispered Uncle when I came to his bedside at night to fix the mosquito net.

"Fantastic," I said. "I hope Mother gets the message."

"She must have got the message. Just wait for the morning."

Uncle was right. In the morning as I was stuffing my school-bag with books, Mother threw my shorts in front of me after cutting a thread with her teeth.

"I have lowered the hem by two inches," she said. "I wish you to take football a little more seriously. A girl like you without a presentable face has much to gain from this blessed game."

4. The Daily Life of Cameroonian Football

Bea Vidacs

Hungarian-born cultural anthropologist Bea Vidacs has studied the interplay among national identity, colonial legacy, and soccer in Cameroon—the West African nation of seventeen million that is the most successful of Africa's soccer-playing lands. Having won the continental championship four times and reached the World Cup finals five times since 1982, Cameroon's greatest moment came in 1990 when the "Indomitable Lions," inspired by thirty-eight-year-old Roger Milla, reached the World Cup quarterfinals, which they lost to England 2–3 in extra time.

In this excerpt from her doctoral dissertation (City University of New York, 2002), Vidacs combines interviews and firsthand observations from her time in the capital, Yaoundé. Her descriptions showcase a soccer-loving nation where playing styles are strongly tied to national self-perceptions and where the fortunes of the national team, a multiethnic blend from the ten provinces, have significant impact on the mood and hopes of the people. Of special interest is Vidacs's rich description of the scarred and overused playing surfaces, testament to the game's integral role in day-to-day society, and to the players' adaptability to difficult conditions. Vidacs says that after nineteen months' immersion in the country's football, to the point of preparing prematch meals for a third-division team, she began to consider participants in the sport—who call themselves *les sportifs*—"in a heroic light." "They perceive of themselves," she continues, "as wanting to create something: something concrete, something real, a better future, a good team, that everyone will remember and which will be the talk of the town. . . . As an ideal . . . Cameroon football represents an antithesis of the zombification, inertia, and impasse of the postcolonial condition."

Football and its images are ubiquitous in Cameroon: walking around on the streets of Yaoundé one sees young men and boys in faded football jerseys, a little boy of perhaps seven in a faded yellow T-shirt, with a handwritten inscription, "Thomas Nkono No. 1"; bars named "Bar des Sportifs," "Sports Bar," "Siflet d'or," "Bar des amis sportifs"; the many taxicabs that carry Roger Milla's name.

Lest we think that this ubiquity is only limited to the cities, although football *is* an urban phenomenon, Cameroonians, like other Africans, regularly go back and forth between town and village. In July 1997, on the way to a small village in the West Province, I saw a match being played and was told that this was a match between children returning to the village for the school holidays. In the village itself there is no electricity, and very few of the amenities of modern life are in evidence; however, in one of the houses I visited, a faded 1982 calendar from a sports journal displayed that year's incarnation of the Indomitable Lions. In another house, next to a framed photograph and other personal memorabilia, was a photograph of Thomas Nkono from a sports journal and an article about the Lions' participation in the 1982 World Cup in Spain.

Walking around Yaoundé I also saw football being played everywhere. Football people in Yaoundé complain frequently that there are not enough football pitches and, doubtless, in light of the demand, they are right. Apart from the Ahmadou Ahidjo or Omnisports Stadium, which is also "the" national stadium since this is where international and first-division professional matches are played, I have attended matches or training sessions at twelve other venues. My research assistant could enumerate twenty-five; doubtless, there were others he forgot.

In addition, inside the most crowded neighborhoods, where there is little space, ad hoc teams suddenly appear, especially during school holidays, and take over the space for a match or a mini-championship, kicking the ball rain or shine, appreciating the joy of the game. On a little side street in a residential area I once saw a group of children, between six and ten years old, playing with abandon: among them, to my horror, a little girl with an eight-inch kitchen knife in her right hand. Clearly she had abandoned her kitchen duties, just for a minute, to join in the melee. She held the knife down, behind her back, so as to keep it "safe," but the sight was hair-raising anyway.

People stop to watch all games. Neighborhood *inter-quartier* championships gather their own crowds, and the organizers might even be able to collect money from the spectators. Village championships in urban areas also have a built-in audience, since members of the village will come together as much to see each other as to see the game. Spectators of these matches may be asked for a hundred francs, or about twenty cents in American money, to watch. The social nature of these village championships explains why there are almost equal numbers of women and men among the spectators, which is never the case when official teams play.

People will stop to see training sessions, too, especially if a practice match is in progress. The Stade Annexe of the Omnisports Stadium in Yaoundé is constructed along a main road, and it is maybe two to three meters below the road level. Any given morning or afternoon when teams play friendly matches it is common to see people standing on the road, looking down onto the dirt pitch, watching intently. Often a car or two also will stop, the passengers, captivated by the game, getting out to watch. In the summer of 1995, when the football federation was suspended by the Ministry of Youth and Sports and a caretaker committee took over, one of the new committee's first actions was to organize a match between the *anciens gloirs* (old stars) of Douala and Yaoundé. Without any special advertising, Stade Annexe I drew an enormous crowd, people standing three deep at what is primarily a training ground. Another row of people sat atop the fence enclosing the stadium. Looking at the scene from outside, I spotted a pair of crutches propped up against the fence, the owner of the crutches watching the game, perched up high.

The football pitches of Yaoundé, as well as those in the rest of Cameroon, are by all accounts in a terrible state. None of them have turf, meaning that either the players play in dust or glide in mud. I have seen a team with better boots win a match in which they were losing because the other team started sliding uncontrollably. Some football grounds tilt noticeably in one direction, giving a definite advantage to the team trying to score downhill. Fortunately, at halftime, the teams change sides.

Ahmadou Ahidjo Stadium is one of two in the country to boast natural turf; the other is the Reunification Stadium in Douala. A third stadium capable of hosting international matches, in Garoua, has synthetic turf. In the mid-1990s the turf at each of these grounds was in an advanced state of deterioration. In his book *Football et politique du football au Cameroun* (Football and the Politics of Football in Cameroon), André Ntonfo writes ironically about the state of Cameroonian stadiums:

> Under these conditions it is not surprising that a stadium with "real turf" sometimes becomes a handicap for a number of players used to playing grounds that the unsuspecting observer could easily mistake for a wasteland: ill-kept cattle pens, grassless pastures for goats or an inaccessible swamp where two goals have been erected for the occasion.
>
> The first things to master on this type of terrain are the forever uncertain trajectories of the ball. And for players who learned and practiced the craft in such an environment, who know that you have to go left to capture a ball that seems to be going right, who know that a hump or a puddle—like suddenly appearing opponents—can redirect it, for players who take advantage of mud, dust and other wild grasses—playing partners unrecognized by the Confédération Africaine de Football and FIFA—for such players, then, to find themselves on "real turf" can present a sizeable handicap.

Ntonfo is not exaggerating. On one occasion, when two second-division teams were playing a Cameroon Challenge Cup match at the Ahmadou Ahidjo Stadium, the grass had not been cut and had grown so high that one of the coaches instructed his team to forget any tactical advice they had been given. In such high grass, it was impossible to play according to any kind of plan.

5. The Soccer Moms — 1996

David Starkey

The "soccer-mom" phenomenon continues to change with the times. First identified—especially as soccer colonized suburban America in the 1980s and 1990s—as selfless chauffeurs for their children, packing juice boxes and nutritious snacks in coolers and arriving at games in a line of minivans, the soccer moms later became the target of marketers and the intended audience for political stump speeches. By 2000 the stereotype had undergone interesting challenges as a growing number of these women had joined soccer leagues as players, or begun to walk the sidelines as coaches rather than as cheering parents.

In the mind of at least one male writer, the sexuality of the soccer moms must not be overlooked. Writing for online magazine *Salon*, Matthew DeBord confesses, "I am over the supermodel; we're not even friends. These days, most nights, I belong to the soccer mom." What next iteration awaits the soccer-mom phenomenon is hard to guess unless, as David Starkey prophesies at the end of his poem, their final days have come and they have "begun to fade, / to drive their minivans off into the twilit / hinterlands of demography."

> The soccer moms emerged like Venus
> from the foam of their shifting
> responsibilities, they skated
> into public view with grace
> and a lurking amazement that anyone
> should care about their intelligence
> and persistent tidiness, I
> would love to have given them a gift
> of appreciation, an Edwardian tea set,

perhaps, or a subscription
to *Parents* magazine, but the soccer moms
were too busy to accept anything
but brief nods of thanks
as they loaded the kids into Windstars
and Caravans, Previas and Safaris
and Voyagers, negotiating the cunning trails
someone else had laid out between
the thicket of family and the brambles
of work, no worries, though, the soccer moms,
prudent and well-organized, made it home
without incident, I would love
to have had their calm foresight,
their sense of the future
as a tastefully appointed kitchen
with yellow roses in a crystal vase,
a china cabinet and an antique hutch,
the scent of blueberry muffins filling
the warm air, I would love to have believed
they would remain with us forever, taking
classes part-time at the local college,
volunteering weekends at the old age home,
coming quick as hummingbirds
attendant upon our nurturing, but already
the soccer moms have begun to fade,
to drive their minivans off into the twilit
hinterlands of demography, joining
the angry white men, their husbands,
who lately ruled the world.

6. Atiguibas

Julio Ramón Ribeyro
Translated from the Spanish by John Penuel

Peruvian writer Julio Ramón Ribeyro was born in 1929. He studied at the Catholic University in Lima, traveled extensively, and in 1960 settled in Paris, where he lived until his death in 1994. His many works of fiction have been widely translated, and he is considered to be one of the most significant Latin American writers of the twentieth century.

In the following story language plays an important role—in particular the mysterious word *atiguibas*, whose meaning the narrator tries desperately to uncover. Similarly, in the translation of this story two common Spanish words (*zambos* and *negroide*) proved slippery, and the translator had little choice but to adopt the English cognates *sambos* and *negroid*, although as readers of the original will note, neither word is necessarily pejorative in Spanish.

In the main part of the narrative, however, Ribeyro takes us into the crowds, into the second-class wooden bleachers at Estadio Nacional José Díaz in Lima as vendors hawk goods and supporters hurl projectiles and urinate at will. (To compare with an account from a stadium in Buenos Aires, see chapter 12 by María Graciela Rodríguez.) The player referred to as the "Brazilian Black Diamond" is Leônidas da Silva, one of South America's pioneering black players who is also credited with having perfected the bicycle kick. Leônidas died in 2004.

As a child and then as a teenager, I had some unforgettable times in the old José Díaz national stadium—modernized and enlarged now. My brother and I saw the most famous soccer teams of Argentina, Brazil, and Uruguay file in over the patchy turf of that field. And the teams from Peru, too, it must be said, because back then we had great players and teams that performed memorable feats. In the 1936 Berlin

Olympics, for example, we were about to win the gold after beating Austria 4–2. But it displeased Hitler that blacks, Indians, and sambos from a country like Peru could beat blond Teutons; for him it was not only a sporting but also an ideological defeat. FIFA, pressured by the führer, ordered the result annulled, contending that the field was a few meters too short or too long. We withdrew from the Olympics, saving our dignity but losing the gold.

At that time, when a foreign team came, you had to go to the stadium at ten in the morning if you wanted to find a place in the cheap bleacher seats. The main match was at four in the afternoon; so that the spectators wouldn't get bored, there were some ten or twelve preliminary matches: children, adolescents, neighborhood teams, second-and third-division teams. All under a burning sun, because the international season was in midsummer. The fans had to put on visors or make themselves hats out of newspaper. And most of them brought bag lunches if they didn't want to faint from hunger in the middle of the afternoon. So the stands became not only a gallery packed with fanatics but also a huge public dining room or picnic area spread out over the bleachers. And there were vendors all over, because you always needed something to eat, smoke, or drink, and that's where they came in, slithering through the stands, offering meat pies, pork sandwiches, roast meats on cane skewers, cigarettes, beer, and sodas. When the game was exciting, the vendors glided around bent over, almost crawling, because otherwise they became the target of insults and projectiles, if they were not simply lifted up over the spectators' heads and passed hand over hand until they landed at the edge of the field.

Here is one particular incident to complete the portrait of the cheap seats of those days: The second-class seats, where my brother and I went, were cement for the first ten rows and wooden up to the top. There were no bathrooms or latrines. After hours of drinking and watching soccer, the fans needed to urinate. There was no choice but to go up to the last row and urinate over the railing onto the space between the stands and the high walls surrounding the stadium. Whoever chose that moment to walk around in that space was assured a shower of urine. But it was more common that the pissers couldn't climb up to the last row because there were a lot of people or because they couldn't hold it in any longer, so they would look for an opening in the wooden stands and, taking up grotesque positions, put their peter in and relieve themselves amid the jokes and laughter of the crowd. In those days women didn't go to the stadium. Soccer was for real men.

The shout broke the tense silence reigning during a match between the popular local team, Alianza Lima, and the visiting Argentine team, San Lorenzo de Almagro. Alianza had just tied its rivals at one when the voice resounded from high up in the cheap seats:

"Atiguibas!"

It was the first time we heard that shout. The crowd responded with laughter and the game went on, getting tenser and tenser, because the Argentines were constantly threatening the Alianza goal. But every five or ten minutes, we heard the shout again:

"Atiguibas!"

And the crowd relaxed.

Soon the Argentines showed their superiority: the stocky Lángara, San Lorenzo's Basque center forward, scored three goals in a row, the last one a blast from more than thirty yards out. There was nothing left to do—we had lost. We had just left the stands with our tails between our legs when one last "Atiguibas!" resounded throughout the stadium and barely managed to make us smile.

From then on there were no international or playoff matches at which you didn't hear that cry in the stadium, no matter whether the game was boring or exciting, whether we were winning or losing, always provoking laughter in the crowd. Who was doing the shouting? The perpetrator was impossible to find, in one place one day and somewhere else the next. Because we went to the stadium so often, my brother and I managed to pinpoint the source of the shout to the upper part of the second-class bleachers and sometimes in the cheap seats on the north side, but we never spotted the individual himself. His voice was powerful and husky, a drunken, negroid voice. But the stadium was full of drunks and negroids. What did that word mean, anyway? Nobody knew. Everybody we asked, in the stadium or out of it, said they had heard it but didn't know what it meant.

Finally, one evening, and in rather somber circumstances, we managed to spot the loudmouth. It was during a long-awaited match where the local champions Universitario de Deportes—the team my brother and I were rabid fans of—were hosting the Brazilian champions São Paulo. Since both teams had white uniforms, Universitario changed its jerseys for green ones out of courtesy to the visitors. Seeing our team come out with a differently colored jersey gave us a bad feeling. In addition, there was a duel of center forwards: Leonidas, the Brazilian Black Diamond, and Lolo Fernández, the Peruvian Bombardier. As soon as the whistle blew we heard a thunderous "Atiguibas!" that put us all in a good mood. And the good mood got even better when our team scored the opening goal thanks to a free kick by Lolo Fernández. The first half finished with us in the lead, but at the beginning of the second the Black Diamond was unleashed. He was a black man with a high forehead, almost bald, and an emaciated body, but he was diabolically technical, intelligent, and tricky. In barely twenty minutes his plays sowed confusion in our defense, and São Paulo scored five goals in a row. The last acted as a detonator: the crowd climbed over the fence and ran onto the field; no one knew whether it was to maul the Brazilians or lynch the Peruvians. The referee put an end to the game, and both teams, escorted by the police, fled to the locker rooms. That was when we heard a pitiful "Atiguibas!" coming from the quickly emptying stands and were able to see high up in the second-class bleachers—our section—a short, chunky mulatto with a big Afro making a horn with his hands and letting out a last "Atiguibas!" just as rowdy fans started setting fire to newspapers. The wooden stands began to burn, and we were forced to leave the stadium at a run.

It wasn't only the fires that kept us from approaching the shouting mulatto that afternoon but also our dejection. Those who know nothing of the sadness of sporting defeats know nothing of sadness. That time, like so many other times, we left the stadium with a dead weight on our hearts, despairing of life, unable to console ourselves due to our team's failure. We were still too young to seek oblivion in bars and of course not mature enough to take the loss philosophically. We had no choice but to suffer for days, weeks, until time blunted our pain or a win by our team made us happy again.

A win—that would take its time coming—but we got it at last, an unforgettable one a year or two later when Racing Club came from Buenos Aires to Lima, preceded by immense fame. They had just won the Argentine championship and had a twenty-game winning streak going. Everybody on their roster was a star, but their most outstanding players were the goalie Rodríguez, the back Salomón (6'5" and 220 pounds), and the left wing Ezra Sued. Universitario de Deportes, on the other hand, had finished third in the local tournament, and their renowned bombardier, our hero Lolo Fernández, was injured and would remain on the bench.

The game started at four in the afternoon, preceded by a thunderous "Atiguibas!" that came from very close to us this time. Racing was really a scoring machine. In barely ten minutes their center forward Rubén Bravo scored two goals, thanks to precise passes from Ezra Sued. Universitario's offense, led by Beanpole Espinoza, kept running up against the gigantic Salomón. A fearful silence reigned over the stadium, and not even the loudmouth sambo—we saw him a few rows above us—dared launch his cry.

In the middle of the first half the Universitario coach decided to send Lolo in for Beanpole Espinoza. His appearance on the field, with his hairnet on his head and a wide bandage around his thigh, provoked thunderous applause and an encouraging "Atiguibas." And that's when the miracle happened. Lolo Fernández scored five goals, every one of them a work of art, a model of strength, technique, courage, and opportunism. The first one was a shot from some fifteen yards out, fired as he ran to meet a waist-high pass up the middle from the left wing. The second one was a so-called little pigeon right between Salomón's legs, a header off a low pass from his brother Lolín. The third was simply a tap of his heel, his back to the goal, taking advantage of a loose ball just outside the goalie box. In the second half of the match Racing started off with a goal, tying the game three-all and sowing panic in the crowd. The Argentines rushed the Universitario field energetically, determined to defend their honor as the champions of Argentina. But Lolo was having the day of his life: taking advantage of a corner kick, he jumped over Salomón the Giant and sent a header bouncing into the goal. Minutes later, on another counterattack, he took a pass from midfield, ran quickly with the ball, and, without stopping, launched from beyond the penalty area a violent, low kick that cleared the Argentine goal for the fifth time. The goalie Rodríguez, out of pure anger, took off his cap and threw it to the ground. That was a sign of surrender: demoralized, Racing accepted defeat. In the last few minutes they just held the ball in an attempt to prevent another goal. The game ended in the midst of hurrahs, songs, and shouts of joy, among them the infallible and sonorous "Atiguibas!" Since the mulatto was in reach of us this time, my brother and I tried to approach him to share our excitement and at the same time wheedle out of him the meaning of that enigmatic word. But he was surrounded by a crowd of drunk fans brandishing beer bottles, and they disappeared in a noisy tumult down one of the dark stairways leading to the exit.

We kept going to the old stadium for years, more out of habit than passion. Losses still made us grieve, and wins rejoice, but with less intensity than before. We were young men by then, discovering love, art, Bohemia, ambition, a different scope for our dreams, where we could get a different kind of reward. We would go to the cheap seats as a group, drink beer, even make pious fun of our heroes, among them Lolo Fernández, who was approaching forty and was shamefully missing even penalty kicks. And the "Atiguibas!" kept resounding, not so often as before, to be sure, but it kept resounding, provoking laughter in the crowd and stimulating our curiosity. But a kind of fate prevented us from ever approaching the source of the shout, the drunken sambo, even though he was sometimes so close we could see his kinky hair, his crude, slightly crooked nose, his skin more purple than black, like a pawed-over bunch of Burgundy grapes. Confusion, drunks, or the arrival of the latecomers (the fans who flooded through the open doors of the stadium and into the second-class bleachers half an hour before the game ended) always took him out of our reach.

So I ended up not going to the stadium anymore and left the country without ever having discovered the meaning of that shout.

Years later, on one of my occasional trips to Peru, I went down Jirón de la Unión, by then a pedestrian street packed with vendors, moneychangers, bums, and swindlers. I was struggling through the crowd when I noticed a beggar in the atrium of La Merced standing next to the colonnade with his hand out. His face looked familiar: that asymmetric nose, that kinky mane of hair, grayish now, and above all, that skin purplish and violet like slightly rotten meat. Incredible, it was Atiguibas! Finally, the opportunity to approach him, accost him, and get the meaning of the word that for so long I had tried in vain to discover. I made my way out of the river of pedestrians and approached the beggar, who had one foot wrapped in a thick, dirty bandage. When he noticed my presence, he lowered his head and put his hand out further:

"Just a little something for a poor old man."

His hoarse voice was unmistakable.

Leaning over, I whispered into his ear: "Atiguibas."

It was as if he'd been stuck with a pin. He started, looked up, and stared at me with his eyes wide open.

"Don't tell me it's not you," I went on. "I know you from going to the stadium when I was a boy. Way up in the cheap seats. I must've heard you shouting a million times. But now you're going to tell me what 'Atiguibas' means. I've waited more than twenty years to find out."

The mulatto looked closely at me and held out his hand even more.

"Sure, but it'll cost you."

I had a five-dollar bill and a hundred-dollar bill in my pocket. I showed him the five. He shook his head.

"Twenty dollars."

I protested, saying it was robbery, if it wasn't that I was passing through Lima I wouldn't have offered him even one dollar, but the mulatto didn't yield.

"Okay," I said finally. "I'm going to go change these hundred dollars. I'll be right back."

The mulatto stopped me.

"Those changers are a mafia. Come inside here with me. I know the sacristan. He gives good rates."

I went into the church behind the mulatto, who was moving around without much difficulty in spite of his bandaged foot. At that hour the temple, lit by candles flickering in front of a few paintings, was almost empty, just some tourists and pious women inside. We walked in front of several empty confessional booths until we got to a slightly opened side door.

"Do you have the money there? Wait for me just a second."

I gave him the hundred dollars and took a few steps around the tabernacle for a closer look at the baroque carvings on the high altar, but, gripped by a sudden suspicion, I stopped short after a few seconds and headed quickly back to the sacristy. There was nobody in that room, nor in the next one, nor in the one after that, which, through a small door, led back to the side nave. By then it wasn't even worth looking for the mulatto, who was neither lame nor a beggar. Out of pure anger I let out a thunderous "Atiguibas!" that resounded throughout the temple, alarming the old ladies kneeling on the prie-dieu. And I thought I understood the meaning of that word when, leaving the church, I caught myself saying that that crafty mulatto had given me the atiguibas.

7. Why Eleven, of All Numbers?
Football between Carnival and Freemasonry

Erik Eggers
Translated from the German by David Wright

Here German sports journalist and historian Erik Eggers attempts to answer a foundational question—why are there eleven players on a soccer team? Historians say that the number was established early on, before standards such as the size of the ball, a fixed crossbar atop goalposts, and field markings fell into place. Eleven is considered by numerologists as the first of the "Master numbers," symbolizing intuition and spirituality, while in the Tarot deck it represents justice—all qualities that sometimes appear in football. Eggers delves into the connections between the game's early modern history and secret societies such as the Freemasons; in addition, Eggers suggests notions of sin, carnival traditions, and mysteries of the cosmos as possible sources for a solution.

Eggers writes for the *Financial Times Deutschland*, *Frankfurter Rundschau*, *Die Zeit*, and occasionally for the German magazine of football culture, *11 Freunde* (11 Friends). He is the author of books about team handball and Herbert Zimmermann, renowned German broadcaster of the 1954 World Cup final (see chapter 52, "The Sunday I Became World Champion," for more on Zimmermann's famous radio call). Eggers has also written about the shameful role played by the German football association during the Nazi era as Jewish athletes, coaches, and administrators were purged and sometimes murdered.

The fact that a football team consists of precisely eleven, and not ten or twelve players is, like the entire grammar of football, taken for granted these days. The size of the pitch, the dimensions of the goals, the breakdown of the team into goalkeeper, defence, midfield and attack—all of these are beyond discussion. And the number of players is just as uncontested as the fact that athletics races are always run counterclockwise, although, incidentally, they ran clockwise at the 1896 Olympic Games in Athens. Has football therefore now become a universal constant?

In any event, historians have hardly ever bothered to examine the origins of the rules of this sport. And on the question of the eleven players, they have discovered precisely nothing. Of course, this is partly due to the dreadful state of the sources. *The Laws of the Game*, the fourteen original rules laid down in London in December 1863 by the Football Association founded in the same year, have nothing to say about the number of players. Indeed, there are hardly any indications of why certain numbers were chosen. Admittedly, there is a suggestion of the decimal system, with the pitch a maximum of two hundred yards long and one hundred yards wide. The minimum distance at kick-off and free kicks was even then ten yards. On the other hand, the distance between goalposts was and still is eight yards, although the eight feet for the height of the goal was only added later.

It was left to the International Football Association Board (IFAB), founded in 1886 and still today the body that supervises the rules of football, to finally specify the number of players. "The game should be played by eleven players on each side," has been the international football rule since June 14, 1897. That the number eleven was not mentioned in 1863 is easy to explain. The main reason is to be found in the serious rivalry between the factions from Rugby and Cambridge University that continued even after the FA was founded. Both schools of football applied considerable energy in their attempts to push through their rules. It was only with time that the supporters of the Cambridge rules succeeded in penalising the brutal kicking of opponents (hacking) and the handling of the ball.

Around 1870 it had become clear that there would never be any compromise between rugby, with its fifteen players per team, and what was known as Association Football. Another argument is that there was no need to impose eleven players in a written regulation, since this was already the prevailing practice. Indeed, even before 1863, there is evidence of seventeen clubs in Sheffield who played eleven against eleven. A football team was often referred to as an "eleven" in English sporting language around 1860. And this was even the case when the first game was played according to the official FA rules in 1864 between the teams from Harrow and Cambridge, when eleven players faced a team of fourteen. The eleven-a-side principle was first documented in writing in 1841 for a game at the elite school in Eton. English football researchers therefore assume that Cambridge, the decisive force in the creation of the rules, simply took over this feature. However, the sources do not mention why eleven played against eleven at Eton.

As a result the area has become a fertile ground for conspiracy theorists. The FA, the national supervisory body, was founded at London's "Freemason's Tavern" by representatives of eleven clubs and schools. Historians have so far not attached any importance to the place where organised football was founded on Great Queen Street. However, the early activities of English Freemasons at least allow speculation about the involvement of their lodge in the foundation of the FA. The historian Reinhard Koselleck describes how the Freemasons were looking for ways of implementing values such as humanity, tolerance, equality, and freedom of the spirit in the increasingly secular society of the eighteenth and nineteenth centuries, and how they were involved in the foundation of a number of scientific organisations. Is it purely by chance that the world's first football organisation was founded in exactly the same place as the Royal Astronomical Society (1820) or the English branch of the National Geographic Society (1888)? Could football possibly have been regarded as a model for democratisation, a sport that like no other symbolised equality of opportunity for all involved?

Secret societies such as the Freemasons always attached great importance to numbers. The secret of eleven becomes a little clearer if one considers the numerology of the Middle Ages. In the glossaries of the encyclopaedias of the saints and in "allegoresis"—the theological interpretation of biblical texts looking for a hidden meaning behind the words, an approach that blossomed in the Middle Ages—eleven was seen as the number of intemperance and sin. Unlike ten, which was always seen as the figure for the whole and the complete and as the symbol of the circle, eleven exceeds this perfection by one. To be specific, it went beyond the Ten Commandments.

"Eleven! A wicked number. . . . Eleven is sin. Eleven goes beyond the Ten Commandments," to quote Friedrich Schiller's *Piccolomini*, written in 1800. It is no accident that the "eleventh Psalm refers to the wickedness of the world, the disappearance of discipline and order, loyalty and faith," states football philosopher Christoph Bausenwein in his book *Geheimnis Fußball* (The Mystery of Football). However, the decisive indicator is that eleven is the symbolic number for fools—as documented not only in the Rhineland, where November 11 (11/11) has marked the start of carnival since the end of the nineteenth century and where a "Council of Eleven" rules until Ash Wednesday.

Anyone who has the opportunity to attend a game of football during the Cologne carnival will intuitively understand the link between football and carnival. The surprising thing is that this connection is based in history. Many football games in the Middle Ages and in the early modern age were actually ritual elements of licentious carnival traditions. In addition, they were "nothing other than breaches of the law," as the sociologist Norbert Elias has shown. "Wild" games of football, which tended to be more a chaotic free-for-all until the game was codified in 1863, were frequently forbidden by the authorities on the grounds that they endangered public order or led to serious injuries or even fatalities.

The evidence for this is legion. The edict that Edward II promulgated in London in 1314 is famous, prohibiting "the hassling over large balls in the city." The last documented prohibitions on football before the FA was founded date from 1830 (in Burnley) and 1847 (in Derby). By the time the elite schools such as Harrow, Eton, Rugby, and Cambridge University had started to tame this wilderness, eleven had already become a familiar relic from the past. And although the number was tainted with negative symbolism, it was finally laid down in the rules at the end of the nineteenth century. From then on there was no obstacle to its career, making it the most famous number in modern sports.

8. Klapzuba's Eleven

Eduard Bass

Translated from the Czech by Ruby Hobling

The Chattertooth Eleven, originally published as *Klapzubova jedenáctka* (Klapzuba's Eleven), is the story of eleven strapping lads who, under the rigorous training and motivational psychology of their peasant father, become the best soccer squad in the world. Nothing can stand in their way—not bribe-bearing opponents, FC Barcelona, or islanders from the South Seas—as dedication, hard work, fairness, and honor win the day. Written in 1922 by Czech novelist, journalist, actor, and cabaret performer Eduard Bass, the story has enthralled generations of Czech readers—it was made into a film, *Klapzubova XI* (1938), a year before Czechoslovakia came under Nazi control and produced for television before the Prague Spring of 1968.

The genre of football fable has representatives in several languages: British author Nick Hornby contributed a tale of the fictional, microscopic European principality of Champina and its football team to the 2005 children's collection *Noisy Outlaws, Unfriendly Blobs, and Some Other Things That Aren't as Scary.* . . . In Portuguese, Brazilian novelist Jorge Amado tells of a ball falling in love with a suffering goalkeeper in his 1984 work, *A bola e o goleiro* (A Ball and a Goalie). "The keeper becomes unbeatable," writes Alex Bellos in *Futebol: The Brazilian Way of Life* (Bloomsbury, 2002), "since the ball always heads for his arms, where it is kissed and then warmly held to his chest." In French, a 1994 film and related book, *Le ballon d'or* (The Golden Ball), depict a Guinean boy who must work 750 days to save for a leather football. Influenced by the name of the annual award given to the best European player, children paint the ball gold.

In Nether Buckwheat, in the province of Bohemia in Czechoslovakia, there once lived a poor cottager named Chattertooth. He had eleven sons and not a penny in his pocket. He used to rack his brains as to what to put his sons to. At last he decided to make a football team of them.

Behind the cottage was a level piece of meadow; this he called the Playing Field. Then he sold the goat, bought two balls with the money, and set about training the boys. Honza, the eldest, was a maypole of a lad, so he was put in goal. And as the two youngest, Frantik and Jura, were small and wiry, old Chattertooth put them at outside right and left.

He would wake the boys at five in the morning and walk them briskly through the woods for an hour. As soon as they had covered four miles the order would be given, "About turn and back at the double." Only after that did the boys get their breakfast, and then work began in real earnest. And old Chattertooth saw to it that each of them knew his job inside and out. He taught them how to take a ball in midair, stop it, and pass; to feint; to centre; to kick from a stationary position or on the run; to throw the ball in; and indeed everything that a footballer should know.

That in itself was a good deal, but it was not by a long chalk all that the Chattertooth boys had to learn. There was running and jumping as well; they had to cover anything from a hundred yards to five miles, and they soon became as good at pole jumping and at the hop, step, and jump as at high and long jumping. And of course they had to know all about hurdle racing as well, and how to get off to a good start.

But even all this did not satisfy old Chattertooth. When the boys had learnt to shift their weight and throw the javelin and discus to develop their arm muscles, they then had to learn classical wrestling to keep their whole bodies in trim.

Before all else, however, they did breathing exercises with light dumbbells, for old Chattertooth always said that without good lungs and a good heart training of any kind was nothing but murder and sudden death. In a word, they were kept so busy that they stormed the kitchen like hungry wolves at midday, gobbled up their food, and left their plates looking as if a cat had licked them. Then for an hour they lay down in a row, either on the floor of the cottage or on the bare earth of the yard outside, and rested. Hardly a word was exchanged, for each was glad to be able to stretch his bones and do nothing for a while. As soon as the hour was up old Chattertooth put aside his pipe, drew out his whistle and blew it to assemble the lads, and then the fun started again. Towards evening the old man put on his football boots and joined the boys in a six-a-side game. At the end of the day they streamed back into the house, and old Chattertooth massaged them in turn and threw three pails of cold water over each, as there was no shower-bath in the cottage. This was followed by a light evening meal. For a while they talked to each other, but soon they were sent to bed. Next morning the same old routine started anew.

Day in, day out, this went on for three years. At the end of the third year Father Chattertooth popped along to Prague and came back with a signboard, which he nailed to the gate of the field. It had a blue border, and on a white background was painted in red letters:

THE CHATTERTOOTH ELEVEN

In his pocket he had a paper stating that the Chattertooth Eleven had been enrolled in the third division of the Central Bohemian Football League. The boys all raised Cain because they were only in the third division, but old Chattertooth said tranquilly: "Everything in its turn. With God's help you will one day beat the Slavia Club and be top of the League, but you must work your way up to that. I have taught you all you need, but getting to the top depends on you. That is the way of the world."

For a while the boys went on grumbling, but bedtime came, and they all fell asleep except Frantik and Jura, who kept on whispering to each other for a long time before they could agree just how they would get one goal after another against Planička of the Slavia Club of Prague, a remarkably fine goalkeeper.

In the spring the League matches started. The Chattertooths went to Prague. They were to make their first appearance against the Hlubočepy Football and Athletic Club. Nobody had ever heard of the Chattertooth Eleven, and the crowd made jokes about the name and grinned from ear to ear at the appearance of the eleven shy village lads who had never seen a town before. They had lambskin caps on their heads, and as for their trainer, well, this old country fellow with his pipe in the corner of his mouth looked as if he didn't know how many beans made two.

From the moment the whistle blew, however, the Chattertooths piled on the goals, and at halftime led 39–0. That proved too much for the team with the highfalutin name, and they did not appear after the interval. They explained that the League Committee had made a mistake, and that the opposing team certainly did not belong to the third division. Old Chattertooth sat there, with an ear cocked first in this direction and then in that, so that not a word escaped him of what people around him were saying. He smiled to himself in silent amusement, chuckled and shifted his pipe from one corner of his mouth to the other, and his eyes shone like a tomcat's. Finally, when he heard the referee say that there had been some mistake that he would report to the provincial committee, he fetched the boys from the pavilion, patted them approvingly on the back, one by one, and led them off home.

On Wednesday the postman turned up with a fat letter. The letter said that by a decision of the provincial committee the Chattertooth Eleven had been promoted to the second division and was to play the Vršovice Sports Club on the following Sunday. Old Chattertooth chuckled quietly, and the boys gurgled with laughter.

Sunday found them in Vršovice. Thousands of people had collected there, for the news had spread from Prague of what a remarkable team these Chattertooths were. The old man, with the inevitable pipe in his mouth, once more sat there blinking at the boys as they won 14–0. Once again there was a babel of protests, and once more a fat letter turned up—the Chattertooth Eleven was in the first division.

Now it was no longer possible to jump into a higher division. And so they just had to go on beating one club after another: the Headers Sports Club 13–0, the Neck-or-Nothing Athletic Club 16–0, the Cokernut Club 12–0, the Kladno Spartans 11–0, the Czech Karlin 9–0, the Meteors of Prague VIII 10–0, the CAFC 8–0, the Plzeň Sports Club 15–0, the Teplice Athletic Football Club 7–0, and the Victoria 6–0.

In the semifinals they found themselves up against the famous Sparta Eleven. For a week beforehand old Chattertooth put them into light training, massaged them thoroughly, and on Sunday, just before the match, he reshuffled his team. Two hours later he sent his wife a telegram:

MRS. CHATTERTOOTH WOODSIDE COTTAGE NETHER BUCKWHEAT SPARTA BEATEN SIX NIL STOP HONZA FELL ASLEEP IN GOAL WITH BOREDOM STOP CHATTERTOOTH.

On the same Sunday the Slavia Club beat the Union Club 3–2.

A week later the Chattertooth Eleven met the victorious club. There was such a crowd in the stadium that the soldiers had to be called out to close all the roads leading to it. Any other matches arranged for the day were cancelled so that everyone could watch the Chattertooth Eleven.

The boys came by omnibus from Nether Buckwheat to the stadium. Old Chattertooth sat beside the driver and watched the crowd. He led his sons into the dressing room and stayed with them until they were in their football costume. Then he said:

"Well, boys, are you going to show 'em what you can do?"

"Of course," they answered.

Two of the committee came and led the father to the seats of honour, where they placed him next to the mayor of Prague, the chief of the police, and the minister of finance. Smoking was forbidden there, but when old Chattertooth took out his pipe the chief of police gave a sign to the man on duty not to stop him.

When the Chattertooth Eleven appeared there was sudden confusion as sixty photographers charged on to the field to take photographs of the miracle team. At last order was restored, and the referee blew his whistle.

The Chattertooth boys were at the top of their form. The Slavia team, too, played a good game, but at halftime the score was 3–0 for the Chattertooth Eleven. In the second half they got another three, and won easily by 6–0. The boys from Nether Buckwheat were borne back in triumph to their hotel by the crowd, shoulder high. In front of the hotel there was such a crowd that the chief of police had to beg Mr. Chattertooth to address them; otherwise they would have refused to budge. So old Chattertooth went out on to the balcony, took his pipe from his mouth, pushed his lambskin cap on the back of his head, and, once the wildly cheering crowd below him had calmed down, began:

"Well, it's like this. I just said to them, well, boys, I said, you just learn 'em. And they did learn 'em. There's nothing like children doing what they're told by their parents."

And that was the speech made by old Chattertooth to twenty thousand people when his team had won the championship with a total score of 122–0.

9. Holland, a Country of Clubs

Simon Kuper

As Simon Kuper observes, Dutch culture offers ample space for football and, through players and coaches attuned to the best uses of this space, has helped create a playing style pleasing to the eye and satisfying for the intellect. Playing the game in one's head is a characteristic that Kuper attributes to Johan Cruyff, the "Pythagoras in boots" whose nimble playmaking qualities perhaps best represented the great Ajax of Amsterdam teams from 1966 to 1973. Under the guidance of coaches Rinus Michels and Ştefan Kovacs, Ajax won six Dutch titles and three European Cups during that period. With a philosophy that allowed players freedom to utilize space to their best advantage—switching positions as needed and combining to create attractive passing moves—Ajax and then later the Dutch national team placed their stamp on what came to be known as "total football."

In *Brilliant Orange: The Neurotic Genius of Dutch Football* (2000) David Winner provides an enchanting, if speculative, application of Dutch sensibilities regarding art and space-planning to soccer. Winner speaks to landscape architects, photographers, and art historians to tease out how a Dutch penchant for order and inspired uses of space—important in one of the world's most densely populated countries—makes the native football unique. Postmodernist sculptor Jeroen Henneman, for example, calls Holland and Arsenal striker Dennis Bergkamp "a great artist" for space-creating passes that compare favorably to the innovations of Jan Vermeer and Piet Mondrian in Dutch painting.

Kuper's synthesis of insights from anthropology and culture studies, coupled with an on-site reporting style that he pioneered in *Football against the Enemy* (1994; see also the Further Reading section at the end of this volume for more on soccer and the social sciences), has itself been innovative. Kuper writes on sports, politics, and culture for the *Financial Times* and contributes to the Dutch literary football magazine *Hard gras*, among other publications.

He has also addressed lesser-known aspects of Dutch collaboration with the Nazis during World War II in *Ajax, the Dutch, the War: Football in Europe during the Second World War* (2003).

When I moved to the Netherlands in October 1976, I was seven years old and had never previously heard of the country. Only later did I realise I had landed in the middle of a golden age.

My father had taken a job in the town of Leiden, and our new house stood on what I now take to be a typical Dutch street. The tiny terraced houses were fronted by huge windows, through which passers-by could peer in to make sure nothing untoward was happening inside.

On our first Dutch evening my brother and I ventured onto the street to meet the other children. They greeted us by singing what were probably the only English words they knew: "Crazy boys, crazy boys!" But over the next few evenings relations improved. Soon we became regulars in the street's daily football match. I had barely ever kicked a football before. In London, where I had lived before, nobody I knew had. But in Leiden everybody did. The Netherlands in the 1970s was the world's premier footballing country. From Jacques Tati to Rudolf Nureyev, the world watched entranced.

My first memory of watching football is the World Cup of 1978. Holland was then so predictably good that while they were thrashing Austria 5–0, a friend and I got bored and went to kick a ball around on the field behind our house. Holland reached the final. Playing against Argentina in Buenos Aires, in a stadium packed with the armed soldiers who then ruled the country, the Dutch went down 1–0 early on. Then, a lanky flower seller from the northern Netherlands named Dick Nanninga headed the ball into the confetti-strewn Argentine net. I can still hear the cheer erupting from our neighbouring houses. But Argentina won, 3–1.

I left the Netherlands in 1986 and now feel Dutch in one regard only. I root for Oranje (as we call them in Holland). So does practically the entire population. Even this summer, when Holland appeared at the 2004 European Championships in Portugal with a team of sated has-been multimillionaires, their big matches were watched on TV by two-thirds of all Dutch people. No other European team regularly draws such a proportion of its population.

Not only the Dutch support Oranje. So do millions of other people from Jakarta to Timbuktu who barely know that the Netherlands is a country as well as a football team. The reason is not merely that the Dutch tend to win, although they do: Marco van Basten, below only Cruyff in the pantheon of the country's football idols, is currently building a new team worthy of the orange shirts.

The important thing is that the Dutch play the beautiful game. No other country its size has produced players to match Cruyff, van Hanegem, van Basten, Rijkaard, Bergkamp, or van Nistelrooy (with van Robben rising fast). Of the larger countries, only Brazil has. In the seventeenth century the Dutch produced great and distinctive painters. Now this overcrowded country of just sixteen million people manufactures footballers. Why? At the risk of giving away the secret, I will explain.

Soon after my arrival I discovered that every Dutch boy belonged to a football club. In Leiden, which then had just over one hundred thousand inhabitants, there were dozens. Some of them fielded twenty senior teams, seven teams of under-eights, and so on. Not to play football was not to exist. My brother and I joined the Ajax Sportman Combinatie (ASC), a club founded in 1892, which had once been one of Holland's best and still possessed a genuine grandstand with terracing. ASC was no longer any good, but that never deflected me.

As a child I would rise each Saturday at 7:00 a.m. and race to the ground. The gates would still be locked, but my teammates and I would rattle them until someone, at last, unlocked them around 8:00 a.m. Then we would play on ASC's gravel pitch until our match kicked off. Afterwards we would hang around the ground hoping for a game with another team. Then we would go to someone's house to play football. When football was rained out—a time of bleak despair in the Kuper household—we would race to the ground anyway, where we would be taken to a hall to play indoors or be shown videos of the 1974 and 1978 World Cups.

Most Dutch boys spent their youth this way. Of the fourteen million people living in Holland in the seventies, one million played football at clubs like ASC. No other country had a higher proportion of registered footballers. Franz Beckenbauer said he finally understood why Dutch players were so good when he flew over Holland in a helicopter and saw that it consisted chiefly of football grounds.

No wonder we all played. My parents paid ASC about fifty pounds a year, and in return my brother and I were allowed virtually to live at the club. Twice a week we were trained by coaches who had completed long courses for the privilege. One had played professional football. We played on pitches obsessively watered and mowed by the local council. Dutch football, in fact, is a testament to Dutch social democracy.

In England, when two lovers of football meet, the first question is "Which club do you support?" In the Netherlands the question is "Which club do you play for?" The Dutch are players first, fans second. I once asked Boudewijn Zenden, who plays for Middlesbrough and Holland, which club he had supported as a child. None, he said. Nor did he have posters of idols on his walls. Zenden played.

When I later returned to England, I met people who loved football, watched their team each weekend, but never kicked a ball. I discovered that in Britain it is hard to get the chance. Between 1981 and 1997, under the Conservative governments of Margaret Thatcher and John Major, about five thousand British playing fields were sold and turned into houses or supermarkets.

Albert Camus, the late goalkeeper and sometime novelist, said, "All that I know most surely about morality and the obligations of man, I owe to football." Well, all that I know most surely about Holland, I owe to football. Playing the game was an education in the country. We encountered teams from seaside villages where the people were so devoutly Protestant they didn't play on Sundays. They lived on brown bread, fish, and dairy products, so that even in the under-elevens many of them stood well over 1.8 metres tall. Edwin van der Sar, Holland's giant goalkeeper, comes from one of those clubs.

In villages further inland, where the local farmers had become millionaires selling flowers to the world, the local teams drew crowds of several thousand. The best players received such lavish under-the-table payments from the farmers that many refused offers to turn professional, saying they couldn't afford to.

Each club we played against had a distinctive culture: Protestant or posh, bulb-farming or Dutch Caribbean. The Netherlands is a country of clubs. The Dutch have the time for it. They work an average of thirty-two hours a week, less than any other country in the Organisation for Economic Co-operation and Development. Most Dutch offices are deserted by 5:00 p.m. My father usually returned home at lunchtime and spent afternoons skulking indoors in case a colleague saw him. When he went outside, my father used his leisure time to play cricket. Most people used it for football.

But playing was only one way of passing time at the club. Many Dutchmen think that their real job is chairing their football club or its materials committee or coaching the fourteenth team. Club culture in Holland is universal. Ajax Sportman Combinatie was one of the country's worst clubs, yet it was recognisably related to the best, which also happened to be called Ajax.

When Ajax of Amsterdam was founded in 1900, its board asked my club's permission to use the name Ajax. We granted it, but said we would review the matter a century later. Ajax agreed. Sadly, by the time 2000 rolled around ASC had mislaid Ajax's letter. The Amsterdammers have thus retained their name.

In the 1970s Ajax of Amsterdam was still a neighbourhood club rather like ASC. It just happened to be the best neighbourhood club on earth. Ajax won three consecutive European Cups between 1971 and 1973, with a team consisting mainly of local boys who would provide the nucleus of "total football."

Of the forward trio, Sjaak Swart (the outside right) and Piet Keizer (the outside left) each grew up a short walk from the old Ajax ground. Johan Cruyff, the center forward, as a child would toddle up the road to watch the Ajax first team train.

I once met Swart in his restaurant above an ice rink, just behind where the old Ajax stadium had stood. "The other day," said Swart, "I walked into the canteen at the new Ajax ground and Johan and Piet were sitting there. And I come in and I shout, 'There they are again, the great forward line!'"

Then they all had a coffee. I can imagine a similar scene at ASC. So rooted are Dutchmen in club culture that when a star retires, he often instantly finds himself another, lesser club. Swart played nearly twenty years of amateur football after quitting Ajax. Wim Meutstege, an Ajax player in the late 1970s, later joined ASC. Frank Rijkaard, before emigrating to manage FC Barcelona, played for the third veterans' eleven of his local club, Abcoude.

Rijkaard told me: "We have a nice team, a team of friends, and for an hour and a half we chase, run, play football. Well, fantastic! And then you've sweated, you've done something, and you go into the canteen and drink a beer and chat about the game. Often you have a nice opponent, have a joke along the way. I have no aspirations to anything more."

I once watched Rijkaard's contemporary, Ruud Gullit, play for the fifth Saturday team of the Amsterdam amateur club AFC. They were playing the third eleven of a club called OSDO, and there were about twenty spectators, one of whom remarked to his son: "Look, that's Ruud Gullit." "Does he play for OSDO?" the boy asked. The father was shocked: "Ruud Gullit, who played in Italy and for the Dutch team! You know him, don't you?" "Yeah, yeah, you're kidding me," said the boy. One could understand the child's doubts, because by halftime Gullit's side was down 5–0 , though they eventually recovered to lose just 5–3. Yet Gullit looked happy. Once or twice he almost scored, but on each occasion he missed the ball entirely. After the game he shook everyone's hand and congratulated the pygmy woman referee. As he walked off the pitch, he exclaimed to nobody in particular: "The second half was better!" We have all left the field on a Saturday afternoon thinking exactly that.

Gullit has since gained promotion. He now plays for AFC's third eleven, alongside his fellow former internationals Van Basten and Aron Winter.

The mere fact that almost everyone in Holland plays football cannot itself explain the country's success. Until the 1970s Dutch football was mediocre. Holland would occasionally lose to Luxembourg and viewed Belgium as their great rivals.

It was Johan Cruyff who made the Dutch good at football, but it took me a while to realise this. In October 1976, when I arrived, Cruyff was disappearing from the scene. He still played for Barcelona, but had already said he would skip the World Cup in Argentina. He retired from football in 1978. Then, discovering that he had lost his fortune in a pig-farming venture, he began playing again in the United States.

So I only discovered him on December 6, 1981, when he returned to Ajax. This little man, his body wrecked by two decades of chain-smoking and being kicked, astounded me most Sundays for the next three years.

Cruyff shaped all Dutch footballers: Gullit and Rijkaard who played with him, the Dutch internationals of today, and all of us at ASC. He got us talking about football. Cruyff himself, when he later became a manager, would complain: "The moment you open your mouth to breathe, Dutch footballers say, 'Yes, but . . .'" However, that was his own fault. It was Cruyff who turned Dutch football into a sort of academic debating society. "Football is a game you play with your head," he once said. Other countries don't see it that way. I once asked Gullit to compare English, Italian, and Dutch footballers. "In a Dutch changing room," he said, "everyone thinks he knows best. In an Italian changing room everybody probably also thinks he knows best, but nobody dares to tell the manager." And in England? "In an English changing room they just have a laugh."

I have interviewed British chief executives, Argentine generals, and Ukrainian mafiosi, but the most talkative people I know are Dutch footballers. You speak to them for hours, ask every question imaginable, and when you finally turn off the tape recorder they hold forth for another half hour. Sjaak Swart, who told me before the interview that he had no time, said, when I finally managed to cut him short, "Another cup of coffee, boy?"

I always root for the Dutch. But I never expect them to win prizes. That is because the Dutch think winning is irrelevant. I realised this in 1990 when I took my English football team on tour to Holland. We won our first match 8–0, and afterwards, over a beer in the canteen, one of our Dutch opponents said to me: "But of course we played the better football." He meant that his team had combined better, thought harder, played the prettier game, whereas we had merely been brutish. He was talking nonsense, but he was making a common Dutch point: that playing "good football" matters more than winning.

To the Dutch, "good football" is the passing, thinking, balletic game invented by Cruyff. The master himself has taken to saying that Holland "really" won the World Cup of 1974, even though they lost in the final. How so? Well, argues Cruyff, everyone still remembers the beautiful football Holland played, and that is a victory more enduring than any mere final score.

Guus Hiddink, coach of the Dutch side that reached the semifinals of the 1998 World Cup playing beautiful football, said later, "Our style, our philosophy has impressed the world and that's what I'm proud of. I don't know if I'd have been happy with a World Cup won in a bad way." No coach of any other country could have said that. Marco van Basten even has a clause in his contract committing him to playing "Dutch" attacking football. Whatever happens at the next World Cup, though, a few weeks later he will be doing his pirouettes for AFC thirds.

10. Readymade

Álvaro Enrigue
Translated from the Spanish by Anna Kushner

In some ways the search for a club to support resembles the search for home. Novelist Álvaro Enrigue, a writer for the literary magazine *Letras libres*, creates a conundrum as to where allegiances lie in this fictional account—an account that blends real names, places, and occurrences from Mexican soccer. Considering the competing claims of teams that boast nationwide support—Chivas de Guadalajara as well as Club América from Mexico City and Pumas of Universidad Nacional Autónoma de México—Enrigue nevertheless lingers on his character's associations with Atlético Pachuca. The team is based in the capital of Hidalgo state, Pachuca, fifty miles north of Mexico City and part of the Mesa Central, the high plateau on which the Aztec civilization developed in the thirteenth century. British laborers who had come to mine the region's prodigious silver resources created the team in 1901, having taken to playing football in their off hours.

The concreteness of Enrigue's description, which incorporates iconoclastic nicknames, a supporters' group led by sex workers (a circumstance validated by Enrigue's research), and the antiquated wooden seating at Pachuca's Revolución Mexicana stadium, testifies to the cultural depth of *fútbol* in Mexico. Ball games are attested throughout Mesoamerica, dating to the Olmecs of central Mexico some three thousand years ago. Aztecs had developed a prototype for the game, *tchatali*, using as goals decorated stone rings mounted in cavernous ball courts. Estadio Azteca, which hosted the World Cup finals in 1970 and 1986, lies south of the ruins of the Aztec capital, Tenochtitlan, over which the federal district of Mexico City was later constructed.

Enrigue's tale originates from a reading that he gave in Pachuca, where he dined at Juicy's taquería and first heard about Alfonso Madrigal, known as "the Fool." "While Juicy showed me around his very strange restaurant—very ceremoniously," Enrigue writes, "I asked him who that guy was, and how such a pot-bellied guy could have played soccer. Then he told me the Fool's story, which I later confirmed in the local newspaper archive with the assistance of Juan Carlos Hidalgo—writer and avid Tuzos fan—and Carlos Calderón," a soccer historian. Enrigue describes Madrigal as a "found object," yet one with the capacity to execute a bicycle kick. Early in the twentieth century French conceptual artist Marcel Duchamp termed his experiments with found objects "readymades," from which Enrigue takes his title.

For Juan Carlos Hidalgo and Carlos Calderón

1.

Alfonso "the Fool" Madrigal played his first match in Pachuca during the summer of 1966. He went in as a substitute during the second half, wearing the blue-and-white jersey he'd play with for the rest of his career. He hailed from Tepito and his game was true to his neighborhood's stereotype: clever, easygoing, and flashy. He was apt to score unbelievable goals whenever he could keep his balance on the field, something that didn't always happen: occasionally he fell over while fighting for the ball and couldn't get back up again because he was too drunk. He played his last match in 1978. It was in the playoffs—something that would have been unthinkable for the Pachuca Tuzos, always debating between first, second, and even third division, before he joined their ranks.

2.

I was born in 1969, when the Fool was already a central figure in the Pachuca lineup. When I was born in Guadalajara, my father already knew he was being transferred to the nation's capital—each of my siblings is from a different city. At first, we lived in the Diplomático Hotel. The neighborhood had a market and a supermarket, a bullring, and an American football stadium. There was a stationery store, a sewing supplies shop, and a hardware store. There was also a bank and a taco restaurant—no pizzeria, though, because those didn't make it to Mexico until the late seventies. Everything was within walking distance. Since my mother never learned how to drive—she is the last person in Western Civilization for whom swimming and driving weren't part of basic education—they rented an apartment nearby, on Augusto Rodin Street. It was a world with a luster I've never encountered again, as if everything were tailor-made for us.

3.

Madrigal the Fool could be found almost every day in El Churrero cantina—on Morelos Street, in Pachuca—linking the hangover from the night before to the next drunken spree. During the week, he lived in a small house with his wife, no one really knows where. On Fridays he went straight from El Churrero to the El Abanico brothel, in the city's red-light district, from which he didn't emerge until Sunday to meet his enemy on the field. There's no record of his exploits when the Pachuca Club played away games. As a matter of fact, no record of anything exists: we don't know how many career goals he scored despite the fact that there were apparently plenty of them, and mostly impossible ones at that.

4.

It turns out that the Augusto Rodin building had an unspoken soccer connection: the Argentinean Dante "Morocho" Juárez—idol of Necaxa—was one of its original residents: he rented apartment 303 with his wife and four children. On the dining-room wall, where half the building's twenty-four families had a still life and the other half, a Last Supper—sometimes painted on black velvet—the Juárez family had a framed Santos do Brasil soccer jersey with the number 10 printed on the back. Pelé's sweat was preserved beneath the glass, more sacred than the food nature bestows on us, or that Aramaic fellow shown blessing said food with his twelve followers. There was also a framed photograph of Morocho and Pelé, exchanging their soccer jerseys in Maracanã stadium. The photo was signed and the glass protecting it was forever smudged with the fingerprints of the entire building's children—back then being cool wasn't a value, so people bred—who ran their fingers over the autograph with hallowed reverence. The back stroke and open circle of the *p*, the elliptic line of the *e*, the *l* and the *e*, the bold accent mark over the final *e*: ´. Pelé. I can still imitate his signature perfectly. I practiced it tirelessly in all my notebooks at school. The teachers circled them in red ink when they collected and graded them. Some of the notebooks—the ones from my most boring classes, I suppose—looked like they had chicken pox.

5.

All the chronicles from that period, let's call it a quaint period, regarding the Pachuca Fútbol Club note that around the time the Fool started playing for the team, the folks who religiously attended the "Mexican Revolution" Stadium formed the team's first official fan squads. The most famous one of all was led by Juicy, who guided his followers with a blue-and-white pennant. His squad no longer exists, but you can still see him presiding over a fancy taco establishment downtown. On the opposite side of the stadium—across from Juicy's ostensibly decent fans—was the whores' fan squad. On Sundays they descended in a pack from the city heights and filled their section of cheap bleacher seats. If the game was against a lesser team and attendance was poor, the hookers spread themselves out in the stands forming the word "Pachus" with their lustful bodies. They worshiped Madrigal the Fool.

6.

My aunt Nuria got married and moved into the Augusto Rodin building where we lived. She's from Veracruz: clever, easygoing, and flashy—maybe all Mexicans are that way, except me. I thought her apartment was an extension of our own—and I'm not sure this was the case for my siblings as well; probably not, since I was clearly the favorite. Even though they were separated by three floors I don't recall ever climbing the stairs: our green-carpeted home continued into her red-carpeted one—ah, the seventies, so Kubrick. Nuria would cut my hair and then pay me for the cut (one peso), take me to the Giant supermarket and buy me a Tinlarín chocolate bar, then sit me down at her kitchen counter. It had a splendid view that is probably the reason for the meditative paralysis that Mexico City's skies still bring out in me during the rainy season. Moreover, she told me I was from

Pachuca. She would say this, obviously, to amuse herself. I rooted for the Pachuca Tuzos for years because of her.

7.

The coach who brought out the best in Madrigal the Fool was Crooked Candia. The teammates placing the corner kicks he turned into goals were Rodríguez the Bum and Kid Piña. His nemesis from the Atlas—the team they usually contended with on the way down—was Astroboy. Those were the years of Miracle Foot and El Wendy Mendizábal. There's something high-flown and ruthless about these nicknames that makes them memorable. But things were different then, more peculiar: teams like the Leather Tanners' Union or the Farming Athletes were playing first division. Not long ago, I heard a TV commentator dub Guillermo Ochoa, the América's goalkeeper, the Journalist. Allow me to propose something even wittier: let's give Guillermo Ochoa the moniker Guillermo Ochoa.

8.

I doubt Morocho's soccer jersey hangs in Pelé's living room, but his death from cancer still breaks my heart. The last time I saw him, at my sister's wedding, he grabbed me by the back of my neck like he used to—I was already a few inches taller than him, I had already been run out of every school in Mexico, I was already married to my first wife—and he said to me: How's it going, Alvarito? My brain traveled back at lightning speed to those years when the world was perfect even though notebooks had chickenpox; I could discern the smell of chimichurri sauce and empanadas that permeated his apartment, which to us was more like a temple.

9.

There aren't any photographs of Madrigal the Fool in Mexican soccer-history books either, despite his dying young, a martyr to himself, adored by his people. As far as I know, he never entered Pachuca riding a colt, but palms received him at the "Mexican Revolution" Stadium when he descended from the red-light district in a convertible, surrounded by ladies of the night, still fully loaded. His wife welcomed him while his fans cheered.

10.

I doubt my aunt Nuria had ever been to Pachuca when she convinced me I was born there. She would have heard, at any rate, of its reputation for ugliness. But she was from Cordoba, pound for pound a city just as ugly as Pachuca or even more so, despite the splendor of its surroundings. The high-flown and ruthless trick of making me think I was from the state of Hidalgo doubtless originated in how thoroughly bad the team coached by Crooked Candia really was: rooting for the Pachuca Tuzos could only be a joke.

11.

The move that catapulted Madrigal the Fool to fame was a delirious counterattack that took place during a game against Laguna. Its description shows up in more than one contemporary account, so it can't have been mere legend. Apparently, the opponents were ahead, bombarding the Pachuca goal when The Fool had a flash of inspiration, doubtlessly alcoholic in origin. When he was sure no one was looking, he signaled Kid Piña and ran to the corner, hiding behind the flagpole. He remained concealed for some time—no one has been able to explain the sudden invisibility of his notorious belly—until he had the chance. Kid Piña passed him the ball and he ran like lightning, dribbling along the end line. The Laguna players, who were downfield getting ready for what they thought would be a corner kick, couldn't reach him in time. In my humble opinion, the goal of the century was attributed to Maradona—against England, in the 1986 World Cup—only because the Fool's goal against Laguna wasn't broadcast on television.

12.

Probably because of the aura of success Dante Juárez projected during his entire life, many of the South American soccer stars playing in Mexico in the 1970s came to live in our building. There was one who resided there for several years—I'll keep his name to myself. He was efficient and chivalrous: he scored transparent goals, blocked smoothly and forcefully, and placed beautiful assists. His family was adorable: he had a pretty, intelligent wife—just like him—two brilliant and extremely well-behaved children. Soccer balls were suspended in midair whenever the girl yelled to her brother that supper was ready, her emerald-green eyes appearing in the window. One day, when his team narrowly lost the finals, he was knocked down in the goal area and the referee marked a penalty. Words can't describe how long the seconds lasted as we watched him take the shot. He missed. They moved back to Santiago that very same year. In the next decade, the 1980s, my father, who had developed a close friendship with him, went to Chile on business for a few weeks. He searched for him and he found him. He'd become a born-again Christian car salesman, his wife was an alcoholic, his son had run off with the guerrilla fighters, and his daughter was as big as an elephant. Like me, she couldn't hold down a job, and was probably doing drugs as well.

13.

In the "Mexican Revolution" Stadium, games were played on Sunday afternoons, so there were stands in the sun and stands in the shade, just like at a bullfight. The stands were constructed only along the sidelines, so as the fan base grew larger, seats were added in the end zones in a more or less improvised fashion: they were made out of wood and lower than the ones in the rest of the stadium, which was squat per se: next to it was Cubitos Hill, where the match was watched by whoever didn't have money for tickets or by those who preferred to picnic while they watched. The Las Avenidas River ran by one of the end zones, so when a player sent a ball over the goal area, it frequently fell into the river and floated away.

14.

I never recovered from not having been born in Pachuca: my parents' insistence on the fact that I was from Guadalajara was not unlike being cast out of a Paradise. Ever since then, I've been a socceristically disoriented person: I never really warmed up to the Chivas, whom I tried to support with all my heart, forget about the Atlas or the Tecos. Later on I settled in with the Pumas—the local team in Copilco, where I've lived since I was fifteen—but I had a son with my third wife who's an América fan.

15.

Madrigal the Fool could by no means endure all ninety minutes of a match. Given that on his best days he was still drunk when he went in—and on the worst he was hung over—Crooked Candia tended to treat him like a secret weapon, with the mantra—sometimes the plea—that he hold on until the end of the game. If Pachuca was losing by the second half, the crowd generally asked for him, yelling, "Fool-Fool-Fool," led by the hookers' fan club and seconded by Juicy's squad. Then Candia would look at his watch and calculate whether his most imaginative player could handle what was left of the game. If so, he'd give the trainer the signal that Madrigal's turn had come. There are some in Pachuca who say that everyone in the stadium knew the Fool was about to go in when he stood up and danced a few steps like a boxer, which apparently meant he was warming up. Some tell a better, albeit improbable, version of the same story according to which Candia would resist public pressure until the stadium was in an uproar. Then he'd have a word with the trainer, who would get up from his seat, walk over to the cooler, take out a beer, open it, and hold it up like a trophy. The crowd would go wild: their idol was about to step onto the field.

16.

Maybe some Sunday I should go to Pachuca and watch a game at their new stadium. Maybe the world would, once again, be filled with meaning.

11. Soccer Fields, Fort Missoula

Bridget Carson

Finding space to play soccer can be complicated. When the so-called Lost Boys of Sudan wanted to hold practices and games in a park in their new hometown of Clarkston, Georgia, the refugees discovered that soccer was not the only game in town—and not the most favored. The fields were reserved for a different sport according to Clarkston mayor Lee Swaney: "There will be nothing but baseball down there as long as I am mayor." Further up the East Coast in Scarsdale, New York, a group of Hispanic men found themselves the center of a controversy when they organized an impromptu game on a school field, leading to an outcry from residents and the intervention of the school superintendent.

Another form of contested space is evident in the following poem by Bridget Carson. Here the competition lies not with other sports or the perceptions of local residents but with history itself. As the poet discloses in her note on the poem, playing soccer in this space invited the ghosts of the past:

> Fort Missoula, established in 1877 to protect the white townspeople of Missoula, Montana, from nearby indigenous tribes was, among many things, the home of one of four black regiments created after the Civil War and organized into the Twenty-fifth Infantry Bicycle Corps to test the military potential of bicycles, and during World War II, the site of one of the country's internment camps. Once detaining 2,200 Japanese and Italian men, it is now home to several soccer fields managed by the Missoula Parks and Recreation Department. One hundred years since its inception, I began playing soccer there in 1977 at the age of four.

> The flight of the players
> counter-weighted
>
> shifting through a century

over clawed earth
the foot dreams

lifts the stampede

the worn rush
of bicycle wheels

a faded line of fence
washed from view
like ink in sunlight

here is war bent inward
here are birds

living in underbellies
tossing shins at shins

here is a flat rock
cast out over flat water
passing through a mirror

sun caught in cleats
overloads the stiff pines

moves through treetops

a lemon sliced open
on a pale knee-cap

the strikers
searching for a way through air

find the answer kept
in a ricochet

in the first touch
on that uprooted

flash of day.

12. "Get Him a Body Bag!" (A Brief, Enthusiastic Account)

María Graciela Rodríguez
Translated from the Spanish by Miranda Stramel

María Graciela Rodríguez, a specialist in popular culture at the University of Buenos Aires, indulges in the informal *crónica* (chronicle) form to describe her attendance at a match in 1996 between intercapital rivals River Plate and San Lorenzo. Shaping her narrative into brief scenes, Rodríguez recounts the alienation encountered by a woman attending her first *fútbol* match. She enhances the psychic distance from the overwhelmingly male crowd by sitting with the visiting supporters of San Lorenzo or Los Cuervos (Ravens). San Lorenzo is based in the working-class neighborhood of Boedo, one of forty-eight *barrios* (districts) in Buenos Aires. Rodríguez mentions her upbringing among fans of River Plate (from the Nuñez *barrio*)—two-time winners of the continental championship, the Copa Libertadores—who nevertheless have adopted the somewhat derogatory nickname Las Gallinas (Hens).

In her formal research into women at football stadiums in Argentina, Rodríguez studies a case of gender relations in extremis. Periodic violence and ritualized homophobic chanting, as studied by anthropologist Eduardo Archetti, create space for acting out one type of masculine ideal: "The affirmation of masculinity," Archetti wrote, "depends upon depriving the other of his masculinity." Several of Rodríguez's own interview subjects (both women and men) contend that women lack the expertise and innate passion to understand football's significance, transmitted through elaborate rituals and chants and carried somewhere within the male body. One twenty-eight-year-old man says simply, "Football is a manly thing and is played by men." Archetti has also argued that the lyrics of classical tango are another area of male identity formation in Argentine culture; appropriately, Rodríguez begins with a quotation from Enrique Santos Discépolo, a renowned composer of tangos in the 1920s and 1930s.

Your presence is a torment
that tortures without killing
DISCÉPOLO

Scene I: The Initiation

Not long ago I went to the soccer field to see River Plate versus San
Lorenzo. Although I'm a *gallina* (hen) by birth (one doesn't question
these inheritances), I put on the hat of the visiting team with a fan of
San Lorenzo, who instructed me not to yell for any goals that weren't
made by a *cuervo* (raven). My lack of experience with going to the field
and my less than passionate allegiance to River were my saving graces:
River played masterfully and won 4–0. And not only was I floored,
but by the end I was suffering as much as my friend.

I went to have fun, with the spirit of the noninitiated. I went to take
notes of the things that happened to me. I went without the pressure of
hard work but knowing that the experience would surely be reflected in
my worldview. I asked Ramiro, the lucky friend that fancied taking me,
about the codes of the crowd. I delighted in the cheers (they had told
me that San Lorenzo has the most creative fans), and, fundamentally,
I dedicated myself to observing the spectacle of fans, including the
moments in which I was too distracted to watch the game at all.

Scene II: The Observation

I anticipated that the first thing I would notice was the absence of
television, and I wasn't wrong: I missed knowing the names of the
players, seeing their faces, having access to distinct angles of a shot,
the replay of a goal, and so on. Television organizes perception in a
determined manner, observes for you, classifies the details, puts the
plays into a hierarchy.

But in some ways this makes you lazy: In little time I realized that if
I followed the ball, I missed the referee's calls or the fouls or the fights.
In a way I had to unlearn a form of constructed observation thanks
to the work of the cameras in order to begin to see the players and
the surroundings, the trajectory of the ball and its destiny, the signals

of the referee and what was occurring around him. Something that, obviously, Ramiro knew how to do, as I suppose all those accustomed to converging in the stadiums know.

To go to the field and to watch the match on television are two distinct, perhaps complementary ways, of watching soccer. The illusion that at a live match there is a more "free" view is debatable: The supposed freedom of my view impeded me from seeing some central matters, such as a potential penalty or something that may have led to a goal. Maybe the trained view of Ramiro isn't any more "free" than mine?

Scene III: The Codification of Passions

This organization of perception that television creates for us, those of us that don't go to the field, was something predictable, although I should confess that its absence was significant. That I, a River fan (though not the type of fanatic that would permit real emotional liability), was in no time cheering for San Lorenzo was what was unpredictable. There was this *gallina,* in the middle of the visiting fans, yelling things like: "I can fight! I'm insane! I'm from Boedo, and I take coke!"

Just as the television organizes perception and makes it lazy, being a fan controls one's emotions and makes one biased. With a foul, for example, there are only two possible feelings: (1) "Motherfucker! Take back that red card!" if it is against our team, or (2) "Kill the son of a bitch! You deserve it, cheater!" if it is in our favor. Or, more poetically: "Get him a body bag!" as one fan yelled.

Scene IV: Identification of the "Other" . . .

Passions, when they are unpredictable, as mine were, are influenced by the rhythm of a crowd that tells you who is the tyrant and who is the victim, when someone is an animal because he throws the ball at the stands and when he does it because of hard luck, where the enemy is (there, on the other side of the stands, yelling lies) and where the friend is (here, in our enclosure, which we occupy for a little while).

None of this makes sense without the other, without the enemy that marks us, that tells us who we are ("from Boedo"). I remember watching a teenager, who was a few feet below me, converse with a River fan at a distance. They were talking, gesturing, and reading each other's lips. They communicated: "And what do you have to say now . . . ?" "Sit down, sweetheart, I don't want to hear it." "Yeah, right, look at you guys." If the other didn't exist, who would you yell "asshole" at?

Scene V: . . . and the "Supporter"

Yet the presence of the other becomes untenable when we are losing, although, at the same time, without it, one can't exercise the martyrdom of defeat. His presence isn't accidental—it's at the same time necessary and intolerable, essential and distressing. As Discépolo wrote, "Your presence is a torment that tortures without killing."

San Lorenzo, visiting and down to ten players, is losing 0–2, already half an hour in. River is dancing on the field. And in the stands ten thousand guys dressed in red and white wave their T-shirts and chant little songs in unison that insult the *cuervos*. I am there, in the middle of the San Lorenzo fans hoping that Ramiro will let me know the party is over and that we are going. None of that. One must suffer the endless halftime to demonstrate to the other side that we aren't quitters.

In my own flesh, and for the first time in my life, I understand what "supporter" means: it takes a lot of balls to sit in the stands, quiet and stoic, the humiliation of the River fans' cheers inflamed by a dance that will end 4–0. I comment to Ramiro that the "endurance" is a true torment in the most strict, monastic sense, a comment that to him, a passionate supporter of San Lorenzo, seemed obvious. Then, at the same time, I realized that it is a very masculine feeling, almost exclusive to men. Because the "endurance" is to support a symbolic death without saying a word; it is to demonstrate a manliness from which one gains added valor.

Scene VI: The Rematch

We leave, finally, with hanging heads, a few minutes before the end of the game, while at our backs millions (or was it only thousands?)

of these *gallinas* who are pecking at us, champions of the Copa Libertadores, yell like giants. And I make a promise to Ramiro that the next time we go to see a home game San Lorenzo will almost certainly win. To be able to feel the euphoria of victory. If it is against River, even better.

Part 2. Improvisation

Soccer is . . . the athletic equivalent of stream-of-consciousness writing, and its all-time greatest artists . . . practically scribbled *Finnegans Wake* in the sod with their cleats. — REED JOHNSON, *Los Angeles Times*

Introduction

Footballs made out of rags, out of plastic bags . . . pickup games on the street, the beach, in a backyard or an abandoned lot . . . gym bags or crumpled coats to serve as goalposts . . . playing in sneakers, boots, street shoes, or barefoot . . .

Almost any orb can be pressed into service. Dropped onto a thigh and juggled in the air, it becomes a football. On the roadside, a soda can. I see it and squash it under my foot, then kick it to you. You kick it back. Suddenly we're in the middle of a game of football. I'll be Pelé. You be Zinédine Zidane. They were never teammates, but now they are.

Football, as many have noted, is a game characterized by improvisation.

In this section we include works that celebrate this theme, whether by isolating a single player juggling a ball after practice or by tracing a series of seemingly random passes that lead to a sensational goal in a European Cup final. Some of the pieces take unusual angles (a popular musician playing a concert while hearing backstage rumors of his team's possible, impossible comeback) while others are so common as to be universal (a boy listening to a balky radio with his ear pressed to the receiver). From the autobiography of a legendary English player, we hear of a spontaneous lie that grew over years with fans and fellow players colluding in the lie. Still other entries represent innovative forms of writing, such as an Argentine writer's surreal depiction of football under military dictatorship.

Common among these selections, however, is the spirit of improvisation—the desire to make something happen out of the time-bound and limited resources of the moment.

13. Young Shoots

Lady Murasaki

Translated from the Japanese by Arthur Waley

The following excerpt comes from chapter 34 (entitled "Wakana, Part One" or "Young Shoots") of Lady Murasaki's eleventh-century Japanese masterpiece, *The Tale of Genji*. The passage depicts a game called *kemari*, a recreation of Japanese courtiers—part of a family of noncompetitive East Asian ball games—that featured clusters of players in formal court regalia "juggling" a deerskin-covered ball. Tracking the "score" in *kemari* was possible and based on several aesthetic criteria that emphasized beauty. The four goals described are trees that occupied designated corners of the ball-playing courtyard. Customarily these were a black pine, a cherry tree, a willow, and a maple, which the translator, Arthur Waley, indicates were "growing in tubs."

Kemari features elsewhere in Japanese literature as well, particularly within the traditional Noh theater and in the journals of renowned *kemari* players of the royal courts. In his summaries in *The Nō Plays of Japan* (1921), Waley refers to the journal of twelfth-century football player Fujiwara no Narimichi. After celebrating his thousandth game, Fujiwara describes a visitation by three "football sprites" who identify themselves as "Spring Willow Flower," "Quiet Summer Wood," and "Autumn Garden." "Pray remember our names," the sprites tell Fujiwara, "and deign to become our *Mi-mori*, 'Honourable Guardian.' Your success at *Mi-mari*, 'Honourable Football,' will then continually increase."

During the third month there was a spell of delightful weather, and on one of these bright, still days Prince Sochi and To no Chujo's son Kashiwagi called at the New Palace. "I am afraid things are very quiet here," Genji said to them. "At this time of the year, when there are no public or private festivities of any kind, it is harder than ever to keep people amused. I wish I could think of some way to distract you. . . .

Yugiri was here just now. I cannot think what has become of him. I suppose we shall have to watch some more of this shooting on horseback; though I confess that for my part I am sick to death of it. I expect Yugiri caught sight of some of the young men who always clamour for it, and that was why he vanished so soon." "I saw Yugiri," someone said. "He is in the fields near the Race-course, playing football. There are a lot of them there. . . ." "I am not myself very fond of watching football," said Genji. "It is a rough game. But I feel that today we all need something to wake us up . . ." and he sent a message to Yugiri asking him to come round to the front of the house. The young man presently appeared accompanied by a band of courtiers. "I hope you have not left your ball behind," he said to them. "How have you arranged the teams?" Yugiri told them how they had been playing, and promised to find a fresh ground where the game could be seen from the windows of the house. The Crown Princess having now rejoined her husband, her apartments were vacant, and as there was a large stretch of ground not intersected by rivulets or in any other way obstructed, this seemed the best place to set up the posts. To no Chujo's sons, both young and old, were all expert players. Neither the hour nor the weather could have been bettered, for it was the late afternoon, and there was not a breath of wind. Even Kobai abandoned himself with such excitement to the game that Genji said: "Look at our Privy Counsellor! He has quite forgotten all his dignities. Well, I see no harm in a man shouting and leaping about, whatever his rank may be, provided he is quite young. But I am afraid I have long passed the age when one can go through such violent contortions without becoming ridiculous. Look at that fellow's posture now. You must admit it would suit a man of my years very ill."

Yugiri soon induced Kashiwagi to join in the game, and as, against a background of flowering trees, these two sped hither and thither in the evening sunlight, the rough, noisy game suddenly took on an unwonted gentleness and grace. This, no doubt, was in part due to the character of the players; but also to the influence of the scene about them. For all around were great clumps of flowering bushes and trees, every blossom now open to its full. Among the eager group gathered round the goal-post, itself tinged with the first faint promise of green, none was more intent upon victory than Kashiwagi, whose face showed clearly enough that there was a question of measuring his skill against that of opponents, even in a mere game; it would be torment to him not to prove himself in a different class from all the other players. And indeed he had not been in the game for more than a few moments when it became apparent, from the way in which he gave even the most casual kick to the ball, that there was no one to compare with him. Not only was he an extremely handsome man, but he took great pains about his appearance and always moved with a certain rather cautious dignity and deliberation. It was therefore very entertaining to see him leaping this way and that, regardless of all decorum. The cherry-tree was quite near the steps of the verandah from which Genji and Nyosan were watching the game, and it was strange to see how the players, their eye on the ball, did not seem to give a thought to those lovely flowers even when they were standing right under them. By this time the costumes of the players were considerably disordered, and even the most dignified amongst them had a ribbon flying loose or a hat-string undone. Among these dishevelled figures a constant shower of blossom was falling.

14. A Boy Juggling a Soccer Ball

Christopher Merrill

In anticipation of the 1994 World Cup finals, hosted for the first time by the United States, poet Christopher Merrill published a prose memoir entitled *The Grass of Another Country: A Journey through the World of Soccer* (1993). In its pages he hoped to describe not only a sport but a way of life, "one foreign to most Americans." Referring to his book as "a chronicle of exploration into soccer," he defined his purpose as making "the game understandable and interesting to readers who may join the rest of the world in watching World Cup 1994."

In the following poem Merrill—himself a former player and coach who grew up in soccer-rich New Jersey—continues to make his subject both understandable and interesting. Focusing on a lone soccer player juggling a ball after a day of practice, Merrill reveals the universal urge to test one's limits and the sheer joy at pulling off one trick after another.

> after practice: right foot
> to left foot, stepping forward and back,
>   to right foot and left foot,
> and left foot up to his thigh, holding
>   it on his thigh as he twists
> around in a circle, until it rolls
>   down the inside of his leg,
> like a tickle of sweat, now catching
>   and tapping on the soft
> side of his foot, and juggling
>   once, twice, three times,
> hopping on one foot like a jump-roper
>   in the gym, now trapping
> and holding the ball in midair,

balancing it on the instep
of his weak left foot, stepping forward
    and forward and back, then
lifting it overhead until it hangs there;
    and squaring off his body,
he keeps the ball aloft with a nudge
    of his neck, heading it
from side to side, softer and softer,
    like a dying refrain,
until the ball, slowing, balances
    itself on his hairline,
the hot sun and sweat filling his eyes
    as he jiggles this way
and that, then flicking it up gently,
    hunching his shoulders
and tilting his head back, he traps it
    in the hollow of his neck,
and bending at the waist, sees his shadow,
    his dangling T-shirt, the bent
blades of brown grass in summer heat;
    and relaxing, the ball slipping
down his back . . . and missing his foot.
    He wheels around, he marches
over the ball, as if it were a rock
    he stumbled into, and pressing
his left foot against it, he pushes it
    against the inside of his right
until it pops into the air, is heeled
    over his head—the rainbow!—
and settles on his extended thigh before
    rolling over his knee and down
his shin, so he can juggle it again
    from his left foot to his right foot
—and right foot to left foot to thigh—
    as he wanders, on the last day
of summer, around the empty field.

15. Fallen from the Sky

Javier Marías
Translated from the Spanish by Miranda Stramel

Spanish poet, novelist, and translator Javier Marías, writing in the Madrid newspaper *El País*, comments on a game-winning goal from Zinédine Zidane—a left-footed, swivel-hipped strike on a looping cross from Real Madrid defender Roberto Carlos—that in May 2002 helped the "Madridistas" win their ninth European Cup 2–1 over German Bundesliga opponents Bayer Leverkusen at Hampden Park in Glasgow, Scotland. Marías makes no claims to objectivity—the title of his 1992 novel, *Corazón tan blanco* (A Heart So White), alludes partly to the white shirts of Real Madrid.

As a statement of the improvisational capacities of one of the greatest players, Zidane's goal earned high marks even in the arts community. Richard Holloway, a former Episcopal bishop appointed head of the Scottish Arts Council, called the moment "pure ballet." He continued: "I'm not a great football supporter but I had a rhapsodic moment watching that."

Among memorable goals, there are good ones, there are great ones, there are wonderful ones, and there are supernatural ones. The latter always seem somewhat (or very) chancy, improvised, unexpected. A dead-ball goal will never be in this category. Nor will an intentional goal, which is to say when the play is set up for a goal, or, let's say, when the player or players who assist pass it with their heads so that it can be kicked, bodied, or butted into the net. Supernatural goals have an air of gratuity, of the unthinkable, of gift. Not in the common sense in which one talks about a gift from the rival team, of a mistake or blunder in one's favor, but in another more noble sense of the word: they seem like gifts fallen from the sky.

Zidane's goal was wonderful because it took place in a European

Cup final, because the victory was icing on the cake, because it involved enormous difficulty and beauty, because it made him a star and not a secondary. But even then it wouldn't have been supernatural if it hadn't been unexpected by everyone, including Zidane, until almost the last instant. Madrid pulled one of their players from the game. From that substitution up to Zidane's last volley the Madrid players got in fourteen touches, most of them to keep possession of the ball, with which they had not had much contact during the now concluding first half. The Spanish television commentators talked about other things, not paying attention to which way the ball was going, not offering any play-by-play. Míchel (wiser and quicker than his dull partner, who always had his head in the clouds) noticed a pass by Solari. "Nice," he commented, distracted. That pass was the first with intent, not directed toward the goal, but toward the open field. Roberto Carlos ran, received the ball, and drove it without stopping toward the center of the penalty zone to see what would happen, almost backwards, more worried about losing it to the defense that was closing in on him than about involving anyone in the situation. His pass turned out to be unintentional. The ball rose very high—a balloon, like a defender's clearance. It never occurred to anyone that this might end in a goal. Not to the goalie or Leverkusen's defense, who didn't have time to be alarmed. And not to Roberto Carlos either, or even Zidane. He didn't look for the ball, as I said, nor did he go to the spot where he anticipated it was going to fall. No, he circled the edge of the penalty zone, and while the clearance-balloon went up and up, very high, the idea of a goal still didn't enter his mind. When did it come? When did it finally become intentional? Exactly when the ball stopped rising and hovered in the air. It was then that Zidane, who knows gravity and speed, understood that there was no other route in the air than the vertical toward the ground. And he saw that it would fall exactly where he was. Only then did it occur to him, only then did he decide it (if this last verb can be applied to what was never medi-tated—not by the German players or the Madridistas). Only then did Zidane understand the chance, the improvised, unexpected nature of the ball: it was supernatural, a gift fallen from the sky. He did the rest. At times he also seems to have fallen from the sky. That's how he rec-ognized it, and the gift became flesh, and then verb.

16. Combing over History

Stanley Matthews

Short and wiry, Sir Stanley Matthews was an "outside right" (winger) who from his first league match at seventeen until his last, thirty-three years later, exemplified the sportsman's ideal. A predecessor of Garrincha of Brazil and George Best of Northern Ireland, Matthews was hailed as "the wizard of dribble," having perfected the art of sudden speedy sprints, head and body feints, and accurate passes to streaking teammates, accompanied by a prolific finishing touch. He was celebrated for his loyalty (playing only for Stoke City and Blackpool), fair play (never having been booked), work ethic, and modesty—preferring always to give credit to his mates. This last attribute was evident after one of his greatest individual performances in what was later termed the "Matthews Final" in the 1953 FA Cup. With Blackpool trailing Bolton 1–3, Matthews, at age thirty-eight, displayed tenacity, skill, and poise in goal-setting to help ensure a 4–3 victory for Blackpool.

Matthews played his last international match at age forty-two and final first-division game at age fifty. Shortly before the latter occasion, in 1965, he became the first English player knighted for performances on the field. After retiring he served as an ambassador for the game, traveling widely and spreading a message of professionalism and sportsmanship. Matthews died in 2000 at age eighty-five. The following episode, which begins during an international friendly in Turin on May 16, 1948, comes from his autobiography, *The Way It Was* (2000).

Italy had been considered the best side in Europe. For England it was a famous victory, and the story of one incident from the game was to follow me around the world for years, turning out to be arguably football's longest-running shaggy dog story.

Towards the end of the game, with the scoreline 4–0 in our favour, I received the ball out on the right touchline and took it towards the corner flag to kill the game and frustrate the Italians. I turned to face Italy's left-back Eliani, who was giving me a little too much space from his point of view. The heat was unbearable, and the perspiration was streaming down my face, so I wiped my hand on the side of my shorts before quickly wiping away the perspiration that had gathered on the hair above my brow. It was all done in a flash. I quickly brushed my hair back with the fingertips of my right hand when I was suddenly aware of a gasp from the terraces. Believing the crowd had seen something off the ball, I thought nothing of it and the incident disappeared from my mind for years, only to resurface twenty years later when I was living in Malta.

I was with my second wife, Mila. It was in the late sixties, and we were living in Valletta. One morning Mila said she was going to the hairdresser's and asked me to pick up some meat from a local butcher's. The butcher employed an assistant who was a football fanatic. As I entered the shop, the assistant recognised me straightaway and immediately engaged me in conversation about football. During our chat the assistant said he had been in Turin in 1948 supporting England, and the highlight of the game for him was when I took the Italian left-back to the corner flag and, with the ball at my feet, produced a comb with which I proceeded to comb my hair before dribbling past my opponent.

"I have never seen such an amazing thing before or since on a football field. It was fantastic."

I didn't have a clue what he was talking about. It was only later when thinking of the game itself that I remembered wiping the sweat from my hairline and the gasp of the crowd. It clicked that they must have thought I'd had the audacity to produce a comb and do a bit of grooming out there on the pitch against, of all teams, Italy.

Even then I thought nothing of the incident, but a few weeks later the story cropped up again. A Maltese pal of mine came to see me to say one of the ministers in the government had heard I was on the island and would like to meet me. I readily agreed to go along and meet the minister in question, and during the course of our conversation he told me he had been in Turin in 1948 and I had given him his most abiding memory in football.

"What is that?" I asked, not having a clue.

"Which one?" the minister said rising to his feet with a look of amazement on his face. "The one the whole of Malta talks about. Against that great Italian team, when you had the temerity to pull a comb from your pocket and comb your hair! What a thing to do with the ball at your feet and an Italian defender confronting you! It was fantastic."

I attempted to play down the so-called incident, but the minister interrupted.

"Stop being so modest, Mr. Matthews. I see it all with my own eyes. Are you trying to tell me my eyes deceive me? I know what I see and thousands of others see it too!"

I have to say I nodded meekly and, not wanting to further embroil myself in the tale, changed the topic of conversation.

Some years later, on another trip to the same butcher's shop, the owner's young son, now a teenager, was standing behind the counter with the assistant, whom I had got to know quite well over the years.

"Here he is!" exclaimed the assistant on seeing me. "Stanley Matthews, the comb man!"

It was no good trying to deny the comb story to him, and I was grateful that after the initial reference to it he busied himself with my order. Just as I was leaving, however, the owner's son, who if my memory serves me right was called Charlie, sidled up to me.

"Mr. Matthews," he said in a soft voice.

"Yes."

"Is it true?"

"Is what true, Charlie?" I asked, knowing only too well what was to come.

"Is it true that once when playing for England against Italy, you stopped with the ball at your feet, pulled a comb from the pocket of your shorts, and combed your hair?"

I was on the point of denying it, but when I looked at the lad his face was full of wide-eyed expectancy. I glanced over to the assistant who was smiling and nodding his head, urging me to confirm the story.

"Yes, son," I said. "But it was a long time ago."

I was intending to say it was a long time ago and people's memories can play tricks, but I never got the words out.

"There! What did I tell you?" the butcher's assistant blurted out and clapped his shovel-like hands together in great satisfaction. "I was there," he continued, suitably proud and relieved that my confirmation had released him from years of being a Walter Mitty character in the eyes of the boy. "Against Italy I see Stan Matthews comb his hair. Now you hear it from the man himself, just like I tell you!"

It is one of the most amazing things in my life that this story, untrue as it was, followed me around the world. I was in Hong Kong in the sixties, playing a series of exhibition matches and coaching local youngsters, when I was asked to attend a reception held in my honour at the headquarters of the Hong Kong FA. At the start of his welcoming speech the president of the Hong Kong FA introduced me by saying, "We have great pleasure in welcoming the man who played league football in England until he was fifty. The first footballer to receive the CBE from Her Majesty the Queen. The first to be knighted and the player who, during a game against Italy, was so particular about his appearance, he paused with the ball at his feet to comb his hair."

The reference to the comb made me cringe with embarrassment, but in time I got used to this apocryphal tale that had attached itself to my football career. During one of my many trips to South Africa to coach youngsters, I was driven into one township in an open-topped Land Rover to be greeted by lines of schoolchildren, some of whom waved Union Jacks, while others held aloft old combs.

When the time came to leave Malta, I found an old comb of mine, knocked out some of the teeth and made a last visit to the butcher's shop in Valletta. I thanked the owner, his son, and their assistant for their friendship and service and said I had a special presentation to make to the assistant. I then produced a small wooden box containing the comb and handed it to him. I told him it was the comb I had used to comb my hair in the famous win against Italy in Turin in 1948. It was meant to be a bit of light-hearted fun, and I never for one moment expected the effect it would have on the assistant. He gently opened the box, stared down at the comb, and for a few seconds said nothing.

Then his face welled up and tears came into his eyes. Still holding the box and comb in one hand, he threw his hands around me, hugged me and cried unashamedly.

"I cannot believe this," he sobbed. "I'm only a humble butcher's assistant, but now I got a piece of football history. I will treasure it for ever. I will pass it on to my son and the son of my son and he to his son. How you say? A family heirloom, yes?"

I never expected him to take it so seriously, but there was no way I could then say it was all a joke. I had to go along with it. In true *News of the World* fashion, I hastily made an excuse and left.

Some years later a Maltese pal of mine told me the butcher's assistant had mounted the comb in a glass box, and it had pride of place in his living room. As far as I know it's still there. At the time, I did think about having a small brass plaque engraved with the message "Parting is such sweet sorrow," which, considering the present was a comb, I thought appropriate. Looking back, I'm glad I didn't.

The comb story got the better of me in the end. So many people asked me about it, it was easier to go along with it, and over the years I almost began to believe it actually happened—until a trip to South Africa in 1976.

I had been coaching young boys and girls in various townships including Soweto, and as with all such trips there were a number of civic and formal presentations to attend. On one such occasion I was asked to attend a dinner at a golf club not far from Johannesburg. Following the dinner, my South African hosts asked if I would pop in to the kitchen, as the head chef, Carlo Loppi, was a member of the Italian squad the day England beat Italy in 1948. They felt it would be good for us to meet up again and had arranged for photographers to be present to capture the moment for the local newspapers.

Loppi was delighted to see me. It had been thirty years since the Italy game; he hadn't actually played in the match, and I didn't recognise him. Despite that, we greeted one another like old friends and were soon bouncing conversation off one another about the old days.

"Valentino Mazzola, your captain that day," I said. "A great player and a gentleman."

"'Ee was fantastic. 'Ee could make ze ball almost talk. But what about Finney and Lawton? They were brill-i-ant. You and Mannion, too. Always a 'andful, even for as great a team as Italy."

"Remember Gabetto's shot that hit the bar?" I reminded him.

"Si, 'ee hit it with such power, that crossbar is still shaking now. Remember Mortensen's goal? 'Ow he score from such a place I don't know. It seem impossible, but 'ee did it. A great goal."

"Remember those two headers from Carapellese?"

"Si, we were on our feet in ze dugout. Each time we think, 'Goal!' but Swift, he make two great saves. Stan, remember Menti and the goal he score?"

"A great goal, but he was offside," I reminded him.

"So the referee say, but I dunno. Remember your battle with ze great Eliani?"

"How could I forget?" I said. "He was one of the finest full-backs I ever played against. Great skill."

"Si, I remember Eliani and you running the length of the pitch shoulder to shoulder, then you back heel the ball, turn, and centre for Lawton who just 'ead over the bar."

"Yes, I remember it well," I said, aware that the conversation was becoming reminiscent of a scene from *Gigi*.

"Remember Eliani boxing me into the corner?" I ventured, carried away with the excitement, "and me pulling a comb from the pocket of my shorts and combing my hair?"

"That story is famous," Loppi said. "All round the world people talk of that. But it is rubbish. It never 'appen. Your memory is starting to play tricks on you, Stan."

17. Encomiastic Arts of Our National Gamesmen

Antonio Skármeta
Translated from the Spanish by Malcolm Coad

Soccer can be a source of boundless joy, but it has also been used by dictators and military regimes to further their own agendas, most noticeably during the Nazi and Fascist periods in Europe and more recently when juntas have come to power in Argentina, Brazil, and Chile (see also chapter 27, "Generals and Fools," for a comparative perspective from Burma). As the two commentators in this excerpt from Chilean writer Antonio Skármeta's 1975 novel *Soñé que la nieve ardía* (*I Dreamt the Snow Was Burning*) speak superficially of a botched penalty call, subtler references to the Chilean military's use of the national football stadium in 1973 as a prison and torture center become apparent. "What happened happened and the whole stadium saw it," Skármeta writes, before adding in the voice of one commentator that "certain moral coordinates . . . must not be violated if the very integrity of the spectacle is to be maintained." The bleak history hinted at here has been recorded in the documentary film *Estadio Nacional*, directed by Carmen Luz Parot (2001).

Born in Chile in 1940 and raised in poverty, Skármeta studied literature and philosophy and, in his late twenties, began publishing stories, screenplays, and newspaper articles. After the 1973 coup, which brought Augusto Pinochet to power, he first moved to Argentina and then later to West Berlin, returning to Chile in 1989 when democracy was restored. He is best known for his 1985 novel *Ardiente paciencia* (Burning Patience), adapted for the screen as *Il postino* (The Postman), a story of both the friendship between Chilean poet Pablo Neruda and a young postman and of the importance of poetry and love—life's improvisational qualities—in the face of political repression.

Soccer features elsewhere in Skármeta's work. In his 1998 children's book *La composición* (The Composition) a poor youth dreams of a real white-and-black ball, and the game becomes a vehicle for political resistance. The whole of *Soñé que la nieve ardía* concerns a young man who comes from the provinces to

Santiago, the capital, with the dream of becoming a professional player, but who instead learns important lessons of human solidarity and love.

over to you then, Facus, tell me how you see the action so far, poised over it like a wild beast lying in wait for its prey, mouth hot, watchful falcon's eyes infinitely, millimetrically alert

many thanks, Marquez, for your overflowing generosity in employing epithets of which I am unworthy as I'm no more than a human being who has the joy of being able to serve our listeners through my humble eyes which are as fallible as any others and at times more so due to the professional incapacities caused by their irritated pupils being worn out by the flirtatious dance of the ball

very well said, Facus, I've always been of the opinion that what your eyes miss your tongue sees, that eloquence which is worth a ton of good Spanish in its exaltation of the encomiastic arts of our national gamesmen

thank you, Marquez, as far as I'm concerned, given that anything you say is law, and without going any further, if you'll forgive this emotional outburst, I'm reminded of that biblical phrase so widely diffused in our schools where future patriots are being formed, I'm referring to that phrase which goes "in the beginning was the word," I imagine that God must have been thinking of that word when your good parents brought you, via the stork, into this world

well, Facus, I feel you're exaggerating, a professional of language such as I is set neither below nor above other mortals and precisely what you have just quoted should be the motto that guides our conduct as narrators of events; not feeling privileged because effort or chance ordained that this magic apparatus called a microphone should have fallen into our nervous hands to bring joy, culture, and entertainment to thousands of listeners, and now, Facus, if it's not indiscreet, what did you think of that move, in your view was it a penalty?

listen, Marquez, a penalty as such it wasn't because the referee didn't order one, and if the referee didn't call it then unless by some miraculous art the world were turned backwards like a gigantic grinding machine in space which pulls things back to their points of origin, that violation can never now be called by anyone, so Flecha fans will have to carry it in their hearts like an abortion or a dark black crow pecking at their most sensitive organs, so any discussion about whether it was a penalty or wasn't a penalty would be a mere gallimaufry, Marquez, Byzantine, and we can't have that

quite right, Facus, quite right, nevertheless for our listeners' information how did the incident appear to you?

well, Marquez, for the sake of shedding light on the matter and for the record of this championship I'll give you my judgement: penalty, Marquez, penalty that's all there is to it! Garcia made a short pass down the inside edge of the field near the corner flag looking for Santillana, who returned sideways to Garcia, which allowed the player, as he opened up, to see Arturo's frenetic entry from the centre of the pitch, and shoot level towards the centre, way forward, as if he'd set his kick by the compass, to the precise point on home territory where Arturo was to arrive; so the Flecha star made contact with the ball, bringing it to earth with a blow of his boot which to many sounded like a corpse being thrown into a grave, eliminated the threat of Navarro with a dribbling manoeuvre, and upon confronting the goalkeeper, man to man alone, the latter hurled himself not at the ball, but straight at Arturo's legs preventing him from moving his lower extremities freely and thus from turning into reality what nestled in the hearts of the fans neither as intimation nor intuition but as certainty that the ball was about to go to the very back of the net and, naturally, as this was not to be its destiny, the fans experienced first the ravages of anger and immediately then the bitter undertow of desperation, do you follow, Marquez?

I follow, and as always, from my commentator's box on high, am with you, Facus, however far from home base your mission as a journalist may take you, and was just about to say to you myself that with respect to myself that with respect to the manoeuvre in question I received a similar impression, that is to say that the goalkeeper annulled the mobile capacity of the lower Arturian limbs with the malintentioned vigour of someone who is no longer content just to defend, wouldn't you say?

yes, Marquez

but more than to defend, to paralyse, bury, grind his opponent into the turf rather than let him achieve his destiny of a goal, Facus

exactly, Marquez, exactly, there was the first fragrance of a goal in that move, and rapidly that aroma which a fan's discriminating nose recognises when his skin tingles and his body seethes on the terrace, became the penetrating perfume of a super-goal because the entire galaxy saw that *that* was a penalty, the entire galaxy apart from the ref; I respect the gentlemen in black and short pants even though they are often treated like vultures of evil omen, but it is a fact, Marquez, that the Football Association does at times make available to rival teams gents in black who appear to be dressed like that as a kind of visiting card indicating utterly clouded brains, and please don't see in that remark any racist allusion nor any discourtesy towards the splendid black race

black is beautiful, Facus!

yes it is, Marquez

after all, I, less than anyone, with my considerably sunburned complexion, have any right to let slip a single anti-democratic word and you can testify to my spirit as a man of libertarian ideas, Facus

I so testify, Marquez, here, on the pitch, before an attorney, or in church before God if necessary

I thank you and continue, Facus, as I was saying among these gents in black who frequently distort the inherent spirit of the game with their inopportune whistles there are many who suffer from serious visual difficulties, Facus, advanced cases of astigmatism and cataracts; I've seen some of them in the privacy of their own homes using glasses for something as simple as observing the television from a distance of no more than a yard; without mentioning others who long since left behind the gym and the *mens sana* on the bar cardtable among full houses and royal flushes and pairs, and leaving aside altogether the Sunday lunches which many of them swallow down before epiphanizing on the pitch to direct the match, true bacchanalia of good pasta, excellent ravioli, superb sauce, fine cheeses and, why not spell it out clearly, the marvellous wines which have always characterized this land, none of which would have any importance on the spectators' benches, let's say, or for commentators like us who make more use of our tongues than our legs, and if you'll excuse the figure of speech without imagining that there's any allusion intended to your slight paunch, Facus

no offense, Marquez, those in glass houses, you know, Marquez, nor can the pot call the kettle

but to call things by the names used on the terraces, if you have to move from here to there following the sallies, feints, and dance of the ball, it does matter if you're weighed down by a belly, and when that black speck is left cut off from the action and the move ends up in a penalty which was seen by the whole stadium, and how I'd like to have an action replay here so that the amateurs won't doubt my word, the natural anger of the crowd is aroused and the players', and then the heads start to get hot and then hands and, well, you know how these to-do's end up

in effect, Marquez, they end up like this one ended up, to parody that verse by the poet Parra where he says "the party was good, it lasted until it ended"

exactly, Facus, exactly, and among other things, if anything came to an end here it was Arturo's reputation, always so long as you don't see in my words any conclusive and negative judgement regarding the young Flecha star, because I have the impression that his expulsion from the turf occurred just as he was putting the final touches to his first great ingenious move in a match which at that time was thirty minutes into its second half

apropos, Marquez, we're now thirty-eight minutes into the second half and Flecha are attacking. Lux, for youthful skin!

thank you, Facus, I repeat that if we were to pile the eighty minutes of play onto one side of the scales and on the other the dross of mistakes committed and opportunities squandered by Arturo, the scales would murmur, supposing it was one of those speak-your-weight machines in Diana's Entertainments, the scales would murmur gravely in their operatic baritone: nothing, demonstrating in its vertical tension its verdict on the actions of him who was a star but is one no longer, who can never again be a star except in that very moment of glory which justly earned him his being sent off, I don't know, Facus, how you saw that sequence of events which led referee Molina to take the drastic step of pulling up and censuring Arturo with the red card, and I assure you that I and all your listeners await your version of the facts so that it may be recorded in the book of definitive and unappealable judgements

thank you, Marquez, thank you *señores* listeners, for such unlimited trust, I can only say with all my heart that your confidence moves me so deeply that I can do no more than respond with a truthful, brief, and exact synthesis of the unhappy facts which culminated in Arturo's being sent off; a confused incident took place in the region of the corner flag from which Garcia emerged in possession then touched short to a teammate, receiving the ball straight back again, and then estimating the lightning speed at which Arturo was burning down from the very centre of the pitch like a comet blazing its trail across the green heavens of the turf, Garcia delivered the ball to him at an obtuse angle of some twenty degrees, and as ball and Arturo's boot now clung together in secret adultery both sporting items moved forward together and when the goal-bells were already sounding in those lovely cathedrals of the fans' hearts goalkeeper Pizzuti took possession of both Arturo's legs with the evident purpose of obstructing his translation forwards; as a result of this incident, and as a natural physical consequence, Arturo's body was precipitated towards the ground, and the sound "penalty" came together in its three syllables in mouths throughout the stadium at which the player sat on the ground condemned to await the sanctioning whistle, while the spectators sought out the sombre shadow of referee Molina in the large expanse of the other team's half, we commentators and professionals of the microphone waiting for the finger of the referee to signal pointedly from the other end of the pitch towards the critical location at the end of twelve regulation paces (and it would be true to say that everyone, even Pizzuti himself, was beginning to crouch down between the three poles which like the three masts of a caravel floated in the unfading blue sky of this Latin American homeland) when something happened which no one suspected: the referee waved his right hand in front of his face, not exactly to fan himself, but to indicate with that traditional gesture *no, nothing doing, gentlemen*, but, Marquez, facts have an irreversible mechanism and what happened *happened* and the whole stadium saw it; however much room for subjectivism football may allow there are certain moral coordinates which must not be violated if the very integrity of the spectacle is to be maintained; here, the referee, like a tiny black insect, like a diminutive David hurling from the catapult of his authority the pebble of an error at the face of that many-faced Goliath which is the national public, the most gentlemanly in the Americas, broke the limits of all prudence, and so how can one not justify, although it has no justification, that Arturito, wounded on this day of low grey clouds, should get up from his position on the turf, upbraid him with his fist and then finally convey the latter with singular violence towards the referee's jaw, laying him out instantaneously, what do you say, Marquez?

I say that's right, Facus, that that's exactly how things were, and by my watch we're now forty-five minutes into the second half and the game will be stopped at any moment with Flecha down by one goal to nil, Miquel's goal after fifteen minutes of the first half, and the ever-moving hands of the clock are looking to make reputations at exactly forty-five minutes, and it's all nearly over, *señores*, with just the last few agonising seconds to live through, and before these microphones are discharged of the precious energy which feeds them and together with the noble players we set off for a well-deserved rest I'd like to hear your valuable final summary of the game, away we go, Facus

well, Marquez, the conclusion to be drawn from this match can be summed up in three simple words: *same as always*, another fever of high hopes produced in the lower divisions by a prodigy which, if you'll permit the metaphor, snaps on his second outing onto the pitch like a fragile branch in autumn; an attempt to impress all and sundry sailing on the tempestuous ocean of the poor clubs, but which finishes up with a reputation accumulated in the hold lost in the cold salt sea where no fine fruit can grow; we came to see the launch of a rocket to fame and what we witnessed was the shipwreck of a row boat, because Arturo's performance can merit no other judgement from the experts; lazy in its take-off, unprepared when it came to retaking defensive positions, tangled up in fancy dribbling while the wings were waiting for long passes, in short, all the typical ills and endemic evils of our Latin American talents which augur disaster in the World Cup in Germany for the chances of a continent which once upon a time was the cradle of Pele, Labruna and the immortal Tucho Mendez, whom Armando Bo put onto the silver screen in his deeply felt *Ball of Rags*, in short, it's high time the lads who debate with the ball and the trainers who coach them woke up to the fact that it's all very well to be trained in building castles in the air and lighting up the night with firework displays, but they should realise that the castles collapse and the fireworks fade away in the night of passing time leaving joy among the naive, to be sure, but no real foundations for an edifice which could give this Latin America, so much loved and so much our own, as many soccer stars as those which shine in its young sky, what do you say, Marquez

that's it, Facus, that's it, I add my signature to what you have written, you have been generous and God willing Flecha's ambitions will lead to a good end and what happened this evening will be no more than a gaffe, a nightmare at the edge of a dream, a grease stain on the albion shirt of the sport and that next Sunday they will have fully recovered, and that Arturo remembers once and for all, now that his punishment has been dished out and taken on board, that he was the spermatozoa that engendered so many hopes in his club and, why not be honest about it, in you and I, who are nobody but who a month ago placed in him the hopes which seemed appropriate; now back to the studio for our signature tune

18. The Longest Penalty Ever

Osvaldo Soriano
Translated from the Spanish by Miranda Stramel

At first unsure whether to pursue a career as a footballer or to make a career by writing about the game, Osvaldo Soriano ultimately chose the latter, much to the delight of his readers. When the Argentine journalist and author died in 1997, the Osvaldo Soriano Football Club formed in Italy to honor him.

The penalty kick, around which the following story is built, has inspired other fiction writers, such as Peter Handke in his 1970 novel, *Die Angst des Tormanns beim Elfmeter* (The Goalkeeper's Anxiety at the Penalty Kick). Like Handke's character, Soriano's goalkeeper (el Gato) suffers in his decision over which way to dive. In fact, the parallel between the two works is striking when one compares the scene in the present story, in which el Gato speaks with the club president, to the following passage from Handke: "A penalty! The goalkeeper wonders into which corner it will go. If he knows the opposing player, he knows the kicker's favorite corner, but the kicker knows he knows. So the goalkeeper wonders if he might choose the other corner this time. But the kicker knows that, too, so maybe he'll go for his favorite. And so on and so on." Both works were later made into feature films, Handke's in 1972, using the original German title and directed by Wim Wenders, and Soriano's in 2005 (*El penalti más largo del mundo*), directed by Roberto Santiago.

The most fantastic penalty I've ever heard of was suffered on a Sunday afternoon in 1958 in an empty stadium on a forgotten parcel of the Black River Valley in Argentina. Polar Star was a pool hall full of poker tables, a drunk's dive on a dirt road that dead-ended at the riverbank. Polar Star had a soccer team that played in the valley league because on Sundays, when the wind dragged dust from the fences and pollen from the farms, there was nothing better to do.

The players, or their brothers, were always the same. When I was fifteen they were thirty and seemed ancient to me. Díaz, the goalie, was almost forty and had the hair to prove it: white hair that fell across his Araucanian Indian forehead. Sixteen teams played in the championship, and Polar Star always finished lower than tenth place. I think in 1957 they came in thirteenth and went home singing, with their red shirts folded neatly inside their bags, because those were the only ones they had. In 1958 they started out by winning over Chilean Shield, another miserable team.

Nobody noticed. A month later though, when they had won four consecutive games and were the leaders of the tournament, people started to talk about them in all twelve towns of the valley.

The victories were all won by one goal, but that was enough, because Belgrano Sports, the eternal champion—the team of Padín, Constante Gauna, and Tata Cardiles—was left in second place, one point behind. They talked about Polar Star in school, on the bus, in the plaza, but still no one imagined that by the end of autumn they would have twenty-two points against our twenty-one.

The stadiums filled with people hoping to see them lose good one time. The Polar Star players were as slow as donkeys and heavy as furniture, but they played man-to-man and squealed like pigs when they didn't have the ball. The coach, a black-suit type, with a trimmed little mustache, a mole on his forehead, and a cigarette stub between his lips, ran along the sidelines and urged them on with a wicker rod when they passed him. The crowd had a great time with this and we, who played Saturdays because we were younger, didn't understand how they could win if they were so bad.

They kicked and received with such loyalty and enthusiasm that they left the stadium on each other's shoulders, the crowd applauding their 1–0 victory and reaching out to them with bottles of wine that had been cooled in the humid earth. At night they celebrated at the Santa Ana brothel, and the fat Leticia complained that they had eaten the rest of the chicken she had put away in the freezer.

They were stars, and in the village they got away with anything. The old men collected them from the bars when they drank too much and got into fights, the storeowners gave them free toys or candies for their children, and at the movies their girlfriends consented to caresses above the knee. Outside of their town nobody took them seriously, not even when they beat Atlético San Martín 2–1. In the middle of the euphoria they lost, like everyone does, and at the end of the first round they fell behind—Deportivo Belgrano put them in their place with seven goals. We all thought, then, that normality was beginning to reestablish itself.

But the following Sunday they won 1–0 and continued with their long litany of laborious, horrible triumphs, reaching the spring only one point behind the champion.

The final confrontation was historic because of the penalty. The stadium was full, as well as the roofs of the homes nearby. Everyone hoped that Deportivo Belgrano would repeat the seven goals of the first round. It was a cool and sunny day, and the apples were reddening on the trees. More than five hundred Polar Star fans took one stand by storm—the firefighters had to bring out their hoses in order to settle them down.

The referee that called the foul was Herminio Silva, an epileptic that ran the local numbers and that everyone knew took a nice cut. Forty minutes into the second half they were tied at one and still Silva hadn't made any calls, except when Deportivo Belgrano headed the ball into Polar Star's penalty box and did some somersaults and juggling to impress him. With a tie the home team would be champion. Herminio Silva wanted to keep some self-respect, and so he didn't call any fouls because there hadn't been any infractions.

But everyone's mouth fell open when, at forty-two minutes, Polar Star's left wing drove in an open shot from way out and put them up 2–1. Then, yes, Herminio Silva thought of his investment. He stretched out the game until Padín entered the box, and when Padín had barely approached a defender, the referee blew. Right then he whistled stridently, spectacularly, and called the foul. In those days the penalty spot wasn't marked with a white dot and you had to count out twelve feet. Herminio Silva didn't have a chance to pick up the ball because Polar Star's right back, Colo Rivero, had knocked him out with a bloody nose. The fighting went on until nightfall, and there was no way to clear the field or to wake up Herminio Silva. The police chief, with a lantern, suspended the game by firing a gunshot into the air. That night the military commander declared a state of emergency, or something like that, and called in a train to carry off anyone from the town that didn't look like they lived there.

The league court met on Tuesday and ruled that there were twenty seconds left to play from when the foul was called, and that the match, now between Constante Gauna the kicker and Gato Díaz the goalie, would take place the following Sunday in the same stadium behind closed doors. Therefore the penalty lasted a week and was, unless someone can tell me differently, the longest in history.

Wednesday we skipped school and went to the next town to snoop. The club was closed, and all the men had gathered on the field under the storm clouds. They formed a long line to take turns kicking toward Gato Díaz, and the coach, with his black suit and his mole, tried to explain to them that this was the best way to get the goalie ready. In the end everyone took their shot, and el Gato stopped quite a few, because they were kicking in sandals and street shoes. One tiny, quiet little soldier in the line delivered a kick with his combat boot that almost uprooted the net. At dusk they returned to town, opened the club, and started playing cards. Díaz didn't say a word all night, pulling back his rough, white hair until, after dinner, he put a toothpick in his mouth and said:

"Constante kicks to the right."

"Always," said the president of the club.

"But he knows that I know."

"Then we're fucked."

"Yeah, but I know that he knows," said el Gato.

"Then dive to the left and be ready," said someone at the table.

"No. He knows that I know that he knows," said Gato Díaz, and he got up to go to bed.

"El Gato gets stranger all the time," said the president of the club, watching el Gato leave pensively, walking slowly.

Tuesday he didn't come to practice, or Wednesday either. Thursday they found him walking along the railroad tracks, talking to himself, a dog with a clipped tail following close behind.

"You gonna stop it?" the clerk in the bicycle shop asked him, anxiously.

"I don't know. What would that change for me?" he asked.

"Then we'd be recognized, Gato: we kicked those Belgrano faggots' asses!"

"I'll be recognized when the blonde from Ferreira wants to be mine," he said, and he whistled to the dog as he turned to go home.

Friday, the blonde from Ferreira was helping at the dressmaker's when the mayor of the town came in with a bouquet of flowers and a smile as wide as an open watermelon.

"Gato Díaz sent you these and until Monday you're going to say that he's your boyfriend."

"Poor guy," she said with a grimace, without looking at the flowers that had been traveling on the bus from Neuquén since ten thirty.

That night they went to the movies together. During the intermission el Gato went out in the hall to smoke, and the blonde from Ferreira stayed alone in the dimmed lights with her purse on her lap, reading the program a hundred times without looking up.

Saturday afternoon Gato Díaz rented two bicycles, and they went riding along the bank of the river. At dusk he wanted to kiss her, but she turned away and said maybe Sunday night, after he stopped the kick, at the dance.

"And how do I know?" he said.

"How do you know what?"

"Which way I need to dive?"

The blonde from Ferreira took him by the hand and led him to where they had left the bicycles.

"In this life you never know who's tricking who," she said.

"And if I don't stop it?" he asked.

"Then that means you don't love me," responded the blonde, and they went back to town.

The Sunday of the penalty kick twenty trucks full of people left the club, but the police stopped them at the entrance to the town, and they had to stay on a shoulder of the highway, waiting in the sun. In that time and in that place they did not have television or radio broadcasts or any other way to find out what was happening in a closed stadium, so the Polar Star fans established a post between the stadium and the road.

The clerk from the bicycle shop climbed on top of a roof from which he could see Gato Díaz's goal, and from there he narrated what was happening to another guy that had stayed on the sidewalk, who in turn passed it on to another guy twenty yards away, and on and on until each detail reached the place where the Polar Star fans were waiting.

At three in the afternoon, the two teams left for the field dressed as if they were going to play a real game. Herminio Silva was wearing a black uniform, faded but clean, and when they were all gathered in the middle of the field he went right to the spot where Colo Rivero had thrown the punch the previous Sunday and had been sent off the field. The red card still hadn't been invented, so Herminio pointed to the tunnel entrance with a trembling hand from which his whistle hung. In the end, the police removed Colo by force, who wanted to stay to see the penalty kick. Then the referee went to the goal with the ball tight against his hip, counted twelve steps, and put the ball in its place. Gato Díaz had combed his hair with gel, and his head shone like an aluminum saucepan.

We could see them from the thick wall that surrounded the field, just behind the goal, and when he put himself on the white line and began to rub his bare hands together we started to bet on which way Constante Gauna would kick.

On the road all traffic had been stopped, and the entire valley was hanging on this instant: Deportivo Belgrano had not lost a cup or league championship in ten years. The police also wanted to know, so they permitted the chain of informers to grow two miles long, and the news traveled mouth to mouth, hardly slowed by the spaces between breaths.

Right at three thirty, when Herminio Silva had managed to get the directors of both clubs, the coaches, and the live forces of the town out of the stadium, Constante Gauna went to familiarize himself with the ball. He was skinny and muscular, and his eyebrows were so thick that they seemed to cut his face in two. He had kicked penalty kicks so many times—he counted them all later—but he would return to this kick at every moment of his life, asleep or awake.

At a quarter to four Herminio Silva put himself halfway between the goal and the ball, raised the whistle to his mouth, and blew with all his strength. He was so nervous, and the sun shone so brightly on the nape of his neck that when the ball went toward the goal, the referee felt his eyes shaking, and he fell onto his back spewing foam from his mouth. Díaz took a step forward and lunged to the right. The ball flew spinning in circles toward the middle of the goal and Constante Gauna knew immediately that Gato Díaz's legs would carry him right to where he could deflect it to the side. El Gato thought about the dance that night, in his belated glory, and about how someone should run to block the ball at the corner because it was still in play.

Little Mirabelli arrived before anyone else and kicked it away toward the fence, but the referee, Herminio Silva, couldn't see it because he was on the ground, rolling around in an epileptic fit. As all the Polar Star players were piling on top of Gato Díaz, the line judge ran toward Herminio Silva with a flag, and from the wall where we were sitting we heard him yelling: "It doesn't count, it doesn't count!"

The news spread from mouth to jubilant mouth, Gato's stop and the referee's collapse. Then on the highway everyone opened their bottles of wine and started to celebrate, even though the "doesn't count" was arriving, stammered by messengers with astonished faces.

Until Herminio Silva got up, rattled from the attack, there was no definitive answer. The first thing he asked was "What happened?" and when they told him he shook his head and said that they had to start over because he hadn't been there and the rules said that the game couldn't go on with a passed-out referee. Then Gato Díaz separated himself from those that wanted to punch the Deportivo Belgrano raffle merchant, said that they needed to hurry because that night he had a date and a promise to keep, and went back to his place under the goal.

Constante Gauna must have lost faith in himself, because he passed the ball to Padín and right afterwards he went back to the ball while the linesman helped Silva stay standing. Outside you could hear Deportivo Belgrano's party horns, and the Polar Star players began to retire from the field surrounded by the police.

The ball went left and Gato Díaz dove left with an elegance and confidence that he would never have again. Constante Gauna looked up to the sky and then began to cry. We jumped from the wall and went to look at Díaz up close, the old guy, the champion, staring at the ball he had between his hands as if he had caught the ring on the merry-go-round.

Two years later, when he was a ruin and I was an insolent teenager, I ran into him again, twelve immense paces away, crouching on his toes, with his long fingers spread. On one hand he wore a wedding ring, not from the blonde of Ferreira but from Colo Rivero's sister, who was just as Indian and old as he was. I avoided looking him in the eye, and I shifted my weight; then I kicked to the left, low, knowing that he wouldn't stop it because it was pretty hard, and the glory weighed on him. When I looked for the ball inside the net Gato Díaz was getting up like a beaten dog.

"Nice, kid," he told me, "Someday, when you're older, you're going to go around talking about how you scored a goal against Gato Díaz, only by then nobody will remember me."

19. Fretting while the Scarlet Tide Make History

Elvis Costello

Born Declan Patrick Aloysius McManus, singer-songwriter Elvis Costello recalls the machinations necessary to follow his beloved Liverpool FC during a university gig that happened to correspond with the 2005 European Cup final versus AC Milan. In charting the game's unlikely outcome, Costello, writing for the *Times* of London, calls on both his natural creative impulses and those of the football supporter who must improvise when events require. He also sketches a history of England's most successful team, which the London-born Costello began to follow when he moved to the Merseyside seaport with his mother after his parents' divorce.

Since its first game in 1893, Liverpool has won the league championship eighteen times, the FA Cup seven times, and the European Cup five times. Among the many players who have worn its red uniform, with the city's liver bird as a badge, are such greats as Roger Hunt, Kevin Keegan, and Kenny Dalglish. Despite the growing international influence of recent years, Liverpool holds firmly to its working-class origins and cherishes the period of dominance enjoyed under managers Bill Shankly and Bob Paisley. The main grandstand at Anfield, the home ground, is called The Kop to honor a Liverpool battalion's heavy losses at the Battle of Spion Kop in 1900 during the Second Boer War.

Costello also recalls more recent wounds, including a 1985 European final match at Heysel Stadium, where 39 died and 454 were injured before play began between Liverpool and Juventus of Italy. Liverpool backers were held responsible in that they rushed a section of Juventus fans before a restraining wall collapsed at the decrepit stadium. Less than four years later, in April 1989, 96 Liverpool fans were crushed to death before an FA Cup semifinal at Hillsborough Stadium in Sheffield. With his reference to "crimes . . . committed with words in newsprint," Costello alludes to allegations made by *The Sun*, a national tabloid newspaper, that Liverpool "hooligans" were to blame. An official inquiry, however, pointed to basic flaws in crowd control and resulted in the elimination of standing terraces from many English stadiums.

I was on a narrow road through ancient woodland when the awful news came over a crackling connection: "He's left out Hamann and he's playing Kewell!" My heart sank. I knew we were doomed. Minutes later I arrived at the University of East Anglia, where I have played concerts since 1977. I was booked to perform just as Liverpool were taking the field in their first European Cup final in twenty years.

I had tried everything to re-schedule the concert, remembering what Paul McGrath had once told me about an Albanian trip with Ireland: "I might pull a hamstring . . ." I had suggested a teatime show or even a late-night show, but the best we could manage was to announce through the local radio and newspapers that the start would be delayed until the end of the ninety minutes. This way I would still have sufficient time for a complete set. I had remained quietly confident that it would not take very long for Liverpool to subdue an overconfident AC Milan. That was until I heard the team news.

Now I thought it might possibly require extra time. If so, I would have to get on stage and face the unusual torture of having the score relayed to me by semaphore or hand-printed cards. The last time we attempted this was in Glasgow during the infamous Michael Thomas game at Anfield in 1989. I played the longest song in my repertoire, while keeping my gaze from the wings, knowing that by the time I finished the tune, with the score at "0–1," Liverpool would be champions. As the applause began, I looked round to see my stage manager holding up "0–2."

The travelling musician often ends up following an important game in unlikely circumstances, listening to the World Service via an aerial hung from the curtains in a Hamburg hotel, or maybe that was in Nagoya. Then there was the 7:00 a.m. rendezvous in "The Mad Dog in the Fog" pub in Haight-Ashbury, San Francisco, for Liverpool's Cantona-inspired defeat in the FA Cup Final of 1996 and realising that Ray Davies, of the Kinks, was sitting at the next table. Perhaps, more pertinently, there is the memory of staying up all night in Australia to watch the broadcast of Bruce Grobbelaar's "Spaghetti Legs" defeat of AS Roma in 1984.

So, in contrast, a large-screen TV in a university common room was an unimaginable joy. Then the game started. The absence of Hamann was immediately felt as no one picked up Maldini, even though his powerful downward half-volley might have been saved by a goalkeeper who had been on the park for more than fifty seconds. Things went rapidly downhill. Players who had performed superbly during the season—or at least when they hadn't been confined to the treatment table—such as Xabi Alonso and Luis García, looked like boys against Milan's men. Liverpool's most improved player of the season, Djimi Traoré, was suddenly returned to the nervous and accident-prone form that he had shown under Gérard Houllier.

At twenty-three minutes, with the midfield being totally overrun and the Reds' usually resolute defence looking vulnerable, Rafael Benítez's big gamble finally paid off: Kewell pulled up. Now, Australian Harry may be a very fine human being, but he has the misfortune of appearing to many fans as the epitome of the spoilt modern footballer who places his agent's agenda ahead of that of the club.

The commentator reported that Kewell had "asked" to come off. In Liverpool folklore you do not ask to come off in a final . . . or any game, unless you are dead. For heaven's sake, Gerry Byrne played 117 minutes of the 1965 FA Cup Final with a broken collarbone and still managed to set up one of the goals. In 1956 Bert Trautmann, the former German POW and Manchester City goalie, played in the Cup Final with a broken neck. Did he complain or ask to be taken off? Did he heck. They didn't even discover his injury until three days after the game.

Then there is the matter of the "Alice" band. At the risk of sounding like a fogey reminiscing about the good old days, I honestly cannot remember "Sir" Roger Hunt, the legendary Liverpool striker, ever sporting one of these accessories. Even an Evertonian wouldn't wear one. If big Duncan Ferguson grew his hair down to his knees, it is inconceivable that he would ever pace the Goodison dressing-room saying, "Wee man, does this make me look harder or just like a bit of a Jessie?" There doesn't even seem to be any discernible benefit in wearing the "Alice." Milan Baros has sported one all season, and he still cannot find the goal.

OK, for a short while things did go from bad to worse. Milan continued to cut through the Liverpool defence like a chainsaw through a bucket of ghee. By half-time the scoreboard read 3–0, and I felt a horrible repressed memory welling up from childhood: the morning in 1966 when the paper reported that Bill Shankly's invincible Liverpool side had been crushed 5–1 . . . apparently by a team named after a famous household cleaner. Now this game was also turning into a humiliation too dreadful to witness. I decided to do the unthinkable and go on stage early.

During half-time, as my crew completed the final checks on our equipment, I fielded a commiserating call from my one friend who is a Chelsea fan and a stricken text message from a pal in Istanbul. I began warming up my voice and tried to locate the most reverberant location backstage. This turned out to be the stairwell leading to the now deserted TV room. "Oh well," I thought. "I might as well see the first few minutes of the second half." I found that Didi Hamann was on the field, as he should have been at the start, and that Liverpool were on the ball, looking far more organised. I pulled up a chair just in time to witness Steven Gerrard's magnificent header.

I affected a nonchalant air and strolled back downstairs to indulge in the strange rituals and superstitious practices that precede every performance. "Well, they've made it look a bit more respectable," I said, to no one in particular, as crew members hurried by in every direction. My stage manager called out "five minutes," and I decided to use two of them by taking another quick peek at the screen. It couldn't hurt.

A member of the university staff was the only person in front of the television. He had a startled look on his face. The score read "3–2." I heard someone bellowing down the stairwell, "Hold on" . . . and it was me.

The crew quickly deserted the stage and burst into the room just as Gerrard burst into the box and was flattened. You could see from Alonso's eyes that he wouldn't put away the penalty, but he is twenty-three and much quicker to the goalkeeper's parry than Milan's veteran defenders. Unbelievably, Liverpool had levelled the score in just over five minutes. The members of the Imposters (my band) now joined the television audience. Collectively they know as much about football as I know about lacrosse. However, they tolerate my football-related monologues with the indulgence of an elderly aunt humouring an eight-year-old attempting to explain the mythology of *Star Wars*. Soon they were swept up in the drama.

When a substitute was seen pacing the touchline, doing menacing neck rolls like a boxer in a title fight, Pete Thomas, the drummer, let out a comic shriek of "Who is *that?*" I was inspired to a ludicrous bout of deadly serious Motson-like myth-making. "That is Djibril Cissé, and he has recovered from a career-threatening double fracture of his leg in record time, and he is destined to win this competition."

Our American bass player, Davey Faragher, remarked that, with his dyed yellow hair and strange tattoos, Cissé looked more like a character from a superhero comic strip. Frankly, if the commentator had told us that he was part amphibian and had webbed feet, it would have seemed quite credible then. However, by the time the striker was introduced, Liverpool's most talented playmaker, Gerrard, was filling in at right back, and García and Alonso seemed too exhausted to lift the ball over the head of Jaap Stam, who would have otherwise been left in the dust by Cissé's astonishing acceleration.

Normal time concluded without a conclusive result, and we could delay the show no longer. Steve Nieve, the pianist, who had just had the rules explained to him, confidently predicted that Liverpool would prevail in any penalty shoot-out. An ominous rumbling finally penetrated our theatre of football. We approached the stage to the sound of a slow handclap and catcalls. The promoter had spent the second half cowering backstage rather than taking responsibility for any coherent announcement explaining the ongoing situation. This was left to one of my soundmen, who is an Arsenal fan, and you know how they like to lie doggo and then win with the last kick of the game.

I can't say that our entrance to the stage was greeted with wild acclaim. The lights finally went down, and the booing actually increased. The lights came up and at first glance the people of Norfolk seemed to be divided into two sub-groups. Those who like to eat biscuits and go to bed early after a little light jiving and a handful of the kind of untamed flatlanders who are sometimes portrayed in seventies horror films brandishing flaming torches at a lynching.

It had been suggested by my Chelsea-supporting friend that I might further ingratiate myself with a Norwich crowd by echoing the recent emotional outburst of Delia Smith. So my opening remark was "Let's be having you," and I promptly received a glass of water across the neck of my guitar.

Now I have had many things thrown at me over the years, but none of them has been less terrifying than half a glass of lukewarm water. At least it could have been some beer, preferably still in the bottle. I've had people seriously intent on killing me, and not just in the late seventies, when a man came dressed with a hatchet in his head at a couple of our more lively gigs. As recently as "Woodstock 3," in 1999, Nieve and I faced down what looked like an irate mob of method actors auditioning for a remake of *Apocalypse Now*. Once the audience have their faces painted green and twigs in their hair, you know you are in deep trouble. Those crazy kids seemed to want to maim us for no other reason than that we were older than them. They were throwing full cans of lite beer and Diet Coke at us, but we pressed on regardless and managed to get out of town unscathed before they started to enact any of the more grisly scenes from *Lord of the Flies*.

Back in Norwich it started to become apparent that some people had not got the message about the late start. The drunk who threw his glass of water was ejected by security, but not before I identified him, in strictly literal terms, as "a tosser," along with a couple of other adjectives that might have offended some *Daily Mail* readers, even if they are not usually that prominent at my shows, because I hate their guts. The offender was promptly taken outside and beaten to a pulp . . . by his girlfriend, who was angry about missing the show.

Once we got rolling, the boisterous start gave a different flavour to the show, although the Imposters played with their customary swagger and panache, not unlike the Liverpool team of the Hansen/Dalglish era. I tried my best to keep my eyes from the TV screen over the bar at the back of the room, but the words "Oh s***, he's missed" might have accidentally crept into the lyrics of "Good Year for the Roses."

And suddenly it was all over. I could see people in the bar area punching the air, and a rolling cheer overwhelmed the applause for

"Kinder Murder." Our security man, Paddy Callaghan, capered in the shadows at the edge of the stage with a balletic grace that belies his frame, and this was all the confirmation I needed to cue "You'll Never Walk Alone," a song that we had never performed before as a band.

The audience took up the anthem like a mini-Kop and saluted the Liverpool victory with the massed illumination of their mobile phones. It was a bizarre and moving sight. I managed to make only a couple of football-related dedications during the rest of the two-hour set. I'm not sure that Benítez would really appreciate "The Delivery Man," but you can guess what I meant by it. We had already played "I Don't Want to Go to Chelsea," so I couldn't dedicate that one to Gerrard, but we did end with "The Scarlet Tide."

The next day I had to check the headlines to see that it wasn't all some kind of crazy dream. Liverpool made the first edition, and our antics made the late-night final after a couple of "Angry of West Runton"–type people decided to get their names in the paper. Our promoter demanded four hundred pounds to compensate for the sixteen souls who had asked for their money back, the cheap swine. He's never had more publicity in his life. On the other hand, I was happy to offer free tickets for our next Norfolk show, if such a thing should ever occur, in the event that a ticket-holder had to catch the last bus home or relieve a baby-sitter.

Now I've seen kids wearing Liverpool shirts everywhere from Addis Ababa to Anfield and maybe, years from now, some of them may be able to reel off the names of this team, as I can still recite Lawrence, Lawler, Byrne, Strong, Yeats, Stevenson, Callaghan, Hunt, St. John, Smith, and Thompson. If so, they should start with the name of Jamie Carragher, even though Jerzy Dudek was the hero of the shoot-out.

Or maybe it will be another glorious trail that leads nowhere, like Houllier's treble-winning season in 2001. Still, I wouldn't trade that famous afternoon in Cardiff or one insane evening in Dortmund any more than all the Liverpool fans in Istanbul and around the world—which still includes Norwich, when I last checked—are ever likely to forget last Wednesday night.

Bill Shankly's famous aphorism, "Football isn't a matter of life and death. It's much more important than that," was made macabre by a shameful night in Belgium twenty years ago and utterly stripped of its almost innocent power to inspire by the terrible crimes surrounding the Hillsborough disaster. Some of those crimes were committed with words in newsprint, and they should never be forgotten or forgiven.

Football may not be more important than life and death, but this match unexpectedly proved that, despite the greed, vanity, and vile bigotry that lurks within and sometimes overwhelms the game today, it can still be magical, confounding, and create a dramatic scenario that would be rejected as too fantastic if written as sports fiction. For those two hours or so it was certainly more important than rock and roll and getting to bed early.

20. Streaker Disrupts Iceland vs. Albania

Einar Már Guðmundsson
Translated from the Icelandic by Bernard Scudder

International football matches provide rare opportunities to peek behind the curtain of totalitarian regimes, and Icelandic poet and novelist Einar Már Guðmundsson avails himself in these musings concerning a notable 1990 European qualifying match. With Albania shaking off more than four decades of extreme isolation, trips to trendy European capitals meant almost certain culture shock. Analogues in football's past include North Korea's journey to England for the 1966 World Cup finals. As depicted in the 2002 documentary film *The Game of Their Lives*, the North Korean players charmed the Teesiders in Middlesbrough, and building on their popularity they shocked Italy 1–0 to reach the quarterfinals. Yet never having been exposed to Western religious imagery, the players said they were unnerved by Christian statuary in a retreat house in which they received last-minute accommodations. They lost the next match to Portugal 3–5.

Picking up on this theme of strange encounters, Guðmundsson sketches the odd, but factual, tableau of Albania's national team being confronted by another archetypal symbol of Western cultural expression—the streaker. Streakers and football formed a strong enough association over the years that manufacturers of the popular table-football game Subbuteo, seeking to add a touch of sideline realism, produced nude figurines in plastic.

The match between Iceland and Albania took place on May 30, 1990, not in June as Guðmundsson writes. Iceland won 2–0, but neither side qualified for the 1992 European Championships. Democratic elections also occurred in Albania in 1992, seven years after the death of Communist Party leader Enver Hoxha.

In the summer of 1990, Iceland and Albania played a football match. It was a momentous event. This was a qualifying game for the European

Cup and one of the first portents that Albania intended to join the community of nations in its work and play. The country had been isolated for decades and hardly visited except by a handful of admirers of its dictator, Enver Hoxha.

Nothing is told about the Albanian national team until they arrived at Heathrow Airport in London. They made a stopover there on their way to Iceland and the players can be expected to have found it quite a novelty to venture beyond their country's borders. It was a sunny Sunday afternoon in June. No news reached Iceland until the evening, when it was reported that the Albanian football team had been taken into custody at Scotland Yard. The players were suspected of shoplifting duty-free goods by the armful.

During questioning, the Albanians referred to the "Duty-free" signs that were hung up everywhere in the terminal, besides which it was a Sunday and various goods there, for example beer, were free in their country that day. For all they knew, this was the custom in other countries as well.

But even though the Albanians escaped the clutches of Scotland Yard, their dealings with the eagle-eyed authorities were far from over. On the Albanian team's arrival in Iceland, an extensive customs search was made through their luggage and they were kept almost under house arrest afterwards until the time for the football match came around. So the Albanians' weak attempt to break their isolation with the rest of the world took on a very peculiar form.

Nonetheless, the football match began. The teams entered the pitch and lined up to hear their national anthems being played. But no sooner had the stadium brass band played a few notes than a naked Icelander, male, came running out from the spectators' stand and started hopping around in front of the Albanian team. At once, six brawny policemen appeared on the scene. They rushed for the naked man, rugby-tackled him and piled on top of him in a heap. But the naked man was slippery as an eel and slipped out of their clutches. He ran past the Albanian football team, waving his genitals at them. At that point the police managed to overpower him. They were last seen carrying him away.

But at that moment everything went wild. The brass band had stopped playing and one of the stadium groundsmen had switched on the microphone and was reciting an impromptu verse in celebration of the incident.

I have often wondered what it would have been like if an Albanian writer had been sitting in the capital city Tirana, a year or two before the football match, imagining it taking place and describing everything that actually happened. He would have smashed every rule known to socialist realism and imposed by the Albanian Writers' Union on its members, because reality often outdoes fiction, and nothing is so poetic that reality has no place in it.

This Albanian writer has suddenly become very real. I visualise him, and his position demonstrates two things. Firstly, how ridiculous it is to subject mental activity to rules, or rather, to social goals; and secondly, how unrealistic it is to intend to be realistic, in particular when a predetermined definition of reality is used as a yardstick for truth.

Reality is always catching realism by surprise.

21. Football at Slack

Ted Hughes

Ted Hughes, a former poet laureate of Great Britain, was born in Mytholmroyd, Yorkshire, in 1930. As in many of his poems, the evocation of nature in rural places plays a prominent role in this description of a football match. The moors and crags seen here are distinctive to Hughes's native Calder Valley and served as inspiration for his 1979 collection, *Remains of Elmet*, from which this selection comes. The poem's title refers to the town of Slack in West Yorkshire, four miles from Mytholmroyd.

Biographer Elaine Feinstein in *Ted Hughes: The Life of a Poet* (2001) observes that Hughes himself took little interest in football growing up, although Hughes's father, William, was a player and watched avidly. "Male Yorkshire society is a powerful one," writes Feinstein, "and a boy who grew up in it would be expected to demonstrate some prowess in games." Hughes, a tall man who enjoyed small-game hunting, opted instead for the discus. His Yorkshire childhood remained a popular theme in his poetry, and Hughes would return to football as a subject in 1995, three years before his death. In a limited-edition poem, "Football," bound with illustrations by Christopher Battye, Hughes appears to allude to his father's fascination with the game and to his own dislike. The poem begins, "I was sick of football / before I understood / What the game was."

> Between plunging valleys, on a bareback hill
> Men in bunting colours
> Bounced, and their blown ball bounced.
>
> The blown ball jumped, and the merry-coloured men
> Spouted like water to head it.
> The ball blew away downwind—

The rubbery men bounced after it.
The ball jumped up and out and hung on the wind
Over a gulf of treetops.
Then they all shouted together, and the ball blew back.

Winds from fiery holes in heaven
Piled the hills darkening around them
To awe them. The glare light
Mixed its mad oils and threw glooms.
Then the rain lowered a steel press.

Hair plastered, they all just trod water
To puddle glitter. And their shouts bobbed up
Coming fine and thin, washed and happy

While the humped world sank foundering
And the valleys blued unthinkable
Under depth of Atlantic depression—

But the wingers leapt, they bicycled in air
And the goalie flew horizontal

And once again a golden holocaust
Lifted the cloud's edge, to watch them.

22. Dead Radio

Charles Simic

In her poem "The Ripest Rankest Juiciest Summer Ever," Hsia Yü writes that "compared to a soccer broadcast live hardly anything exists." Such is the feeling conveyed in poet and essayist Charles Simic's recollection of trying to listen to the radio transmission of a match from the 1950 World Cup finals. The match was between his country of birth, Yugoslavia, and the host country, Brazil. If we are not present to experience the game as it happens, whether in person or through radio, television, or Internet broadcasts, has the game taken place? Do the strange rituals we enact at important moments of a match affect the outcome?

The mediated experience of football, in particular at the quadrennial World Cup finals, has become a phenomenon of which FIFA boasts, brandishing extraordinary numbers to show the fruits of its stewardship. FIFA, not troubled by counting people more than once, says that 26.3 billion viewers in 214 countries watched the 2006 World Cup finals on television. Broadcast rights for radio, television (both standard and high-definition), and broadband Internet are parceled to each country, from Albania to Peru to Vietnam, for untold billions in revenue. In some countries viewers must pay for the privilege of watching the games live—a long distance from Simic with his ear pressed to a dead receiver.

Simic, who teaches fiction writing at the University of New Hampshire, has lived in the United States ever since emigrating, at age fifteen, from Yugoslavia in 1953. Through visits to the library, he developed an early obsession for reading and writing poetry. To date he has published more than sixty books of poems, essays, and translations. He won the Pulitzer Prize in Poetry in 1990 for *The World Doesn't End: Prose Poems*, and in August 2007 Simic became America's fifteenth poet laureate.

Is anyone still upset about the loss of Yugoslavia to Brazil in the 1950 World Cup? Probably not, but I am. I was twelve years old at the time, but already a fanatic football fan. I read the sports pages of newspapers and weekly magazines, listened to games on the radio, went to some with an uncle, talked about football endlessly with my friends, and for lessons in higher wisdom sat in a local barbershop where old men reminisced about our glorious past. I heard about a Serbian player from the 1920s who had a shot so powerful he killed a couple of goalies when they tried to stop the ball. Every time he stepped up to take a free kick they would rush to get a coffin ready. Finally the football association gave him a choice: let doctors remove some of his leg muscles or quit football. I forget what supposedly happened next.

The World Cup that ruined my life took place in Brazil. Yugoslavia had already beaten Mexico and Switzerland in their group when Brazil, which had defeated Mexico too, surprisingly tied Switzerland. Only one team was to advance into the final round, so all Yugoslavia needed to do was to tie the host nation. As we had a strong team, this should have been a cinch. There was one problem, however. The games were broadcast past my bedtime, so officially I was supposed to be in bed and not huddled in our dark living room listening to the radio with the sound turned way down. My mother had absolutely no interest in football. When neighbors ran into the street shouting because of some great victory or threw their radios out of windows because their team had lost, she went around demanding to know what was wrong with everybody.

The night of the important game with Brazil I went through the charade of going to sleep. Instead of sleeping, I laid in bed trying to visualize the two teams warming up in the Maracanã stadium in Rio. Poor mother, not only was she ignorant of who Barbosa, Augusto, Juvenal, Zizinho, Jair, Chico, and Ademir were, but she didn't even know the names of our players. When I finally snuck up to the radio the game had already started. I remember the noise of the crowd, the excited voice of the announcer as if a penalty had already been called or a goal scored. All of a sudden our radio went dead. I fiddled with the dials, checked the plug and the fuse box in the kitchen, but I could do nothing. I sat for a long, long time with my ear against a dead radio hoping for a miracle. The next morning I rose before anyone else did and ran into the street to get a paper. It took me a while to find an open kiosk and an eternity to find the page with the score. My first thought was, *I'm still asleep*. What I saw shocked me as much as seeing a pile of rubble after a bombing raid where a building used to stand. Brazil had beaten Yugoslavia 2–0. With the great players we had and the strategy I had devised for our team during the night, this could not happen. I still don't believe it ever did. I know what the record books for the 1950 World Cup say, but somebody ought to get to the bottom of this and verify if the score of that game was reported correctly.

23. Fahrenheit 1976

Rogelio Ramos Signes
Translated from the Spanish by Toshiya Kamei

The following meditation by Argentine writer Rogelio Ramos Signes has as its background the coup of March 24, 1976, when Argentina's armed forces overthrew the government of Isabel Martínez de Perón. Thereafter the military maintained tight controls on football, particularly over the 1978 World Cup finals played in Argentina (see chapter 39, "Boycotting the World Cup," for further commentary on the event).

The improvisational nature of Ramos Signes's imagery evokes a telling contrast with the game as dominated by generals. "They called it soccer" is the refrain. "How intense those days were," recalls journalist Ezequiel Fernandez Moores in Jimmy Burns's *Hand of God: The Life of Diego Maradona* (1996). "Football had become the center of everything in Argentina. One couldn't, because one wasn't allowed to, talk or write about anything else. There we were, in a dictatorship, with footballers surrounded by soldiers." David Winner, in *Brilliant Orange: The Neurotic Genius of Dutch Football* (2000), quotes Dutch player Johnny Rep as saying of Holland's 1–3 loss to Argentina in the final: "It was not a good atmosphere. It was too hot. All the *militaire*. It was too heavy. It was *kokend*, boiling." Detainees at the Escuela de Mecanica de la Armada (Navy Mechanics School), a clandestine detention and torture center, reported hearing the cheers from Estadio Monumental less than a kilometer away.

It wasn't the soccer I liked. It wasn't soccer at all, but they called it soccer anyway, and it was the only sport they played. The ball, made of transparent glass and elongated like a chorizo, was carried from field to field in an apron pocket. You couldn't touch it with your feet (and if you did happen to touch it, you got an automatic prison sentence);

the penalties were decided by how the dice fell into a swimming pool; hanging from a helicopter, the goalies scored the goals, heading the ball, and only if it was raining.

It wasn't the soccer I liked, I tell you, but they called it soccer, and it was the only sport they played there back then. In spite of everything, I ended up being the leading scorer of the tournament, which everyone thought was an affront to the nation. That's why I was condemned to *write a tree* ("Graciela loves Antonio" was what I wrote), *plant a son* (in the backyard of the Department of Justice and Confiscation, as it's known), and *have a book*. That's what ruined me, because the military (again) had overthrown the government. So they cut the tree (because it was blocking a traffic light), took my son away to an unknown destination, and burned the only book I had in my library.

Part 3. Challenge

Soccer offers an ambiguous
middle ground between words
and blows. — TIM PARKS,
author of *A Season with Verona*

Introduction

The challenge of a game begins with the referee's whistle and the opening kickoff. The team without the ball struggles to take it away. A winger rushes down the flank with the ball and crosses it into the box. A striker leaps into the air to head it, joined by a defender hoping to clear it, but both of them are outdone by the goalkeeper, who has risen higher than them both and punches the ball away from danger—for the moment.

But there are more challenges in football than those intrinsic to the game: Teammates compete with one another for starting positions. Coaches fight to keep their jobs. Owners must find ways to make a profit. Fans struggle to buy World Cup tickets. Merchants hope to run successful businesses without incident. The media juggles reporting on tight deadlines and delivering live broadcasts to a large audience.

In this section we look at some of the challenges that place football at risk. In an excerpt of a novel from Hungary we meet a youth-team coach who likely represents the cruelest manager in the history of the game. From Iran we read the words of female football fans who see their exclusion from watching games as a challenge to their rights. From Brazil a short story centers on the years-old guilt one player bears for his nasty challenge that ended the career of a would-be star. And from Israel we learn of the challenges that come up when politics enters the game and everything becomes more complicated, beginning with the selection of players.

Most of these entries highlight the challenges between individuals or between individuals and social forces. Others, however, explore internal struggles, such as Günter Grass's account of a jailed spy who watches a televised match between East and West Germany and finds himself torn by loyalty to both. Which, he asks himself, is his country? Which could possibly be his rival?

The works collected here remind us, if we needed reminding, that for all its potential to bring diverse people together—as the theme of the 2006 World Cup declared—the game is not always just a game, and the challenge to avoid corroding effects is always present.

24. Dreaming of Sunday Afternoons

Giovanna Pollarolo

Translated from the Spanish by Toshiya Kamei

Grim reality lurks behind the text of Peruvian poet and screenwriter Giovanna Pollarolo. This poem duplicates household rhythms of large sections of middle-class Latin America, in which *fútbol* influences family dynamics and domestic routine.

Beatriz Vélez, a sociologist from Colombia, says in a personal correspondence that such routines—men playing, watching, or discussing soccer while women work—helped influence her course of research at Universidad de Antioquia in Medellín. She has conducted extensive field studies into the novelty of girls playing with boys in publicly backed Soccer for Peace programs, drawing the conclusion that girls and women still exist on the periphery of a game that reinforces male dominance. Vélez evokes the transformation of Colombian city streets on weeknights and weekends into improvised stadiums, "where men of all ages vent their aggressive impulses and psychic eroticism." In a culture where female physical-education students were banned from playing soccer until 1986, Vélez herself has had ample opportunity to experience firsthand women's position at the margin.

"My only brother was not required to help out around the house, but was encouraged to go out and play football with his friends," Vélez remembers. "Often he would come home with his clothes and football cleats full of mud, and it did not seem to bother him to leave a trail of dirt and grime across the floor which I had cleaned. This infuriated me, and I asked myself why he had the right to mess up what I had worked so hard to clean, and why he and his friends never ceased to tell a thousand and one times the same old stories about their games and the goals they scored."

The announcer spits out his words
at each play he screams "no goal"
Inca Kola the national drink
Is your car burning up?
Bring it to Rivarde Body Shop
before it's too late.
Sunday afternoons
Dad lies in bed barefoot
in his BVDS
the radio at full volume
Mom irons and grumbles
I hate Saturdays
and Sundays . . . I detest them.
After family lunch
washed down with wine we don't drink
with dishes coming and going
we just wait for the click of the radio
to exile us to the kitchen corner
where we clean up the party's mess.
I swear, when I grow up
I won't be like Mom
And the man I don't know yet
won't be like Dad
When my day comes there will be no ironing
or soccer or deep sighs.
Sunday afternoons
only the announcer gets to talk
Dad gasps at a goal
forgets about love
Mom just grumbles
I dream of my glorious Sundays.

25. A Fine Fla-Flu

Nelson Rodrigues
Translated from the Portuguese by Albert G. Bork

Nelson Rodrigues, considered Brazil's greatest playwright, "gave Brazilian football its clearest voice," in the words of Alex Bellos, author of *Futebol: The Brazilian Way of Life* (2002). Rodrigues's short stories about football and daily life featured regularly in Brazilian newspapers. "Nelson's columns took football-writing into a new dimension," writes Bellos. "For a start, he made up characters and situations. Perhaps he felt the freedom to do this . . . because he was not a sportswriter—he was a famous playwright. An equally likely reason was because he was so short-sighted that he could hardly make out events on the pitch." Rodrigues's support for Fluminense FC of Rio de Janeiro was unabashed. "I'm Fluminense, I always was Fluminense," he says in Bellos's book. "I'd say I was Fluminense in my past lives." The "tricolor," as Fluminense is known, has its greatest rivalry with another Rio team, Flamengo (the "red and black"), based in a residential area, Gávea, in Rio's southern quarter. Hence their competitions are known as "Fla-Flu."

The match described below took place on October 13, 1968, in one of the world's best-known football arenas, the Maracanã—the shared home ground of both teams. Constructed for the 1950 World Cup finals, with an original capacity of two hundred thousand, the Maracanã's official name is Estádio Jornalista Mário Filho. The name pays tribute to Rodrigues's older brother, a journalist and inspiration behind the stadium's construction. Despite associations between Brazil and "the beautiful game," Rodrigues evokes the physical contest that results when intra-city rivals with a long history meet. Casualties are plentiful, and players drip "epic drops of sweat."

Friends, because of an ill-fated habit we have acquired, we of the dailies write that any game was "technically faulty." If literary criticism were as harsh, Shakespeare would be a pompous mediocrity and Dante a second-rate poet. But woe to us, woe to us. Our limitations are no more than an almost comical affectation. But I, who am not ashamed to admire, or praise, will say that yesterday's Fla-Flu was a remarkably fine spectacle.

We cannot yet demand that Flamengo give its all. It was seriously banged up. There was an instant when we could say, "Gávea is a hospital." A hospital and almost a morgue, so plentiful were the casualties. But yesterday the red and black team held its head high, and its spirit was not to be denied. I have nothing but warm praise for its players. And I repeat that the team deserves its fans' warm encouragement.

Of course I cannot gloss over the goal. When Wilton, taking advantage of a long pass, scored a goal, the entire Mário Filho Stadium filled with a red and black roar: "Hand! Hand!" And, in fact, our worthy striker, yes, in his eagerness to score, used his hand. That's what I saw. And that was also what Marcelo Soares de Moura, Swede the Sailor, and Francisco Pedro do Couto, who were with me, saw. Everyone saw hand, except the referee and the linesman. I'm certain, however, that the goal was credited because, really, neither of them saw anything.

But that was not the entire game. I must praise the tricolor team. I would have no criticism whatsoever of our first half. First off, let us praise our players' fighting spirit. How they strove, heart and soul, and how they dripped, from the first to the last second, epic drops of sweat. They say that against Palmeiras, Fluminense had its worst ground game. But yesterday, in the initial period, we played marvelously. That isn't to say that the second period might have been disappointing. It was well played. But in the first one our euphoria was frightening. It was aggressive team soccer, a game in which everybody helped everybody. In soccer slang, they say a player "put on a clinic." Well then, yesterday, in the first period, we, physically, put on a clinic.

Fast soccer, but note: it wasn't the poor speed, the obtuse speed of the Europeans. No. It was an intelligent and irresistible speed. Running all out, the player would fake, pass, make a play. In the Fla-Flu we saw that one of the keys for the tricolor team was the long ball. We have Wilton, who is exceedingly quick as a striker. He needs to be set free like Paulo Borges on the old Bangu team. And if it can't be

Wilton, then another who shoots forward for a pass, in goal-scoring position. Be that as it may, Fluminense yesterday displayed tactical flexibility that we hadn't seen in its last matches.

And so it was that our fans left Mário Filho Stadium in a state of euphoria. Victory is sweetest and holiest when its technical level justifies the feeling and when the fighting spirit gives it a broader dimension. It's very well that we saw, on the field, a Flamengo that fought nobly, never dejected. Therefore, a great Fla-Flu.

26. Escaping with the Ball

Luiz Vilela

Translated from the Portuguese by Christopher Finney

Luiz Vilela was born in 1942 in Ituiutaba, Minas Gerais, the large southeast Brazilian state where Pelé was born two years earlier. Vilela began writing when he was thirteen years old. In 1966, he made his debut with the short-story collection *Tremor de terra* (Earth Tremor), which won the Prêmio Nacional de Ficção—the Brazilian national book prize for fiction. Vilela also won Brazil's most prestigious literary award, the Prêmio Jabuti Prize ("Tortoise"), for his 1973 story collection, *O fim de tudo* (The End of Everything).

Here Vilela explores the violent side of football and, in particular, the guilt one player carries for injuring another player, even years after the event. The two erstwhile foes in this one-sided dialogue represent an explicit and real form of challenge. Dangers associated with the profession can bring suffering and financial ruin, especially at lower levels of the game in less-developed areas.

Pelé recalls in one of his many biographies—*Pele's New World* by Peter Bodo and David Hirshey (1977)—that once his father, a semiprofessional player, had suffered a career-ending knee injury Pelé had to start working to bring in extra money. Pelé describes selling newspapers at age ten, working as a shoemaker's apprentice, and collecting cigarette butts to resell as handmade cigarettes at football matches. Pelé's mother and grandmother were so concerned for his safety that they rarely watched him play. "In all her life," Pelé says of his mother, Celeste do Nascimento, "she come to see me play at the stadium maybe three times. . . . She always prefer to stay at home and pray."

Was that him? God, he looked terrible! Gray hair, skinny, wrinkled . . . But, no doubt about it, it really was him. So he just walked into the bar and went to the table in the back, where the other man was, the only client at that time in the afternoon, and stopped in front of him:

"Canhoto . . ."

The other man looked at him. When he recognized him, a sudden and intense expression of hate passed over his face—a hate that came from those times and had crossed all those years and erupted on his face now like an explosion.

He had expected a hostile reaction, it was only natural, just not so strong. He felt confused and didn't know what to do next. But the determination that had brought him to that place and that moment made him pull himself together, and he said,

"How's it going? . . ."

The other man barely shook his head in response.

"Can I sit down?"

A vague wave of the hand, indicating the chair. He sat down.

"This won't take long, just a quick chat; I just wanted to talk to tell you some things."

The other man took another drink of rum without looking at him, still with the same sullen face.

"I heard you lived here; I asked around and found out. So I took this trip. I came just to see you."

Then the other man looked at him with a trace of surprise on his hostile face.

"I'm thirsty, I'm going to get a beer . . . Have one with me?"

The other man answered with a gesture to his glass of rum. He looked at the waiter and ordered a beer and another glass.

"What do you do around here?" he asked, trying to start some small talk.

"Some things."

"Yeah . . . I have a store in Belo Horizonte, a clothes store. It's no big deal, but it's a living; I can raise the family on it—the wife and three kids. Things get tight once in a while, but we get by . . . "

The other man didn't say anything.

"Sometimes I think 'Man, what about Canhoto, what's he up to?' I always ask around about you, but nobody really knows. Back then, when it happened, I watched the whole thing: the operation, the treatment, the complications you had later, the talk about another operation, the financial troubles the team had, that you had; I watched it all. The day I found out you couldn't play anymore, I was really sad, really sad. I wished for that not to be true, for there to still be some way for . . . I wished . . . "

He looked at the other man, who remained silent, his eyes fixed on the cup; he held it as if, at any moment, he would crush it with his hand.

"Sorry, Canhoto, I'm sorry about being here saying this stuff. I know it's not fun for you, I know. I bet you would really rather I wasn't here. Well I promise, I promise I won't come back, I promise you that. But I had to come this time, I had to come talk to you. It's been sticking in my throat for six years . . . "

He poured more beer into the glass.

"You really don't want some? . . . "

"No."

"You know, I admit it, I was a coward. I should have visited you right after, those days even, and talked to you, told you how it happened. It wouldn't have helped much, but . . . I don't know, at least . . . I didn't mean to do it, Canhoto, I really didn't; I swear. It's that . . . you remember, we had to win that game, we had to win no matter what; our ranking depended on it. There were just three minutes left, the fans were already celebrating. When I saw you escaping with the ball on that counterattack, our whole defense beaten, I went crazy. I knew you couldn't miss. I only had one chance: stop you. There wasn't any other way. So I went. I went all out. But I didn't mean to . . . I'm not a violent guy, I never was. You know, I was the team captain, the guy with the most self-control. But right then . . . "

The other man lifted the cup to his mouth and threw down the rest of the rum.

"We won the game; yeah, we won . . . And then came the best times for the team, and we won the championship. Those were my best times too: I had never played so well. They even talked about me for the national team. Can you imagine? Me on the national team . . . that would have been the greatest joy of my life. That was my greatest dream. It's every player's greatest dream, yours too probably . . .

Actually, you had a better chance than me: you had more soccer in you, you dribbled better, and you had a shot—man I'll tell you . . . it was a bomb. I'm not saying that just to make you feel better either. I always thought so, lots of people did, you know: out of the teams around here at the time, you were the biggest star, no question. 'Tiago, watch that kid,' I remember Maia told me that day, before the game, in his instructions: 'Watch that kid, he's a demon: don't take your eyes off him for a second.' It was a real show, our duel at midfield."

And he sat remembering, his gaze lost in the table. He remembered other games too, the excitement of the goals, the cheers of the crowd . . . That was all over—why remember?

Outside the afternoon was dying; vague noises drifted in from the calm street of the small town.

"But the other thing I wanted to tell you," he continued, "was that . . . I couldn't forget it, I couldn't. I always remembered. And the better I did, the more they talked about me in the papers, the more I remembered. It was like it was all happening just because of that day. I mean, if it wasn't for that day, none of it would have happened. So on the field, on game day, I would go in and remember; one time I even saw you in there. Just so you know how I was. It felt like I was really going nuts. And that's when my trouble started. Everything started to go wrong for me: I blew passes, lost balls, missed shots, everything went wrong. 'What's going on with you?' they would ask me. Did I know? 'What's wrong with you?' How was I supposed to know what was wrong with me, all I knew was that everything was going wrong, that's all I knew. I even tried voodoo. Did it help? Like shit. Then it came time to renew my contract. No way they were going to renew . . . But I knew they were right. Renew like that, with that lucky streak? . . . That's when I went to a little team—Esporte—with a shitty little salary, just to have something to do. I went. The streak went too. Everything stayed the same, the same bad luck, God damn it. I've never seen anything like it. And then one afternoon, after a loss when I missed two goals, I looked at the field, I looked at the field like this, and I said, 'Goodbye, brother.' I turned my back on it, and I never set foot on a soccer field again."

He finished the bottle of beer.

"My glorious career over, I worked on getting my little life out there together. I bought the store, lost money on some bad deals, but everything came together bit by bit. Everything, except for one thing . . . That couldn't be helped. I had thought that, far from the field, it was going to fade away. Right . . . it didn't fade at all. I reached the conclusion that it would never fade: it would just stay in my memory like a scar. One night, before bed, I talked to my wife—I told her the whole story. I had never told anyone. She listened, listened carefully, then she said, 'Why don't you go find him? Why don't you go tell him what you told me? . . . ' She was right, that was exactly what I should do. I had already thought about it, but then I thought 'Who do I think I am to walk up to him? Who do I think I am to go tell him all that?' . . . But then, all of a sudden, I decided 'I'm going to go there, I'm going.' I found out where you lived, got the bus, and here I am. Here I am, in this town I had never even heard of before; here I am now, telling you all this . . . "

He picked up the cup and took a slow drink of beer. There was a prolonged silence.

"What about you? Aren't you going to say anything? I wanted you to say something, anything. Even if you tell me to go to hell. But say something."

"Say what?" said the other man, his voice tired. "You ruined my life, can't you see that? It wasn't just my leg you broke, it was my life. I was going to be great, I was going to be one of the greatest athletes Brazil ever had. You destroyed it, you destroyed it all that afternoon."

"I tried to explain it to you."

"It was a nightmare, a nightmare day and night. Hell, thinking I could never play again was worse than death. I wanted to die. I started drinking, drank like crazy, to keep from thinking about it. So I ended up ruining my health. I had a bunch of problems. I needed my parents' help, my siblings' too. I went through all their money—it was one disgrace after another. Now I'm what you see: a loser, a failure, half a man. Talk. What do you want me to say? Huh? What do you want me to say?"

He stopped, his breathing suppressed.

"I'm sorry Canhoto, I didn't know. I didn't know so much had happened. I swear I didn't know. I could have guessed some of it, but . . . I'm really sorry. I really am. I tried to explain to you, I told you how it was. One thing you can be sure of: I regretted it all these years, I regretted it a lot. But it was like I told you: a moment of insanity. It was something I normally wouldn't do, something that happened to me, but it could have happened to anybody, even you. That's what I wanted you to understand. I wanted you to understand that in a way I was a victim too, that both of us were victims of the same thing, something bigger than us. I don't know what. Maybe that crowd, maybe that clock, maybe that crazy wind that gets in your head all of a sudden . . . That's what I wanted you to understand. That's why I came here, why I traveled those thousand miles. I wanted you to understand and . . . for you to forgive me."

"There is no forgiveness for that."

Then he stood up and, without saying goodbye, walked over to the bar, dragging a leg, paid, and left.

He stayed at the table alone, alone with that past and the regret that didn't find forgiveness. What else could he do? He did what he could. He couldn't do anything else. But, if you thought about it, it was right. Yeah, it was. Wasn't he a victim too? So he should drag that regret around for the rest of his life, like the other man dragged his leg.

That's how it was and that's how it should be he concluded on his way to the bar, where, surprised, he learned the other man had paid for his beer.

27. Generals and Fools

Andrew Marshall

Throughout the world football stadiums often exist as places in which to challenge political and social norms. Academics have drawn on Russian philosopher Mikhail Bakhtin's theories of the carnivalesque to suggest that crowds reenact, in ritual chanting and insults, a challenge to authority implicit in the pre-Lenten Feast of Fools. In repressed societies—as in the following example from Burma, excerpted from Andrew Marshall's book *The Trouser People: A Story of Burma in the Shadow of the Empire* (2002)—being part of a football crowd offers privileges denied at other times. One of these privileges, according to the magazine *The Irrawaddy*, published by Burmese expatriates in Thailand, is to "shout angry words at military teams when a civilian footballer is fouled."

Marshall, a journalist with expertise in Asia, devised his travelogue in part to retrace the missions of J. George Scott, who in 1878 introduced football to Burma, then part of the British Raj. The Burmese people took to the game quickly, playing in native dress, the *longyi*, gathered and tied between the legs to allow freedom of movement.

Like other areas of Burmese society, the modern game has come to be dominated by the military junta. The junta has governed since 1962, and domestic football has a military flavor. Marshall's guide at one point complains that land for rice paddies has been converted by the military into football pitches for soldiers. "Now the people have nothing," the guide says. Still, authorities make sure that the sometimes unreliable flow of electricity remains steady during major events like the World Cup finals. "Even Burma's generals seem to realize," Marshall writes before the 2006 World Cup, "the dangers of denying a long-suffering people this simple joy."

Later I learned why we had received extra power that night. A week or so before, Lieutenant General Khin Nyunt had lectured a meeting of coaches, sportswriters and retired footballers on the importance of "uplifting the standard of Myanmar soccer." How, he asked, could the national game return to its post-war golden age, when Burma had been one of the strongest teams in Asia? None of the assembled experts pointed out that the golden age of Burmese football died along with democracy after the 1962 military coup. At one point in the 1960s official neglect of the sport was such that the entire country ran out of footballs.

National trials to select Burma's best players were now under way, and were being televised in full. Last night's game had run over, thus the extra fifteen minutes before lights out. But Khin Nyunt's sudden passion for soccer alarmed some people I knew. What was he up to? What did he *want*? It wasn't as if the generals even *liked* footie. In 1962 the only people allowed through the cordon of tanks and troops encircling Rangoon were golfers—the city's best course lay on the other side. But Khin Nyunt wasn't interested in the game itself. For him it was a potentially valuable tool for what he called "enhancing the nation's dignity."

The trouble was, Burmese football was not very dignified. George Scott's students had loved it for being "just like fighting," and little had changed since. In the post-war period, matches often progressed through player punch-ups into full-on stadium riots in which even Buddhist monks were known to put the sandal in. Matches between universities and the military—bitter political enemies off the pitch—were notoriously prone to violence. Students were now banned from competitive football, but the Burmese game was still robust. I saw a match in Mandalay where the referee showed his yellow card thirteen times and sent five people off. As far as I could work out, this was considered quite normal.

Burmese league football was bad, but the national team was worse—possibly the worst in South-East Asia. Its consistently dismal performance abroad was a source of acute embarrassment to the generals. Two years before, when Burma was trounced in a match in tiny Brunei, all reporting about the national squad was banned when a disgusted senior general declared that he "didn't want to hear another word about it." Later, when Burma conceded a crucial goal during a nationally televised game against Indonesia, the state-run TV Myanmar actually went off air for a few minutes—in shame, apparently. Interestingly, the manager of the national team was an Englishman called David Booth. His pedigree was unknown, although one Burmese trainer described his management style as—ironically enough—"very dictatorial."

After Khin Nyunt's golden-age lecture, an editorial in the *New Light of Myanmar* reminded readers that supporting Burmese football was a way of "expressing their patriotism." To which your average Burmese soccer fan, drawing on his nation's rich stock of peasant vocabulary, might respond, "My arse." No one I talked to had a good word to say about Burmese football today. But go to a match—particularly a match between two military teams—and you realize that that's the whole point. Gatherings of more than five people are technically illegal in Burma, and even an innocuous remark can lead to a spell of hard labour. But a thousand football supporters can sit together and scream abuse at the players until they're hoarse, and if there's a five-star general in the VIP box they shout even louder.

I had discovered this for myself a few weeks before, at the final of the Aung San Shield—the Burmese equivalent of the FA Cup. I arrived at Rangoon's Thuwanna Stadium to find about 5,000 people crammed into the shaded west stand. The rest of the stadium was empty, and pariah kites made graceful, swooping orbits above the silent terraces opposite. The spectators were young, male and rowdy. They were squatting Asia-style on the concrete seats, with their sarongs tucked up round their crotches. They were smoking sweet-smelling cheroots, gobbing betel juice between their flip-flops, and passing round hard-boiled quail eggs and dodgy-looking kebabs—just lapping up the pre-match atmosphere. They had each paid about forty pence to see this game, and were expecting to get their money's worth.

I had two friends with me. Sein Da was a cheerful, soft-spoken Arakanese student with a million-watt smile. Tin Mya was his emotional opposite: an intense young Burman whose father, an opposition politician, had spent over a decade in prison. We bought some pumpkin seeds and sat down near the double helping of barbed wire that ran the length of the terrace.

The players trotted on to the parched turf and began to warm up. At this point I would like to report that the teams had romantic names like "Mandalay United" or "Rangoon Rovers." But I can't. The team in the yellow strip was the Ministry of Finance and Revenue; the one in blue and white was the Ministry of Home Affairs. It could have been worse: the final of another tournament had been fought out by the No. 323 Supply and Transport Battalion and the Defense Services Orthopaedic and Rehabilitation Hospital.

I asked Tin Mya if teams in Burma had any nicknames. After all, "Ministry of Finance and Revenue" was a bit of a mouthful.

Tin Mya frowned. "What do you mean?" he asked suspiciously.

"Well, for example, Manchester United are sometimes called Man U. or the Red Devils. Don't teams here have similar nicknames?"

"No," replied Tin Mya sternly. "No nicknames."

With a carpet of pumpkin-seed husks at his feet, Tin Mya gave me his pre-match analysis. Basically, he said, Home Affairs was about to get thrashed. Finance was a relatively wealthy ministry where officials had plenty of opportunities for graft. (Most foreign investors in Burma bribe Finance officials at some point—an envelope of hard currency here, a Rolex there.) Everyone wanted to work there, and the ministry picked the best footballers from among the applicants. Finance was the holder of the Aung San Shield. Tin Mya was in no doubt that it would win again today.

A clinical header, a goalmouth scramble, a low, unstoppable volley—Finance was soon three–nil up, and the crowd had grown increasingly raucous. They scented a massacre. They roared with glee when a Home Affairs defender fell from a mid-air tussle into a lifeless, stretcher-ready heap by his own goalposts. They screamed with laughter when a desperately cleared ball almost knocked the Aung San Shield from a taffeta-fringed table near the dugouts. When Home Affairs blundered into yet another offside trap, a man in front of us sprang to his feet and launched into a virtuoso abuse of the linesman.

I nudged Sein Da. "What's he shouting?" I asked.

Sein Da grinned. "He is saying, 'Hey! You! What the hell is going on? Pisses on you!'"

The man in front of us was still screaming. "And now?" I asked.

"Now he is saying, 'Fuck your mother!'"

"You mean 'motherfucker.'"

"Yes, yes," said Sein Da excitedly. "'Fuck your motherfucker.'"

Finance won four–nil—no surprise there. Afterwards, the pariah kites returned to circle above the electronic scoreboard, which registered a flurry of meaningless pixels. A flock of mynah birds descended upon the threadbare penalty area to feast on worms brought to the surface by the relentless pounding of the Home Affairs goalmouth. A portly colonel in uniform stepped out to present the awards, and it was then, much to my surprise, that the jeering really began.

First the Home Affairs team was given its runner-up trophy. This was accepted not by the team captain, but by a uniformed policeman. A growl of annoyance went through the crowd. The policeman accepted the trophy, then saluted the colonel—and the crowd roared with derision.

"There is no need to salute the colonel," explained Tin Mya. "They are just civilians. But that policeman has saluted, and now—look—the whole team has to do the same."

"What a shit!" someone nearby exclaimed in perfect English.

Many more trophies were handed out. One fell apart in the colonel's hands, and the crowd hooted with laughter. Then a player called Aung Moe Oo came forward. He belonged to the much-loathed Defense Services team and was himself a military officer. A low, whooping sound rose menacingly from the terraces. It sounded to me as if the crowd were making monkey noises, but in fact they were saying a Burmese word over and over again, with increasing volume and venom. By the time Aung Moe Oo took his trophy from the portly colonel, that single word was booming maddeningly around the stadium.

"*Ayu, ayu, ayu, ayu, ayu* . . ."

"Fool, fool, fool, fool, fool . . ."

This open ridicule of the military astonished me. But, as Tin Mya explained, beyond arresting 5,000 rowdy fans, the authorities could do very little to stop it. The crowd dissolved into gleeful, schoolboy laughter. Then, almost as one, people got up, retied their longyis, and began filing towards the exits. This bewildered me, too. It all seemed so abrupt. Wasn't anybody going to watch the Aung San Shield itself being presented?

But for everyone else the afternoon was now complete. They had smoked a few cheroots, they had watched some eventful footie, they had hurled abuse at various members of the police and military. For ordinary Burmese, that's just about the most fun you can have in public without getting arrested.

28. 1974

Günter Grass
Translated from the German by Michael Henry Heim

The 1999 Nobel Prize–winning author, Günter Grass, crystallizes the conflicts in identity—"finding one's 'I' doubled"—endemic to a divided Germany in this narrative set during the 1974 World Cup finals. In Hamburg on June 22, 1974, East and West Germany competed in the only official international match between the two sides, with the German Democratic Republic (GDR) prevailing 1–0 on a late goal from Jürgen Sparwasser. Heightening the sense of divided loyalties, Grass takes license to probe, with football as pretext, the curious existential position of the historical figure Günter Guillaume. Exposed in 1974 as an East German spy serving as a personal aide to West Germany's chancellor, Willy Brandt, Guillaume spent seven years in prison before a return to the East; Brandt's chancellorship crumbled following the revelations. The chapter "1974," reprinted here, is one of one hundred—one for each year—in Grass's collection *My Century* (1999).

The match as a proxy for the ideological systems of East and West Germany becomes even clearer from a historical distance. The East German secret police, the Stasi, had extended their spy network into clubs in the GDR and arranged for hundreds of loyalists to be present at this match in the tournament's first round. East Berliner Alexander Osang, writing in *The Thinking Fan's Guide to the World Cup* (2006), remembers jumping "on the dark brown linoleum of my newly built East German flat" with the GDR victory. Even though he idolized the stars from the West—Franz Beckenbauer and Gerd Müller of Bayern Munich—Osang finds himself fueling a strangely satisfying inferiority complex: "They had the bigger country, the better cars, the better chocolate, the better chewing gum, the better sneakers. . . . But on that summer evening in 1974, in Hamburg, we beat them. I beat them."

The result did not prevent West Germany from advancing in the tournament, and it progressed to win its second of three World Cups. Sparwasser, who scored the game-winning goal, defected to the West in 1988. And despite reunification in 1990, the East retains an inferiority complex, particularly in football. During the 2006 World Cup finals, as acknowledgment of the East's soccer past, remnants of the 1974 team played an exhibition in Leipzig. With only a "couple hundred in the stands," according to German magazine *Der Spiegel*, the match "felt like a last hurrah for East German sports."

What does one feel when one experiences oneself double before the television screen? If one makes it one's business to toe a double line, one cannot in fact be upset by finding one's "I" doubled under certain circumstances. Merely a bit surprised. One learns not only from rigorous training but also from life how to deal with oneself and one's double identity.

Having spent four years in a penal institution like Rheinbach and having managed, after a long-drawn-out procedure, to persuade the small prison board here to accord me access to my own television receiver, I am fully conscious of the implications of living a dual existence, but in 1974 I was still in detention at the Cologne-Ossendorf Prison awaiting trial, and when permission to install a television receiver in my cell for the duration of the world soccer championship was granted, the happenings on the screen rent my inner being in many respects.

Not when the Poles played a fantastic game in the pouring rain, not when Australia lost or the match with Chile ended in a tie—no, it happened when Germany faced Germany. Which side was one for? Which side was I or I for? Whom was I to cheer on? What conflict broke out in me, what forces pulled at me when Sparwasser shot his goal?

For us? Against us? Since I was being taken every morning to Bad Godesberg for interrogation, the Bureau of Investigation could scarcely have been unaware that these and similar ordeals were far from alien to me. But actually they were no ordeals at all; they were simply a behavior pattern in keeping with the duality of German statehood, that is, I was fulfilling a double obligation. As long as my duty consisted in making myself the Chancellor's most dependable aide, his dual-orientation conversation partner in off-the-record situations, I could handle the tension involved; in fact, I scarcely saw it as a conflict, especially since the Chancellor was clearly satisfied with my perfor- mance and, according to my contact people, the Berlin office was likewise, my activities having been praised in high circles there. The idea was that between the man who saw himself as "the Chancellor of peace" and myself, who pursued a mission as "the spy of peace," there should be a kind of synergy. It was a good time, one in which the Chancellor's biography fell in with his aide's agenda. We both took our jobs seriously.

But when on 22 June the referee blew the whistle opening the match between the German Democratic Republic and the Federal Republic of Germany before sixty thousand spectators at Hamburg's Volkspark Stadium, I was completely and utterly torn. Neither side scored during the first half, but when in the fortieth minute that lithe little Müller nearly put the Federal Republic in the lead, but in the end only hit the goalpost, I nearly screamed "Goal! Goal! Go-o-o-al!" in ecstasy and would have celebrated the lead of the West's separatist state just as I was ready to break out into a cheer when Lauck, outplaying Overath by far (he shook off the great Netzer later on in the match), nearly scored against the Federal Republic.

Back and forth, back and forth. One found himself reacting even to the Uruguayan referee's decisions with tendentious commentary favoring now one, now the other Germany. I felt undisciplined, split, so to speak. Yet while Chief Detective Federau was examining me that morning, I had managed to stick to my prepared text. The questioning concerned my links to the rather extreme Hessen-Süd branch of the Social Democratic Party, whose members saw me as a hardworking but conservative comrade. I enjoyed making them think I belonged to the rightist, more pragmatic wing of the Party. But then I was confronted with my darkroom equipment, all of which had been confiscated. The thing to do in such a case is to pooh-pooh the accusations. One points out one had been a professional photographer and pulls out one's holiday snapshots to show photography is still a hobby. But then the prosecution produced a sophisticated super-8 camera and two rolls of extremely fast film, claiming them to be "perfectly suited to undercover operations." I dismissed them as mere circumstantial evidence. Secure in the knowledge that I had not contradicted myself, I looked forward to returning to my cell and watching the match.

Neither here nor there could anyone have suspected I was a soccer fan. I myself had no idea that Jürgen Sparwasser had been a stalwart of our very own Magdeburg team. But now I kept my eyes on him after Hamann passed him the ball. He trapped it with his head, brought it to his feet, raced in front of the tenacious Vogts and, leaving even Höttges behind, rammed it past Maier into the net.

1–0 in favor of Germany! But which Germany? Mine or mine? Yes, I probably screamed "Goal! Goal! Go-o-o-al!" there in my cell, while at the same time lamenting that the other Germany had fallen behind. And when I saw Beckenbauer working to build up his team's offense, I cheered on the West German eleven.

As for my Chancellor (whose downfall was of course none of my doing—I would blame Nollau perhaps and most of all Wehner and Genscher), I sent him a postcard—and kept sending him cards on holidays and his birthday, 18 December—with my regrets for the outcome of the match. He didn't answer. But you can be sure he too had mixed feelings about Sparwasser's goal.

29. End of the World

György Dragomán
Translated from the Hungarian by Paul Olchváry

Author and translator György Dragomán was born in the northern Romanian province of Transylvania in 1973 and moved to Hungary as a teenager. Using autobiographical elements from his childhood in Nicolae Ceauşescu's Romania, Dragomán, whose name means "interpreter" or "official guide," describes in his short stories and novels a world of cruelty, terror, and totalitarianism in which people still attempt to find meaning and beauty.

His 2005 novel *A fehér király* (*The White King*), from which this excerpt is taken, is narrated by a precocious eleven-year-old boy whose father is arrested and sent to a forced-labor camp near the Danube. The boy, known as Djata, and his mother struggle to survive in a world where lies and violence poison every interaction. Even soccer is a source of danger, when a ball is the cause of a bloody battle between two youth gangs. The physical and mental tortures of Coach Gica, depicted below, represent a perverted form of challenge within a society where football participates with military, political party, school, and religion in a struggle for hearts and minds.

Football in the service of the state also existed in Hungary under communism. During the 1950s the national team put together a thirty-two-game unbeaten streak before losing to West Germany in the 1954 World Cup final. Jonathan Wilson, author of *Behind the Curtain: Travels in Eastern European Football* (2006), writes that Hungary was "not merely the best in the world but probably the greatest team there had ever been." Yet suppression of the antiauthoritarian revolt that began in October 1956 helped persuade many of the best players to defect, including the entire Under-21 youth team and Ferenc Puskás, who would leave for fame at Real Madrid.

Coach Gica tended to us goalies specially, he made us show up at every practice an hour early and mainly had us do speed drills, plus we had to jump a lot and dive, too, jump and dive, jump and dive, and he had this goalie-terrorizing machine, he came up with it himself and the workers at the ironworks made it for him, a soccer ball was put on the end of this long iron pipe, the ball was filled with sand, and that's what he shot at us, the whole contraption was built onto an axle and revolved around it, throwing that sand-packed ball with no mercy, and Janika and I knew that if we didn't catch it, it would hit us in the head and break our bones. Other kids had already died in Coach Gica's hands, so they said, which is why he became a coach for the junior team, the adult players couldn't stand his heavy-handedness, one time they caught him and knocked half his brains out, and since then he wasn't allowed to coach the Ironworks' adult team but could work only with us eleven- and twelve-year-olds.

That May we were close to being dropped from the league, so Coach Gica held practice every day, he got us passes so we didn't even have to go to school for the first four hours of the day, everyone knew that Red Hammer, the ironworks team, had to stay in the running, no way we could be dropped, Coach Gica even told us that if we didn't beat Breakthrough, the military team, then that's it, it's over, after the game he'd smash everyone's ankles with a crowbar, for him it would be all the same because coaching was his life, and if we fell from the running, then that would be it, and from then on each and every one of us would be going to school on crutches, he even showed us the crowbar, and he even took a swipe with it at one of the planks in the fence, the crowbar tore right into the wood and he said our bones would break apart just like that, in splinters, not a soul would be able to put them together again. We knew he wasn't kidding because by then he didn't have a family, he lived in the junior team's clubhouse, yes, we knew he was dead serious, and so we really did go all out getting ready for that game, everyone went running, no one dared skip practice, everyone was scared stiff about what Coach Gica would do to their legs. I went running too, as much as I could take, even though I knew I didn't stand a chance of playing anyway because I was just a backup goalie, Janika was the real goalie even though he was a Jehovah's Witness, a Jehovist, the truth is he shouldn't have been playing on the Ironworks' team at all because his father didn't let him be a Young Pioneer, but he was so good at keeping goal that Coach Gica paid a visit to the school and worked things out with the top comrade there, the principal, so Janika would be able to play all the same, and sure enough he kept goal in nearly every game because he had a much better feel for the ball than I did, even when he wasn't in top form. So we practiced really hard, seeing how we were afraid of Coach Gica, but we knew it didn't matter anyway, there was no beating Breakthrough, they had the backing of the army, the team was full of army brats, the armed forces give them everything and give the referees everything too, Breakthrough was unbeaten in the playoffs, and so we knew we didn't stand a chance, and we were scared stiff.

Even on the day of the game Coach Gica held a separate practice for us goalies, and as the two of us walked along toward the sports complex so early that morning, Janika, who was even more scared than I was, stopped all of a sudden while we were still outside in front of the complex, pressed a hand to his belly, then he started retching and puked, if I hadn't got a hold of him he might have fainted, and he said that only now, on seeing the entrance to the Ironworks sports complex, did he remember that he dreamed last night about Coach Gica, about Coach Gica smashing apart his ankles, and as he said this I handed Janika my canteen so he could rinse his mouth, and he said that in his dream Coach Gica took such a hard swipe at his ankle with that iron pipe that even Coach Gica was all in tears, even now he could recall the old guy's beet-red, glistening face, and Janika said he didn't care one bit, he was going home, he wasn't coming to the practice because he couldn't take it anymore, and that I should go along too, I shouldn't stay here all by myself, he didn't even care if the team was left without a goalie. "Soccer is only a game," he said, "it's not worth this much." He wiped his mouth, gave me back my canteen, and he said, "Let's go, let's get out of here before Coach Gica sees us."

"Okay," I said, "let's go," and right then I remembered that I had woken up last night too, I had heard a big, thundering bang, that's what woke me up, but then I just lay there all quiet, and for a long time I couldn't get back to sleep, so I now said to Janika, "All right, let's go," but then, right when I was thinking about my dream, we heard this rumbling sound, but it wasn't at all like in my dream, it was much quieter, and I knew exactly what it was, it was nothing but two trucks approaching the sports complex really fast. From a distance you could tell they were painted green, their canopies were camouflage patterned, we just stood there watching them come toward us, and then the drivers hit the brakes and stopped right in front of us, a soldier got out and came over and asked what we were up to here, and Janika was so scared he couldn't get a word out, so I explained, "We've come for practice, we're certified players for Red Hammer's junior team, Janika is the goalie and I'm the backup," but the soldier didn't even pay us any attention. "All right then," he said, "but what are you standing around here for, get going," and so we went into the locker room, but before we did we could see the soldiers unpacking all sorts of big instruments and devices from their trucks.

Coach Gica was there already, slicing and chewing away at his morning slab of roast bacon, he didn't say a thing but only showed us his watch and three fingers, and we knew this meant we were three minutes late and that we'd have to run fifteen extra laps at the end of practice, but I said, "We couldn't help it, we were late on account of the soldiers," and then Coach Gica asked, "On account of what soldiers?" and he told me not to lie or he'd slap me around so good I'd slide on my snot to the goalpost. But I said I wasn't lying, he'd see for himself if he didn't believe the soldiers were here, they must've come to observe the practice so they'd know what to count on, to see how ready we were to take on Breakthrough. Coach Gica then put away his knife and wrapped up the remaining bacon, and he stood up and said, "All right, get dressed," and told us not to waste any more time or else he'd knock our brains out, then he went out and slammed the locker room door behind him.

We dressed in silence, not daring to say a word, scared that Coach Gica was listening in, he liked to know what was said about him behind his back. Janika was white as a ghost when we finally went out, and Coach Gica was there waiting for us by the edge of the field, he was talking with one of the officers, and as soon as he saw us he gave a wave of his hand. The pylons were already set up, and the two pairs of leaded shin-guards were out there too, they were made of leather but could be filled with lead tubes to make them heavier, Coach Gica had had these made too. Anyway, we got them on and then we began running the obstacle course, and after a while Coach Gica left the officer, came over, and began making us jump up and down. At one point Coach Gica hit Janika on the leg with his stick because Janika wasn't fast enough, and Janika fell and hit himself and his nose started bleeding, but Coach Gica didn't let him stop, he had to keep jumping up and down.

Meanwhile the soldiers were there the whole time, the officer was just looking at his men as they walked around the field in strange-looking clothes, pushing around machines full of wires and tubes, their hands also held all sorts of devices with wires and antennas. Just what they were doing was beyond me, maybe they wanted to broadcast the game on the radio, I'd never heard of such a thing, the machines were buzzing and rattling really loud, but we couldn't really pay attention, no, we had to keep running and jumping and diving.

The drills with the ball were the hardest, you had to dive for the ball blindfolded to get a feel for the direction, at one point I fell on the goalpost and Coach Gica kicked the ball right into my gut and I started heaving. Since Janika was always jumping in the wrong direction, I won the diving contest, by then Janika was pure white, he knew what this meant, it meant that today I would be the first one to give a kick-off, because Coach Gica had us practice kickoffs by setting up eleven balls in a row, one of the goalies had to stand ten feet away while the other goalie ran up to each ball and tried to kick it onto the other's head, and you weren't allowed to jump clear of the ball, no, you had to catch it, clutch it, or deflect it, and if we didn't kick it hard enough then Coach Gica took our place kicking off. So you really had to kick, and the one to kick first was better off because by the time the other goalie had his turn he was so beat that he couldn't really kick hard. The fourth ball I kicked sent Janika's nose bleeding again, I didn't want to kick the ball hard but there wasn't any choice, I had to run up to the ball from four steps away, and the balls always let out this huge snap, and by the end of my turn Janika didn't even reach out his hands anymore, he simply jumped right out in front of the ball and fell to the ground together with the ball. The grass was all bloody in one spot, he could hardly get to his feet, it was obvious he wouldn't be able to kick, he was all worn out. Coach Gica came over to him, he was holding a towel and he handed it to Janika, and he said, "All right, wipe your face, for once we're taking a break, get yourselves into the locker room because that comrade over there, the officer, wants a word with you two in private."

Janika pressed the towel to his nose and that's how we went, the officer really was there, I could tell from his epaulet that he was a colonel, my grandfather taught me the ranks a while back, so anyway, this colonel was sitting there on the bench in the locker room, and he motioned with his hand for us to shut the door and then he told us to sit down, and he asked what grade we were in and if we were good students, and I had to answer the questions because Janika's nose was still bleeding. The officer took an apple and broke it in two, he gave one half to me and the other half to Janika, and he said, "Fine then, you're clever boys," he could see how hard and honorably we worked, we could be proud of ourselves, we'd proven through hard work that we sure had earned the Young Pioneers' red cravat. Then he asked us if we loved our country, and of course we nodded, even Janika, though Janika was a Jehovist and Jehovists can't be Young Pioneers and can't love their country, and then the colonel asked if we knew what radioactivity was, and I said, "No, we haven't yet studied physics, but in Homeland Defense drills we learned that if there's an atomic flash you're supposed to cover your face and climb under the table or under the bed, and then you have to report to the Chemical Defense Command for protective gear, and in the Homeland Defense textbook they write about radioactivity too, they write that radiation rays go through everything and cause damage to living organisms." Anyway, after I said all that the officer nodded and said he had two sons just as big as we were, and that's why he was telling us what he was about to say, but if we dared talk to anyone about it we'd wind up in reform school for rumormongering, and they'd send our moms and dads to prison. "Do you understand?" he asked, and we nodded, but he said he wanted a proper answer, and then we said, "Yes sir, Comrade Colonel, we do understand," and Janika even took the towel away from his face and he said it along with me, that's how scared he was. And then the colonel said that last night there was an accident in an atomic power plant in the Great Soviet Union and that the wind brought the radioactivity here, and the fact of the matter was that the game shouldn't even be allowed to go ahead, but they didn't want people to panic, so it would be held after all, but he advised us goalies not to dive and to avoid contact with the ball because the ball picks up radioactivity from the grass, and anyway, we should watch out for ourselves because we were handsome, healthy little lads, and then he gave us each this white pill, saying we had to swallow it here and now. "It's just iodide," he said, "don't be scared," and only after we took the pills did I remember once seeing a movie about the Germans, about how they'd poisoned themselves with white pills like this, and maybe Comrade Colonel wanted to poison us too because he was sorry about telling us about the accident, and I could tell that Janika was thinking the same thing. But then we didn't die after all, the pill did have a bitterish taste but not like almonds, no, I knew poison was supposed to taste like almonds. Then the colonel patted me on the head and said, "All right, then, everything will be okay, take care of yourselves," and he turned and wanted to leave, but then Janika called after him and asked, "Comrade Colonel, if we can't touch the ball or even dive, how are we supposed to keep goal?" And then the colonel turned back around and looked at us and he didn't say a thing, I thought he was about to yell or give us a good slap, sometimes Coach Gica turned all quiet for a second too, before coming at us, but Comrade Colonel only shook his head and said, really quiet, that he didn't know, so help him God he didn't know, then he bowed his head and went out without a word and left us there in the locker room.

Janika had taken only two bites from his half of the apple, so I told him to give it to me if he didn't want it, and he gave it to me without a word, and I was just swallowing the last bite when the door opened and Coach Gica came in. One of the balls was in his hand, he stopped, and he asked us what Comrade Colonel had wanted with us. Janika and I looked at each other again, then he pressed the towel to his nose and I replied, "Nothing," but Coach Gica stepped over and without a word he slapped me so hard that the apple core fell right out of my hand and I got all dizzy, I had to grab onto the coat rack to keep from falling, and then Coach Gica told me not to lie to him, he'd heard every word, besides, he knew everything about us, he knew we wanted to skip out on practice, and he'd heard full well how the colonel had lied to us, and he could tell that we believed the colonel, how could we be such idiots, we'd deserve to have our brains knocked out, to have the coach hammer out what was left of our brains. He'd have us know that the soldiers had come only because that's how they want to guarantee that we'd get creamed, they wanted to scare us so we wouldn't dare keep goal properly, what did they mean by saying avoid contact with the ball? And as Coach Gica said this he got so angry that he kicked one of the benches right up into the air, the coat rack above the bench fell over and almost broke the window, and then Coach Gica got all quiet and shook his head and he said, "Get it through your skulls that the colonel was lying, if there really had been an accident in that reactor, you wouldn't even be alive anymore, besides, the Party wouldn't let the game go on, everyone knows that the country's future is its youth, yes, that's the country's greatest treasure, there's no way the Party would expose this treasure to danger."

Janika then sat down on one of the other benches and took the towel away from his face, his mouth and his chin were smeared all over with blood, and he said, really quiet, that his father had told him the end of the world would come and that it would begin with a nuclear war, with a nuclear strike, and he knew that the colonel wasn't lying because the colonel had said, "So help him God," and soldiers were atheists, they could never say the word "God" aloud, and if they did, why then, even they must sense that the end of the world had come and that nothing mattered anymore.

Coach Gica went over and stood in front of Janika, he snapped the ball to the floor and caught it with both hands, and he ordered Janika to stand up, but Janika didn't move, he only shook his head, at which

Coach Gica snapped the ball to the floor again and shouted, "I won't repeat it, stand up, for Jehovah's fucking sake," and then Janika stood up and threw the towel to the floor, and Coach Gica said all right, he understood if what the colonel said scared us, but we still couldn't be such cowards, and if Janika apologized he wouldn't be angry at him, the others would be here soon, they had to get ready for the game, but Janika shook his head and said that the end of the world was here and that he wouldn't apologize, at which point Coach Gica snapped the ball to the floor yet again, and he reached a hand into his pocket and said he'd wanted to give this to Janika only right before the game, that this here was a pair of real leather goalie's gloves that did service on the national team. Coach Gica said that he himself kept goal with them when he was chosen one time for that team, and then he reached out with the gloves toward Janika. "Here, put them on, these will protect you from the radiation."

Janika shook his head and shouted that he didn't need them, and he spit on the gloves and I could see that his spit was all bloody, and then Coach Gica shouted something really loud, you couldn't even make out what it was, and with all his might he slapped Janika across the face with those gloves, and then he stepped back and he kneed the ball right into Janika's gut and Janika doubled over, and as the ball snapped back I saw that Coach Gica wanted to knee it again, but instead of hitting the ball this time he kneed Janika's face, I heard something crack, and Janika fell onto the coat rack and slid to the floor. And then Coach Gica bent down and picked up the ball, and as he looked at me I saw that his face was all red and glistening with moisture, and Coach Gica shouted, "All right, then you'll keep goal," he was shrieking, you could hardly make out his words, and he shook his head and suddenly he kicked the ball at me, straight at my face, and I jumped forward, reaching out both hands, and I caught the ball, it struck my two palms hard and stung my skin, and when I sprang to the floor and instinctively clutched that ball tight to avoid giving the attacking player an opportunity, just as Coach Gica had taught us, I saw Janika lying on the floor next to the bench, he wasn't moving and there was blood flowing from his ear.

The ball was a little slick, which I knew was from Janika's blood, and as I stood there holding the ball I thought of the radioactivity, but except for that slipperiness the ball felt exactly the same as always, for a moment I shut my eyes and just stayed there holding it in my hands, and when I opened them again, Coach Gica was still standing in the door and Janika was still lying there and not moving, and I thought, maybe he hadn't really died, maybe he'd just fainted, because if he had died there wouldn't be a game and I wouldn't keep goal, and I looked at those real leather goalie's gloves there on the floor next to Janika, and then all at once my tears began to flow, and the ball fell out of my hands, bouncing once and rolling into the corner, but by then Coach Gica was no longer in the locker room.

30. Not So Much a Religion, More a Way of Life

Ian Jack

In this brief memoir we witness an awakening to football—a baptism, really—born of sudden immersion into working-class surroundings at a Scottish Cup final. Former *Granta* editor Ian Jack's memories are occasioned by Glasgow Celtic's loss to FC Porto of Portugal in the final of the 2003 UEFA Cup—the second-tier club competition of the Union of European Football Associations. The recollection affirms that attachments to the game and to particular teams often are born out of rivalry. Thus a boy from an "anti-football family" in the comparatively genteel atmosphere of Fife, across the Firth of Forth from Edinburgh, has a passion stoked by the barbs and challenges of Celtic supporters who "pissed where they stood."

This essay also refers to other challenges within Scottish football, particularly the "fever of hate" that characterizes the derby matches between Celtic and Rangers, Glasgow rivals known collectively as the Old Firm. Sectarianism in Scotland endures to some degree, as Jack suggests, because supporters of Celtic, identified with Roman Catholicism, and Rangers, a largely Protestant-backed team, stoke the embers of centuries-old antagonisms on occasional match weekends. Yet the passions are real. Roddy Forsyth, a writer on Scottish football, points out that the British Geological Survey in Edinburgh records earth tremors when the teams score within a minute or two of each other.

In 2005 Scotland's first minister, Jack McConnell, convened a Glasgow summit, including delegations from both Rangers and Celtic as well as representatives of the Catholic Church and the Church of Scotland, to address what McConnell called a "national shame." One ongoing aim is to end the singing of sectarian anthems at Old Firm matches. Celtic backers sometimes sing of allegiance to the Irish Republican Army (IRA), while one chant among Rangers' fans includes the lyric, "Fuck the pope and the IRA."

There is too much football: no getting away from it. One morning last week my children told me about Beckham's scaphoid bone. A couple of nights before we watched Glasgow Celtic lose to Porto in the UEFA final in Seville. I went to the loo just after half-time and my children came bouncing up two flights of stairs, twice, to pound on the door and tell me of the goals I'd missed as the score changed from 1–1 to 2–1 to 2–2. Back in front of the television, I looked at the thousands of Celtic supporters in the stands, most of them dressed like the Celtic players on the pitch, in strips hooped with green and white. I remember when I first saw a man dressed like that—dressed to imitate a player in the same green and white hoops. He lived at the bottom of our street in the village. He was a Catholic. We thought he was daft. "A grown man, did ye ever see the like . . . " and so on.

Until I was sixteen, I knew nothing about football. In the 1950s it was still possible to be so ignorant. Football, even in Scotland, was a discrete activity. Some people went to watch it, many others didn't. We lived in the east of Scotland and didn't have television. The sectarian-ism of western Scotland and the clubs it supported were just a rumour to me. Teams without some geography attached to their names were a mystery. For a long time I thought "Rangers" must be a Highland team—the name sounded mountainous—and probably located in Fort William. When, at secondary school, our French teacher, trying to be pally, made Monday-morning jokes about the local team's Saturday performance, they flew over my head like the rarer verbs.

I must also admit a more intimate reason. My family were anti-football; they thought it had drugged Scottish working-class life. In what is still the best non-fiction account of Glasgow, *Glasgow in 1901*, a book published to coincide with the city's international fair of that year, James Hamilton Muir wrote: "The best you can say for football is that it has given the working man a subject for conversation." My father, hurrying for the bus to his class at the Workers Educational Association, would have passionately disagreed with that. As far as he was concerned, it was the worst you could say for football. Football was the enemy of enlightenment and decent talk. "It was as if a fever of hate had seized that multitude, neutralising for the time everything gracious and kindly," wrote George Blake of the crowd at a Rangers-Celtic game in his 1935 novel, *The Shipbuilders*, and my father would have agreed with that, perhaps because his own father had once—occasionally and long ago—been one of that multitude, at the Rangers end.

Then in 1961, Dunfermline Athletic won through to the final of the Scottish Cup. They were the local team, the subject of our French teacher's jokes, and until that year completely obscure. Now they had a new manager, Jock Stein, and started a period of unlikely success. Their progress had passed me by. On the Saturday of the final at Hampden Park in Glasgow, I did my usual Saturday things: I got the bus to Dunfermline, borrowed some books from the library, and then sat in the stalls of the Regal to see the afternoon film. Before I went in, I noticed that the High Street was so empty that the sight of tumble-weed rolling down it wouldn't have been a surprise. When I came out there were men selling special editions of the evening papers. Clearly something big had happened. Dunfermline had drawn with Celtic, 0–0.

Schools got the afternoon off to see the replay on Wednesday and we went west on special trains which took unusual routes through the iron forges and steel mills of the Clyde valley. Inside the ground on a moist afternoon—there were no floodlights then—we stood in our school blazers among Celtic fans, men of a Glasgow type which has since disappeared: dressed with no intervening shirt between their vests and their jackets, flat caps, green and white scarves knotted as mufflers, large bottles of McEwan's Pale Ale to hand. They pissed where they stood—I'd never seen that before. Still, they were the metropolitans and we were the provincials: bumpkins, to be treated in a friendly way.

"Did youse milk the coos before ye came, son?"

It all went wrong for them, of course. Dunfermline won 2–0. That night, Dunfermline's High Street was more crowded than it has ever been before or since. The team appeared to wild noise on the balcony of the council chambers with the town's provost. Whenever I watch the video *Dunfermline Athletic: The Golden Years*, I am always surprised to see that the provost is wearing a high wing-collar, has possibly been at the council whisky, and looks like Neville Chamberlain; and that I was there.

My conversion to football had its equivalent in Galilee; it was my first match and I had been witness to a miracle. It was thrilling to discover that I was one of the blessed, the chosen, on account of where I came from. Later that year we got television, and soon after I saw the philosopher A. J. Ayer being interviewed about his enthusiasm for Tottenham Hotspur, pretty certainly along the lines of "Why on earth is a clever chap like you—and posh too—interested in football?"

I followed Dunfermline Athletic for several years and sometimes to the strangest places; East Stirling, Airdrie, Stenhousemuir. For a short while, I even had a job taking money at the turnstiles. But Stein left to transform the fortunes of the team he and his Dunfermline side had so famously beaten. Under his management, Celtic became the first British club to win the European Cup in the final against Inter Milan at Lisbon in 1967. Last week a fact about that team was often repeated: all eleven had grown up within thirty miles of Glasgow. Much the same could be said of Dunfermline then as well: most of the team were drawn from the towns and pit villages of Fife.

Last week the green and white masses in Seville were cheering on a highly paid team drawn from France, Belgium, Holland, Sweden, Bulgaria and England; only two were Scots. The number of Catholics in the team is a question no longer worth bothering with (the Pope himself has said that Scotland can no longer be called a Christian society). And yet Blake's "fever of hate" still flourishes when the two teams meet; as someone wrote recently in Scotland, their rivalry no longer represents "the tip of the iceberg" of Scotland's sectarian divide, it is the iceberg itself.

To use another metaphor, the wealth and influence of these teams make them the upas trees of Scottish football. My father would have seen them as a brake on social progress; many in Scotland still do. To that extent I think he was more right about football than Professor Ayer, though last week I was sorry, unlike in 1961, to see Celtic lose.

31. Kimmel Springs vs. Metula

Ephraim Kishon
Translated from the Hebrew by Jacques Namiel

Playwright, journalist, screenwriter, and film director Ephraim Kishon was one of Israel's most popular authors, selling more than forty million books worldwide before his death in 2005. Kishon, born in Hungary in 1924, survived several Nazi death camps during World War II. He was once spared due to a camp commandant who kept him alive to serve as a chess opponent. He also had the luck of surviving a guard who executed those surrounding him in line, prompting Kishon to say later, "He made a mistake letting a satirist live." He immigrated to Israel upon creation of the modern state in 1949.

The excerpt below comes from *The Fox in the Chicken-Coop: A Satirical Novel* (1971), which tells the story of a midlevel political hack who, after a stroke, finds himself in a mountain village whose political life reflects and mocks that of the Israeli state in its early years. The Labor Party ruled supreme over most aspects of life, and jobs were portioned according to strict political affiliations. Even soccer teams were divided along party lines. Hapoel (the worker) teams were associated with the trade-union movement; Maccabi teams, named after a second-century BCE battle cry invoking God, with the central-liberal bloc; Beitar, the name of a battle against the Romans in 135 CE, with the right-wing nationalistic alliance; and Elitzur (God is my strength) with the national religious grouping. Fierce antagonism among the teams made itself felt in political circles, and politics in turn influenced selection of players who would represent Israel as a whole. Such considerations are evident below with complex personal and power relations coming to the fore as the village decides to field a team.

The last session of the Temporary Council took place in an unprecedentedly charged atmosphere. On the agenda was a tricky question: the village youth had informed the "government" that they wanted to set up a soccer team to compete with the team from the village of Metula beyond Flood Mountain. This preposterous idea would have been considered sacrilege only a few months back, but in view of the changed attitude of the public toward travelling—the council found itself in a quandary. The councillors were therefore not hasty in coming to a decision, but personally went out to the area at the foot of the dams and studied the youngsters' exercises at length until they grew familiar with the rules of the game. After that the council decided in principle in favor of a one-time contest with Metula; but then they got stuck on the issue of picking the Kimmel Springs team.

This was truly a complex matter. The barber, of course, demanded the majority of the team for himself, on the grounds that his bloc of supporters formed the largest of all the village camps. But the cobbler denied the latter claim, stating that the Cobbler's class at school was no smaller than the Barber's, adding that the ball itself was his own manufacture. He therefore demanded for his followers three out of the five "forward" positions. As a result the other representatives demanded secure positions for themselves, based on their status in the village. Moreover, the slaughterer announced that he wished to escort the players in person, in order to keep an eye on them in the tumult of Metula.

"I also know something about ballplaying," said the slaughterer in self-recommendation. "In Hebrew school we used to play a lot until the teacher caught us and pulled out sidelocks."

The councillors consented to the slaughterer's trip since it would be irrational to leave him alone in the village when all the other councillors would be taking upon themselves the burden of escorting the team. But under no circumstances could they agree on the composition of the team. Elifaz Hermanovich proposed the game be postponed until after the elections, since then it would be easier to work out the team according to electoral strength. But his proposal was immediately vetoed because—they claimed—"after the elections there would be no need for such trips."

Tzemach Gurevich's patience finally gave out, and he laid an ultimatum before the full council session in which he demanded the following team structure:

COBB

BARB   SLAU

COBB   COBB   BARB

TAI/PUB   BARB   COBB   COBB   BARB

"The two outside right forwards will play as follows," Gurevich explained. "During the first half Hermanovich's man will play, and Kish's man will play the second half, or the other way round. I'm not prepared to make any further concessions."

Gurevich's audacity infuriated the barber.

"Comrades, you're insane!" he shouted at the cobbler. "Not only do you take five places for yourself, but you include among them the center half and the center forward. Do you want all of Metula to laugh at me?"

"The team must represent the village," insisted Gurevich stubbornly. "More than forty people signed receipts to say that I mended their shoes for free!"

"And I tell you, gentlemen," croaked the barber, "I will make up a team without a single cobblernik on it, with only Sfaradee and Kish by a majority of three votes!"

At this municipal threat Gurevich lost control of himself.

"Tyrant!" the cobbler roared. "A mayor like you should be burned!"

"Burned? So you've let the cat out of the bag?"

"It can crawl out of your belly, too, you slob!"

"Yeah? Well, I'll slit your filthy throat, you slob, if you ever dare darken the doorway of my barbershop!"

"Don't worry! I'll hang myself, slob, before I enter your reeking hole!"

"Go right ahead and hang yourself. I'll just make sure they don't, God forbid, bury me next to you, slob!"

"Please, we can discuss that later," begged Ofer Kish, the village grave-digger, and in his fertile imagination he swiftly divided the Kimmel Springs cemetery—following the educational reform plan—into the cobbler's enclave, the barber's, and those of the other denominations.

32. For the Sake of My Right and Not Football

Anonymous

Translated from the Farsi by "The Brooding Persian"

Some two hundred women protesters managed to force their way into the Azadi (Freedom) Stadium in Tehran, Iran, for a World Cup qualifier against Bahrain on June 8, 2005. Women's attendance at national-team matches in Iran had been an ongoing source of conflict between activists and the Islamic state. Within this broader struggle, football had seemed a suitable place for women to challenge the Islamic republic, at least since Iran's success in qualifying for the 1998 World Cup finals and its surprise victory at that tournament over the United States. Iranian writer Azar Nafisi, author of *Reading Lolita in Tehran: A Memoir in Books* (2003), recalls that some women removed their veils in public during the wild street celebrations.

After several confrontations with women trying to enter stadiums, President Mahmoud Ahmadinejad in April 2006 lifted the unofficial ban, in place since the 1979 Islamic revolution, so the women might help "promote chastity" in the rough-and-tumble of the all-male terraces. Religious authorities, however, overturned the decision two weeks later. The women's efforts, which sometimes included disguising themselves as boys in order to see matches, inspired Iranian filmmaker Jafar Panahi to create a cinema verité comedy about a group of women detained by police while trying to infiltrate Azadi Stadium. "One of the women swears like a fishwife, using just those words from which the women are supposed to be protected," said the Berlin International Film Festival's review of the film, *Offside* (2006).

The anonymous author of the blog "Brooding Persian" below translates portions of a manifesto written by protesters the night before the Iran-Bahrain match in June 2005. The blog writer adds, "In our society of cynics where the self-absorbed, the moneybags, and other assorted Mammon worshippers rule, these principled creatures are indeed (hidden) gems." The bracketed insertions are provided by the translator.

Tomorrow, I want to go to the stadium just like so many men and boys.

Tomorrow, I want to resurrect the right that I might never actually use [again] just like so many women and girls.

I want to remind the Security Force . . . that we too exist just like so many others.

I want to head for the western gate of the Azadi Stadium so I can accompany the other women and girls who show up.

Tomorrow, I want to go watch the game and to sit next to the men who are said to curse and insult and utter so many strange profanities [so I can] cheer [my team] Iran . . . [next to] the very same men and boys who are my religious brothers when we see them in the streets and [yet who], the authorities and the security officials, among so many others, claim, suddenly transform into predatory wolves when they show up to the stadiums.

Tomorrow, I want to sit next to all the predatory men and shout the name Iran, and I consider myself strong enough to defend myself without a shield . . .

I want to go and tell them . . . this is my right. Leave it to me and I will know what to do.

Tomorrow, I want to go earn the right I am told I am being denied on account of my weaknesses and vulnerabilities.

I want to go there so I can declare this to be my right. This is what I desire. It should for me be a most natural choice. You must just give me [the right] and I will decide whether or not to use it.

Tomorrow, I just want to be there . . . simple as that.

33. Let the Games Begin

Subcomandante Marcos and Mássimo Moratti
Translated from the Spanish and Italian by
Centro de Medios Independientes, Chiapas, Mexico

On January 1, 1994, masked rebels emerged from the jungles of Chiapas, Mexico, took over several towns, declared war on the government and multinational corporations, and called for an end to five centuries of conquest. Known as the Zapatista Army of National Liberation (after Emiliano Zapata, the revolutionary of the early twentieth century), or EZLN, one of their most eloquent representatives is Subcomandante Marcos. While the identity of the ski-masked and pipe-smoking Marcos is shrouded in mystery, the Mexican government claims that he is Rafael Sebastián Guillén Vicente, a graduate of Jesuit schools and a philosophy professor radicalized by the massacre of several hundred students ten days before the start of the Olympic Games in 1968.

According to the Mexican government's version of history, Marcos then joined a vanguard Maoist group and moved to Chiapas in southern Mexico, where he helped meld indigenous concerns and experiences with anarchist and postmodern ideas. In interviews all that Marcos has disclosed of himself is that his parents were teachers and that as a youth the writings of Cervantes and Federico García Lorca influenced him. Marcos is playful, articulate, and media-savvy, fond of quoting Borges and Shakespeare. He is also the author of several works, including the children's book *The Story of Colors* (1999), based on a Mayan creation story, and a lover of soccer.

As part of a campaign for a new constitution and regional autonomy, Marcos and his *compañeros* have traveled across Mexico accompanied by "Pingui" (the Penguin), a rooster with webbed feet. The idea for a soccer match between the Zapatistas and Italian powerhouse Internazionale of Milan—called the *nerazzurri* (black and blue) for their colors—was quickly supported by Internazionale players, including popular Argentine captain Javier Zanetti, known for his tenacity and social awareness. The call was also heeded by the team's president, oil tycoon Mássimo Moratti, and then-manager Bruno Bartolozzi, who said, "Soccer is like the fight of resistance—full of surprises." The following is an exchange between the Mexican rebel and the Internazionale president.

Zapatista Army of National Liberation
Mexico

May 25, 2005

TO: Massimo Moratti,
President of the Milan International FC
Milan, Italy
FROM: Subcomandante Insurgente Marcos
EZLN
Chiapas, Mexico

Don Massimo,

We have received the letter in which you inform us that your football team, the International FC, has accepted the fraternal challenge we made to you. We appreciate the kindness and honesty of your response. We have learned through the media of statements by the Inter's management, coaching staff, and players. They are all simply more examples of the nobility of your hearts. Know that we are delighted to have met you along our now long path and that it is an honor for us to be a part of the bridge that unites two dignified lands: Italy and Mexico.

I am letting you know that, in addition to being spokesperson for the EZLN, I have been unanimously designated head coach and put in charge of intergalactic relations for the Zapatista football team (well, in truth, no one else wanted to accept the job). In this role I should, perhaps, make use of this letter to move forward in fixing details about the match.

Perhaps, for example, I might suggest that, instead of the football game being limited to one match, there could be two. One in Mexico and another in Italy. Or one going and one on return. And the trophy known the world over as "The Pozol of Mud" would be fought for.

And perhaps I might propose to you that the game in Mexico would be played, with you as visitors, in the Mexican '68 Olympic Stadium, . . . and the stadium receipts would be for the indigenous, displaced by paramilitaries in Los Altos of Chiapas. Although then, obviously, I would have to send a letter to the UNAM University community (students, teachers, researchers, manual and administrative workers) asking them to lend us the stadium, not without solemnly promising them that we wouldn't ask them to remain silent . . . and then imposing Don Porfirio's word on them.

And perhaps we might agree, given that you would already be in Mexico, that we would hold another game in Guadalajara, Jalisco, and that the proceeds would go to provide legal help for the young *altermundistas* unjustly imprisoned in the jails of that Mexican province and to all the political prisoners throughout the country. Transportation would not be a problem, because I have read that someone here in Mexico, generous as before, has offered his help.

And perhaps, if you are in agreement, for the games in Mexico the EZLN would turn to Diego Armando Maradona and ask him to be referee; to Javier El Vasco Aguirre and to Jorge Valdano and ask them to act as assistant referees (or linesmen); and to Sócrates, midfielder who was from Brazil, to be fourth referee. And perhaps we might invite those two intergalactics who travel with Uruguayan passports—Eduardo Galeano and Mario Benedetti—to do the play-by-play of the game for the Zapatista System of Intergalactic Television ("the only television which is read"). In Italy Gianni Mina and Pedro Luis Sullo could be the commentators.

And, perhaps, in order to differentiate ourselves from the objectification of women that is promoted at football games and in commercials, the EZLN would ask the national lesbian-gay community, especially transvestites and transsexuals, to organize themselves and to amuse the respectable with ingenious pirouettes during the games in Mexico. That way, in addition to prompting TV censorship, scandalizing the ultra-right and disconcerting the Inter ranks, they would raise the morale and spirits of our team. There are not just two sexes, and there is not just one world, and it is always advisable for those who are persecuted for their differences to share happiness and support without ceasing to be different.

Rushing headlong now, we might play another game in Los Angeles, in California, the United States, where their governor (who substitutes steroids for his lack of neurons) is carrying out a criminal policy against Latin migrants. All the receipts from that match would be earmarked for legal advice for the undocumented in the USA and to jail the thugs from the "Minuteman Project." In addition, the Zapatista "dream team" would carry a large banner saying "Freedom for Mumia Abu-Jamal and Leonard Peltier."

It is quite likely that Bush would not allow our spring-summer model ski masks to create a sensation in Hollywood, so the meeting could be moved to the dignified Cuban soil, in front of the military base that the U.S. government maintains, illegally and illegitimately, in Guantánamo. In this case each delegation (from the Inter and from the Ezeta) would commit themselves to taking at least one kilo of food and medicines for each of their members, as a symbol of protest against the blockade the Cuban people are suffering.

And perhaps I might propose to you that the return games would be in Italy, with you as the home team (and us as well, since it is known that Italian sentiment is primarily pro-Zapatista). One could be in Milan, in your stadium, and the other wherever you decide (it could be in Rome, because "all games lead to Rome" . . . or is it "all roads lead to Rome"? . . . ah well, it's the same). Some of the receipts would be to help migrants of different nationalities who are being criminalized by the governments of the European Union and the rest for whatever you decide. But we would certainly need at least one day in order to go to Genoa to paint *caracolitos* on the statue of Christopher Columbus (note: the likely fine for damages to monuments would be covered by Inter) and in order to take a flower of remembrance to the place where the young altermundist Carlo Giuliani fell (note: we would take care of the flower).

And, if we are already in Europe, we could play a game in Euzkal Herria in the Basque country. If "An Opportunity for the Word" couldn't happen, then we'd try for "An Opportunity for the Kick." . . . It looks like there's going to be seven games now (which isn't bad, because that way we can compete for the audience of the European Cup, the Libertadores, and the qualifiers for the World Cup). The one that wins four of the seven games will win "The Pozol of Mud" (note: if the Zapatista team loses more than three games, the tournament will be canceled).

Too many? Fine, Don Massimo, you're right, perhaps it's better to leave it at two games (one in Mexico and the other in Italy), because we don't want to tarnish the Inter's record too badly with the certain defeats we're proposing.

Perhaps, in order to balance your evident disadvantage a bit, I might pass on to you some secret information. For example, the Zapatista team is mixed (that is, there are men and women); we play with so-called miner's boots (they have steel toes, which is why they puncture balls); according to our uses and customs, the game is only over when none of the players of either team is left standing (that is, they are high resistance); the EZLN can reinforce itself at its discretion (that is, the Mexicans "Bofo" Bautista and Maribel "Marigol" Domínguez can appear in the lineup . . . if they accept). And we have designed a chameleon-like uniform (if we're losing, black and blue stripes appear on our shirts, confusing our rivals, the referee . . . and the public). And also we've been practicing, with relative success, two new plays: the "marquiña avanti fortiori" (note: translated into gastronomical terms it would be something like a pizza-and-guacamole sandwich) and the "marquiña caracoliña con variante inversa" (note: the equivalent of spaghetti with stewed beans, but spoiled).

With all this (and a few other surprises), we might, perhaps, revolutionize world football, and then, perhaps, football would no longer be just a business, and once again it would be an entertaining game. A game made, as you put it so well, of true feelings.

Nonetheless, this is just to reiterate to you and your family, to all the men and women of the Inter and the *nerazzurro* fans, our appreciation and admiration for you (although I'm warning you that, in front of the goalposts, there will be neither mercy nor compassion). . . .

Vale. Salud and may the green-white-red that clothes our dignities soon find themselves on both lands.

> *From the mountains of the Mexican Southeast,*
> Subcomanadante Insurgente Marcos (DTZ)

(designing plays on a chalkboard and fighting with Durito because he's insisting that, instead of the traditional 4-2-4, we should present 1-1-1-1-1-1-1-1-1-1, which, he says, is confusing)

FC Internazionale Milano

Dear Subcomandante Insurgente Marcos,

I am exceedingly pleased to have the privilege of writing in response to your extremely pleasant and kind challenge. I am addressing you, and through you to all the EZLN, in order to thank you for the opportunity you have given all of us to experience this special relationship. Allow me also to express my thoughts in response to your very, very kind letter. We will play. We will play our game, and I thank you for that. It will be a great match. Perhaps in a field, like we did as children, perhaps surrounded by giant trees. Or in a stadium, in the capital or on a rectangle drawn out in chalk on the earth, with the dust rising up until it makes us cough. Exhausted, but happy.

Since we are in agreement, we will bring the balls and you the bitter *pozol*. If you accept, we will begin discussing the organization with the respective representatives and managers. We hope we can play soon. I think we could send a good group of players to Mexico; we'll see about the timing. Let us know what location would be best. Whether in Mexico City or San Cristóbal or in a community or Caracol. Football can be an instrument for achieving important objectives, but it is something that turns us all into children and all equals. Dreamers all. We imagine great things, and we take pleasure in the small ones: a dribble, a scissors kick, a header, all make us happy. And we discover later that these small things are made of true feelings.

Dear Subcomandante, I am happy and proud to have known you and to have developed this relationship with the indigenous peoples of Mexico, in the name of the men and women of the FC Internazionale. The Inter peoples, like this football society, will try to always be close to you, exactly as you, with your example, are close to us. The game will truly be a simple and important moment. Every revolution begins from its own penalty area and ends in the opponent's goalpost.

With so very much admiration and affection, I am sending you and all the Zapatista indigenous men and women, my most personal best wishes, as well as those of my wife, my children, and the *nerazzurro* peoples.

Un abrazo,
Mássimo Moratti

Part 4. LOSS

Why didn't we win? Because
we let in three goals, because we
lost, because . . . I don't know.
In football — not just in football,
but in sport — you win and you
lose. . . . We lost. — RONALDO,
AC Milan and Brazil

Introduction

The central reality of football is failure. The vast majority of attacking moves are thwarted. Defenders' lung-bursting sprints into scoring positions typically go for naught; their reward is to run back from whence they came. Many football matches end with no score or, still more maddening, with an inferior side benefiting from a fluke goal or referee's mistake to win against a team with more ambition and aesthetic merit—no doubt the side that you support. Slovenian writer Uroš Zupan recalls defeats that "remain like scars, wounds on the soul, deep cracks on the face of beauty."

With a snugly woven integration into life, soccer brings pain. Emotional attachments lead ultimately to loss and tragic fulfillment, experienced sometimes at the national level. Organized football has accumulated stores of pathos for more than a century and generated a history of hooligan violence, sectarian and racist thuggery, and deaths resulting from overcrowding and negligence. The game has served even as a tool of terror, personified by the perverse concentration-camp guards in William Heyen's "Parity" who force Jewish victims to join in their warped sense of "fun": "*Come*, said the ss, *today / we must play.*"

Some writers below ask what an obsession with football has cost in human terms. Donna J. Gelagotis Lee describes "cheering / that was so fierce the country exploded / with the goal." Hebe de Bonafini and Matilde Sánchez lament that the spectacle of the 1978 World Cup finals in Argentina brainwashed the masses, helping citizens forget heinous crimes. In Gay Talese's "Penalty Phase" the pressures on the individual become too much to bear. After Liu Ying missed a penalty kick in the final of the 1999 Women's World Cup, her twin sister finds herself in a situation where she must apologize for her to bereft Chinese citizens.

Yet soccer has resilience. As ethnographer Paul Richards observes in Sierra Leone, the game's popularity can reinforce respect for rules and the necessity for cooperation despite war. Poet Rafael Alberti, as far back as 1928, discerned such merits in the play of a goalkeeper now forgotten: "because your steady hand came back to the fight, / the wind opened a gap in the opponent's goal."

34. On a Painting of Playing Football

Ch'ao Yueh-chih
Translated from the classical Chinese by Red Pine

Here a literary reference to one of modern football's early variants—the Chinese kicking game, called *cuju*, which involved a feather-stuffed leather ball—already carries a negative connotation. The suggestion in Ch'ao Yueh-chih's poem is that T'ang dynasty emperor Hsuan-tsung (685–762 CE), referred to as "the Third Son," played games while the nation withered. Red Pine, the pseudonym of translator and scholar Bill Porter, writes in his translation of the classical Chinese anthology *Poems of the Masters* (2003) that the ministers mentioned in the third line, Chang Chiu-ling and Han Hsiu, eventually were forced to leave the emperor's service due to their criticism of the administration. According to Red Pine, Ch'ao Yueh-chih (1059–1129 CE), who was a poet and a painter in addition to his duties as imperial scribe, considered the story an allegory to conditions he experienced during the Sung dynasty, which found itself in similar disarray.

Evidence from antiquity attests to the existence of *cuju* as early as the Han dynasty (206 BCE–221 CE). Murals from the period depict stylized female figures kicking a ball within a circle. In 2004 FIFA's president, Sepp Blatter, recognized China as "the cradle of the earliest forms of football." The World Football Museum in Linzi, China, describes two forms of the game: a physical contest popular with soldiers in training and another in which players kept the ball aloft before guiding it through a circular target. By Ch'ao's time the game had evolved to two teams of ten per side. As told in the classic Chinese novel of the sixteenth century, *Water Margin* (or *The Marshes of Mount Liang*), the primary foe of the 108 Sung dynasty demon-princes, who serve as the protagonists of the story cycle, is Gao Qiu (called "Gao-the-Ball"), who ingratiates himself with imperial officials through his skills in *cuju*.

A thousand doors and windows open in the palace
the Third Son is drunk and gives the ball a kick
Chiu-ling is too old and Han Hsiu is dead
no longer are memorials submitted in the morning

35. Beauty Is Nothing but the Beginning of a Terror We Can Hardly Bear

Uroš Zupan

Translated from the Slovenian by Erica Johnson Debeljak

Uroš Zupan, one of Slovenia's leading poets, studied literature at the University of Ljubljana and has published eight collections of poetry and three books of essays, as well as translations of American and Israeli poets. Growing up in the former Yugoslavia during the last decades of Communist rule, Zupan was a fan of Hajduk Split and of the Dutch national team.

While coming from a small country that is, in his words, "a white spot on the map of world literature" and a literary tradition that is full of "heavy melancholy, pessimism, and self-destructiveness," Zupan's work displays in words the elegance that his favorite players Slaviša Žungul and Johan Cruyff showed on the field. Zupan explains in a personal correspondence, "I write to preserve . . . what has gone away into oblivion, to petrify some moments when I was happy and when I was feeling . . . immortal. To put some order into the chaos that surrounds us. But most of all to have fun, to produce something that is without solid meaning, but something that is magic and can touch like music."

Zupan is presently working on a book about each World Cup tournament he remembers, starting with his memories as an eight-year-old in 1970, melding tales about the game and about growing up under a political system that has vanished. Since Slovenia's secession from Yugoslavia in 1991, media reports have referred to the so-called Yugonostalgia—shorthand for the yearning for unity of more authoritarian times—in the six republics of the formerly unified country. Slovenia, for example, has less than two million people and struggles for its own identity. President George W. Bush confused Slovenia with Slovakia. Wire-service dispatches referred to Slovenian Anže Kopitar on his debut in the National Hockey League as a "rookie from Sweden."

There are some years when everything flows smoothly and according to plan, when all the doors you want to go through just open on their own, and all obstacles disappear as if you are sailing on a high wave, on a high tide. The wave carries you on and on, and your feeling of good fortune is immense, almost sinful, but also dangerous because you know it can't last. Then there are other years when everything goes wrong. Those who are inclined to seek solutions in the stars will stare at the sky and say, "It must be the influence of Saturn." Someone else, more down to earth and with more common sense, might say, "It's raining today, but the sun will shine tomorrow. If life weren't like that, we'd soon get bored." But no year is only good, and none is only and exclusively bad. We are always somewhere in the middle. Some things work out. Others don't.

But what actually am I talking about? I could be talking about anything at all. But I'm not. I am talking about a very specific thing. I am talking about soccer. And about all the results of soccer matches and all the matches themselves.

How much of a soccer fan am I? I often wonder. I am not a fanatic, not excessively fierce in my sympathies. Indeed, for fifteen years I almost forgot about soccer. I became a sporadic viewer, watching only the most important matches in the most important tournaments. Between the ages of fifteen and thirty, other more intoxicating, more hedonistic activities drew me in. And certainly as a fan I do not belong to that most extreme category, for whom the ascents and downfalls of one's own life are inevitably compared to the ascents and downfalls of one's favorite soccer club as they go up and down the rankings. This sort of fan sits in front of the television set wearing a soccer jersey, his face smeared with team colors, terrorizing all those in his presence with his metaphysical assumptions, allowing no possibility for contradiction. Moreover I do not compare the career of a professional writer with that of a professional soccer player. That would be, after all, to compare the experiences of beggars with those of the most prosperous, indeed of the sometimes perversely extravagant. But sometimes I watch a match that really moves me, that either makes my day or ruins it, a match that becomes a kind of high-octane fuel that propels me through the next couple of days. These especially sweet or bitter matches are usually the unjust ones during which some sort of soccer god intervenes, if there even is one, among the heavenly dwellers, a being that governs that particular sphere.

Penetrating the surface and going deeper into the experience of fandom, perhaps my version has more to do with a kind of sympathy—a colder, more platonic relationship, which only reveals that I am committing what in soccer is probably the greatest capital sin, if not heresy. I am not sufficiently constant and loyal. And yet a sort of constancy and loyalty has accompanied me from the very beginning, and along with it the denial and rejection of a particular school of traditional soccer. As a child I rooted for the Split team Hajduk (even today, I still know the precise starting positions of Hajduk players in the mid-seventies) and for the Ljubljana team, Olympia. My support of the Croatian Hajduk was authentic and from the heart; for Slovenian Olympia, it was more for "patriotic reasons." It sometimes seemed to me that the soccer world is perennially divided between two poles: foreign and home. And in this division, Olympia was the home home team. As a fan I always had a reserve team. All the boys from the neighborhood had reserve teams. We would say, "I root for Hajduk, but at home I root for Olympia." Because in the end, Olympia was the only Slovenian club that could hold its own (though just barely) in the first league of the federal Yugoslavia, and it only got to play in that league because of Slovenia's status as a republic. Because of the supposed brotherhood and unity of all Yugoslav peoples, it would have been controversial or suspect for the Slovenians—a republic of skiers and mountain climbers, soccer illiterates and ignoramuses—to have no first-leaguers at all. I have been rooting for Hajduk for nearly thirty years. And, regardless of that fact, during the thirty-year period, there were times when I didn't even know whether it played in the former first federal league of the former federation, or later in the Croatian league, and was at the top of the ratings or was on the verge of falling.

Of the foreign clubs, I was, as I child, most enamored with the Amsterdam squad Ajax that reigned over European soccer in the early seventies and represented, in that era of black-and-white television, the very essence of soccer. An absolute miracle. Ajax was a name that was always spoken with great respect. Today I still know by heart the names of almost all of the players who made up the Ajax powerhouse. Indeed, in my mind the club remains the very ideal of a soccer giant and even now when their game and their results are light years away from their game and results from the early seventies, it seems to me that a strong light emanates from those past times, a light so strong and so enduring that it can still illuminate the present.

Maybe in the perception of soccer the childhood tricks of dimension and distance play a role. I speak of the times when something that once seemed enormous and immense, spacious and infinite to a child, turns out, when the child is grown up, to be a very small space or a very short distance. Perhaps it is the same with Johan Cruyff, who I once saw play with Ajax and once with the Dutch national team, and who remains for me the best soccer player who ever ran on the green pitch. I was too young to have seen Di Stefano or Pelé, but old enough for Maradona, Platini, and the others who came to rule the game. But all the same, in my subjective hierarchy, Cruyff still occupies first place. Perhaps this represents a sort of Dantesque encounter with my soccer Beatrice who became the inexhaustible source of light and my guide to all subsequent places. But no doubt what lends Cruyff his magnificence, his all-encompassing quality, is the time of life when I first encountered him—childhood. I certainly rooted for Ajax because of him, the player wearing number fourteen, who wore his red- and-white jersey with ease and vehemence, a player gifted with unbelievable physical skills and elegance of movement, fragile in appearance, easily loping through all the defensive lines of the opposing team, leading the other players, and then scoring the goals.

This kind of soccer story continues today. Each of us has our own red thread and our own rules. I usually root for a club because I like a certain player. Coming in second is the beauty of the total game and the style of the club, which in any case is usually determined to a great degree, even guaranteed, by that one favored player. And in last place comes tradition and loyalty. I have certain preferences among the stronger European leagues. Arsenal in England, Real Madrid in Spain, Girondins de Bordeaux in France, Milan in Italy, and Ajax in the Netherlands. And all of these various squads in all of these various leagues share one thing: one player that defines the squad and puts his stamp on the club. All teams play, or should play to the best of their abilities, beautiful and aggressive soccer. But in the end I don't root for a certain club just because of the kind of soccer it plays, but because I see the squad as a promise, as a continuation in the evolution of the game.

Among the strongest leagues, Germany is blank on my soccer map. For what German club do I root? I have no idea. It would be the most honest to simply say for none at all. That space on the map remains empty. I root for various national teams—the Netherlands, France, Argentina, Brazil—and for various clubs. Only the German national team and the German clubs have left me cold.

What is the source of this principled, almost *a priori* rejection? Does it perhaps also derive from childhood? Did we, as children, sense the rationality, and therefore the lack of beauty, in the style of the German clubs and national team? Did we already then miss the magic and brilliance, the stunts and the finesse to which we were most attentive, for which we hungered with our wide-open eyes? The German accomplishments, which resided instead in efficient and diligent work, in what lies beneath the surface, could never have attracted or charmed us. Or perhaps there is something completely different in this systematic rejection of German soccer, something naive and likewise arising from my childhood. For my generation of Slovenians, Germans have always been the enemy. We were raised in the spirit of distrust toward the principal agents of the Second World War. We had grown up in the era of war films, historical-cowboy epics about the Second World War, of which the two best Yugoslav examples were *Sutjeska* and *Bitka na Neretvi*. There was no greater shame than to have been delegated to play the role of the German in our childhood games. Indeed, we often managed to avoid this problem by making the Germans invisible. We were all partisans with our wooden machine guns. We were Jastreb, Dimnajačar, Prle, Tihi. We were Bata Živojinović and Ljubiša

Samardzić. We were heroes from the television series *Kapelski kresovi* and *Odpisani* (Mountain Bonfires and Renegades, respectively). All positive figures, all endlessly heroic with revolution in their blood and socialistic slogans on their lips. When we were shot with invisible bullets, we died with our gazes reflecting the clouds and the skies above. We were always the good guys, our guys. Nobody ever wanted to be Major Krüger or some other German officer.

The twenty-five-year domination on the European and international soccer scene by German teams began at just about the same time that we were playing these childhood games. Three successive wins of Bayern in the European Cup, three titles each in world and European championships, and that's only to name the high points. Even today, after so many years, it is difficult to forget all of the painful defeats experienced by the teams I was rooting for when they played against Germany. They remain like scars, wounds on the soul, deep cracks on the face of beauty represented by the technical perfection and improvisational flair of the teams that I loved. With the Germans it was all tactics and power and, above all, a fanatical endurance that would not yield, that swept away all beauty and softness. The spirit of the world and the time in which we live today began to be narrated through the game of soccer, indeed through the kind of soccer that was played by the German national team. All of these defeats always took place according to the same scenario. The Germans did not outplay the teams they defeated; they simply ground them down with their endurance. And even if the Germans were not always the first-place winners, they almost always "sweated" their way to the podium.

But who remembers all of the stations of the cross? I shall mention only the most memorable traumas, the most burning wounds. The 1974 final of the world championship when the Dutch team was defeated by the Germans. The semifinals of the European championship two years later when Yugoslavia lost during extra time. The 1982 semifinal of the world championship in Spain when Germany defeated France. I could not quite rid myself of the feeling that all of the defeated teams had been implanted with, before the match and against their own will, the conviction that the Germans always

won any dramatic turnaround or epic battle and that it hardly made
sense to try to make events go a different way. The English attacker
Gary Lineker even came up with a definition of soccer on this theme:
"Twenty-two men chase a ball for ninety minutes and, in the end, the
Germans win."

But there were also sweet moments, though they were far fewer
than the stations of the cross. Yet, precisely because of their rarity, they
were all the sweeter and burn warmer in my memory. The sweetest
of all, at least for me, was the victory of the Belgrade team, Red Star,
over Bayern in a semifinal in Munich in 1991, followed by a tied home
match in Belgrade that eliminated the German champions. That was
the match that reawakened my interest in soccer. To the extent that
it had followed soccer, the game had always left my generation of
fans far from the pearly gates, but Red Star's subsequent victory over
Marseille in the finals took us straight to paradise. Finally a Yugoslav
national team that did not crash and burn, that did not, with a lead after
halftime or a first-match victory, poison its mind with the thought "of
course we're going to win, we're masters of the world." That is exactly
what happened with my beloved Hajduk in the seventies. With Red
Star, we finally had our happy ending, but it was almost as it were a
violation of the fixed standards of the past and the settled order of
the universe, for shortly thereafter punishment followed. Less than a
month later another ending began. The final chapter in the history of a
country that, at least viewed from a distance and from the perspective
of those who didn't pay a high price in the wholesale slaughter—thank
god—finally fell apart. Albeit not before burning and bleeding in a
series of terrible wars.

After the conclusion of the 2000 European Championships, and
even before, after the final match in the Champions League tournament, I thought that a new era was beginning for soccer—a lighter,
more beautiful era, whose path would be better marked and laid out
and that would lead to the creation of what we might call an empty
space, of beauty achieved, of inner light. Events began to unfold in just
the right way. It was one of those years when everything goes right.
Though I must confess that a slightly different framework, a slightly

different result would have demolished the whole metaphysical construct, would have pulled down the whole hierarchical pyramid that carried on its peak nothing other than beauty and sublime appeal. Real Madrid triumphed in the Champions League. The European championship was dominated by teams from countries that comprised the cradle of civilization, Mediterranean countries and not northern countries, the spirits of the latter being inclined toward rationality and logic, systems and discipline. The achievements of power and raw force were nothing next to those of power combined with feeling and finesse. All together it was a sweet dream, something that I imagined might be the extraordinary passage of soccer into the new millennium. But this dream of beauty's triumph lasted hardly a year. The slap in the face came yet again. Or perhaps it was just another stage in the process of eternal growth and decay. In 2001 Munich's Bayern won the Champions League again.

But my infantile behavior, my almost *a priori* opposition to German soccer for a whole range of reasons—my early traumas as a fan, my love of warmth and the South, my enmity for cold and the North (hell is certainly a freezing place)—I could objectivize with an easy spirit and send on a well-earned vacation (since it stinks of prejudice anyway) if Bayern would include the flow of beauty and elegant soccer in its game and place it above formulas and tactics, the heavy concentration of players on one end of the pitch, the "hard" German variant of so-called *catenaccio,* or defensive soccer, the literal definition of the Italian word being *doorbolt.* But no, Bayern decided, as it always had, for the latter.

An event occurred in the sphere of international poetry in the 1920s. When T. S. Eliot's *Wasteland* was published the whole universe greeted it with great fanfare, but the American poet William Carlos Williams believed that it was a catastrophe, that just when the world of poetry was at the edge of a great discovery, Eliot, the refined conformist, had delivered it back to the classroom. Poetry regressed by thirty years.

I felt something similar in connection with the evolution of soccer when Bayern won the Champions League—the return to the classroom, the repeated ascendancy of something that I thought I had already been through. Instead of the top team striking with a frontal attack, outplaying the opponents on the open pitch, and caring above all for the pleasure of the public, tactics prevailed. Bunker mentality. On top of everything Zlatko Zahovič, the golden boy of Slovenian soccer, missed his unique opportunity to have his name written forever in the sky, to become the new hero of sublime and beautiful soccer, to redeem the game, lead it and return it to its rightful track.

Sometimes things really don't go according to plan. But I comfort myself with the notion that some higher, unknown order governs us and all the things that surround us. Despite my disappointment over the defeat of beauty, regardless of whether or not my team prevailed, I often think about the dichotomy between winners and losers. About the situation and reactions of one and the other when, after the referee's whistle, they all remain a while on the green surface, separated by a minimal distance and a small quantity of air. Watching the reactions of the defeated, I can't shake a certain feeling of anxiety that washes over me, a feeling that resembles a sort of communist or early Christian longing: the desire for a better and more just world. A world founded on equality. The losers, sitting on the grass utterly downcast and ruined, remind me more than anything else of people who have survived a plane crash and are mourning their relatives who died in it. There are enough scenes like that in the daily news; I don't want to watch them at the end of a sports event. Of course someone else would make a different argument: that if you give your life to top professional sports then you take the risk that you will be disappointed in defeat. The question is whether a person really knows what he has given his life to and if the risk is so self-evident.

As far as soccer is concerned, the whole thing could be resolved if we started to give grades not only for winning but for the overall artistic impression. Impractical, I suppose. In order to get rid of the bitter aftertaste of bad and uninteresting and, above all, self-serving soccer matches, I should have recorded the most beautiful and perfect encounters on video. I should have collected and preserved them, just as I collect classic works of literature or music. And then watch them every so often, when I want to feel good and preserve my hope and faith in soccer. Watch them even though I know the result and will be robbed of the sense of unpredictability. But matches that leave us breathless, that intoxicate us, are rare. The most frequent participant in matches of this sort in recent years has been the French national team. I remember best the friendly match they played against Portugal a couple of years ago. The first forty-five minutes were probably the best soccer I'd seen in I don't know how long. Such segments in soccer are rare. They happen maybe once, twice a year. The French totally outplayed the Portuguese, but that wasn't what mattered. What mattered was the way they did it. The triumph of beauty, technique, daring, surprise, and elegance. The spirit of deconstruction—the torture of both the ball and the viewers—was nowhere to be found on either side of the pitch, not even a trace. And beauty is, as Rilke wrote in the first of his *Duino Elegies*, nothing but the beginning of a terror we can hardly bear, and we worship it for the graceful sublimity with which it disdains to destroy us. But beauty in soccer has no desire to destroy us; it can only bring light to our lives. What will destroy us are formulas and tactics. But before us, they will destroy the game itself.

36. Playing Football in Secret

Driton Latifi

Kosovar sports journalist Driton Latifi delivered the following address in 2000 at "Play the Game: World Conference of Sports Media" in Copenhagen. Football, in addition to its use for political purposes, has a history of providing solace in war, whether the game is viewed as a distraction on the home front or as testimony to human qualities in insane times. The Christmastime truce of 1914, for example, featured casual games of soccer, cigarette exchanges, and carol singing between British and German troops along the Flanders front near Armentières, France. The truce, which endured only a day or two, is the subject of the book *Silent Night: The Story of the World War I Christmas Truce* by Stanley Weintraub (2001) and the French film *Joyeux Noël* (2005).

In the Balkans, however, long-standing ethnic conflicts have been accentuated through soccer. Contests in the former Yugoslavia between rivals such as Partizan Belgrade and Dinamo Zagreb became proxies for hostilities that led ultimately to war. At Red Star Belgrade the director of the supporters' association, Zeljko Raznatovic—better known as Arkan, as he is referred to in Latifi's text below—also commanded a group of Serbian paramilitaries before he was assassinated in a Belgrade hotel in 2000.

Following conflict in Croatia and Bosnia and Herzegovina, war came to Kosovo in 1999. Under the rule of Slobodan Milosevic, private sporting activity in Kosovo was banned unless participants allied themselves with Serbian sporting federations. "I remember being at a football match, with some two thousand people watching, when a Serb policeman walked out into the middle of the pitch and stopped the game, two minutes before the end," Agim Islami, president of the Kosovo Tennis Federation, told the *Financial Times* in 2006. Ethnic Albanian secessionists, supported by a North Atlantic Treaty Organization bombing campaign, pushed Serb forces from the region in 1999. Although still legally within Serbian territory, Kosovo remained a protectorate of the United Nations until declaring independence in February 2008.

Latifi's text has been edited slightly for sense, punctuation, and spelling.

Dear friends and respected colleagues,

First of all I would like to thank the organizers of this meeting, who have supported my trip here so I could speak on behalf of what has happened to the athletes of Kosova and its journalists in the past decade. My name is Driton Latifi. I'm from Kosova, a country you have known from last year's NATO bombing. Your states are the ones that have helped me to survive physically, although I have to say that there are a lot of athletes that have died, are in prison in Serbia, or are lost, and their relatives don't know anything about them. Maybe you can say that with my twenty-two years I should have looked after my talent some-where else, maybe in football, but in the last years not only me but also all the Kosovar athletes were not allowed to use the sporting facilities in Kosova.

Kosova is a small country with around 2.5 million inhabit-ants, but with 53 percent of its population under nineteen years old it provides a great potential for sport. Like a lot of other countries, we also have a very modest history of sport. You maybe don't know our athletes, but some of them did win gold medals in European championships, world championships, and Olympic Games as well.

These medals in the mid-1980s gave us hope that in the fu-ture we could win more medals. But that didn't continue to be the case after 1989. Milosevic's climb in position in Serbia years before that and his nationalism didn't show any concern for sports, as it didn't care about any human beings in ex-Yugoslavia. FC Prishtina, in 1983, became a member of the first Yugoslav Soccer League. This team for five years had the . . . most supporters. In 1989, after the game against Proleter Zren-janin that ended in a draw (2–2), when the Kosovar football play-ers were arguing with the referee, in one moment in front of more than thirty thousand spectators, the Serbian police got on the pitch and started to beat the Kosovar footballers. The captain of FC Prishtina and the local favourite, Gani Llapashtica, got the worst—his left leg was broken. Even that was not enough for them; they then started to chase the supporters, who were of course whistling to them because of what they were doing to their idols. Also a lot of supporters were arrested, together with the players.

After this day the home ground of FC Prishtina was closed for the Kosovars, and the stadium was guarded by the police force. Then all the stadiums in other cities and all the other sporting places were closed for Kosovars. Kosovar athletes, with the enforcement of Serbian police, were not allowed to use the sporting facilities. In that time, after some days had passed, the players of FC Prishtina got together the members of the executive committee and told them that they wanted to get on with their work, no matter the price. The team very quickly got together, and they held a training session in a forgotten field outside of Prishtina, some ten kilometers away, in a village called Llukar. The Serbian police stopped their game in the stadium with force, but they never did stop the wish and their passion for playing football. After they secured the first equipment from secret channels . . . the Kosovar football players organized the Soccer League of Kosova and played the games in a location secret from the Serbian police. . . .

A lot of games were stopped, and only a few of them were played ninety minutes to allow the joy of winning. The schedule of games and locations was kept secret until the last moment, so sometimes even we journalists missed the games. In its beginning the soccer league had four groups, and the first two teams from the top group were playing in the playoff for the title. In such conditions, with no field, no equipment, no proper balls, and with the police after you, Kosovar footballers still had time to find joy—what this game is supposed to bring to anyone. You could hear stories of Serbian politicians calling someone who just wanted to play football a "terrorist." FC Prishtina won the first league title organized in such conditions, but this was not an international-caliber competition, and it still is not today.

In these years Kosova was active in some of the most popular games; there were twenty-three existing sports federations that assembled more than two hundred thousand active athletes, and all of them were working in that secret system, away from the public eyes and normal conditions. In 1996 there was no force that could stop Kosovar footballers from forming the first Kosova Unique League with eighteen teams. Away from this league, in the sport stadiums, Serbs had a monopoly, although they were less than 10 percent of the Kosova population. They filled the teams only with Serbs, and the games were watched by their few friends. Somewhere in secret areas you could find up to ten thousand spectators watching a football game, and they were sitting on a stone, in a tree, or anywhere they could. In such conditions Kosova had more than 130 football clubs and more than ten thousand footballers, who were all sponsored by private donors or companies. They were all getting the Serbian police at their doors. In this time, ironically, FC Prishtina was headed by the war criminal Zeljko Raznatovic "Arkan." In the beginning of 1998, when the first shots were heard in the Drenica area, football and all the sport activities stopped because of security conditions.

In this year some Kosovar footballers lost their teammates. Driton Ahmeti, a member of FC 2 Korriku from Dobroshec, was murdered in his home with some of his family members. Ahmeti was the first victim and not the last one. After the war his team retired the shirt number 7 that he used to wear. A talented player of FC Liria (Freedom), Perparim Thaqi, was found dead one spring morning in 1998 together with his two friends. The city stadium in Prizren today has his name, the Perparim Thaqi Stadium. The captain of FC Ferronikeli, Rexhep Rexhepi, from the Drenica area, was executed by the Serbian forces in front of his family. It is very sad, but this list just goes on and on, and the Kosovar FA doesn't have an exact number of killed footballers.

Some statistics estimate that more than one hundred Kosovar

athletes were killed from 1998 until the end of the NATO bombing. In this number I did not include those who are in jail in Serbia or those that are lost, of whom their families do not know anything. . . . Please, colleagues, could you just imagine, for example, what if Catalans were to experience the police beating players in the Nou Camp stadium? How would the supporter of Manchester United or a Bavarian supporter of Bayern Munich react?

When Kosovar athletes returned to their sporting facilities, some facilities had been destroyed by the bombings, but also some by the Serbian forces leaving Kosova. The UN administration after the war has formed the Department of Sport, which in fact is doing the work of a ministry and is trying to help Kosovar sports. There is one Kosovar and one international member of the UN that are in charge of the sports department.

Another interesting topic in this history of Kosovar sport is sports journalism. My colleagues and I had the same destiny as the athletes. Writing about sport in the beginning was more dangerous than writing about politics. In that time the population of Kosova had no information about local sport or international sport. There was only one daily newspaper and no electronic media, such as radio or TV stations; these started only after the war. For sport you could write only after the game was over and very little before it. Anyway, in the end, what Kosova athletes and its media need is your help. It doesn't matter in what way the help comes.

Please help in any way the sport in Kosova. Thank you.

37. Why Does My Wife Love Peter Crouch?

Thom Satterlee

For many fans in the United States, soccer represents membership in an international community. Poet Thom Sattterlee recalls watching *Soccer Made in Germany* as a boy in the 1970s to fuel his passion for the game and to broaden his geographical and cultural horizons. Now nearing middle age, Satterlee continues to follow the international game through satellite-television broadcasts.

He writes, "My wife and I watch English Premier League games on the weekend. This poem conflates several instances of watching Liverpool play during the 2005 season. Once we realized the uncanny resemblance between their striker Peter Crouch and my father-in-law, who died recently of Lou Gehrig's disease, watching the games took on an entirely new dimension. Suddenly 'loss' meant more than the game's final score; 'substitution' began to have mystical proportions."

For Kathy

> Why does my wife love Peter Crouch,
>   the tall, gangly striker for Liverpool?
>
> And why, when he scores a goal and the camera shows him
>   bursting with a smile, does she cry?
>
> It's simple: he reminds her of her father,
>   who died now seven years ago
>
> and who, when he was Crouch's age, leaned over her crib
>   and lullabied her with Elvis Presley songs.
>
> It's a gift to grief sent by satellite
>   over an ocean and reaching her here

in her early middle age,
      at the start of her fatherless years,

a comfort to see time bend for her,
      to believe even vaguely in a God

who'd allow or engineer such coincidence
      if it means the healing of one real hurt.

38. The Dynamo Team: Legend and Fact

Anatoly Kuznetsov
Translated from the Russian by Jacob Guralsky

The story of the formidable Dynamo Kiev team and its exploits following the Nazi invasion of Ukraine in 1941 assumed mythic immensity in Soviet accounts of resistance. As Anatoly Kuznetsov explains in this excerpt from *Babi Yar: A Documentary Novel* (1967), the ravine outside Kiev from which he took his title became known more as the place where the soccer players were shot than the location of manifold horrors accompanying the deaths of more than one hundred thousand Jews, Rom, and Soviet prisoners of war. Kuznetsov, born in Kiev in 1929, grew up not far from Babi Yar and describes hearing executions by machine gun, seeing smoke from burning bodies, and walking on human ash following the Nazi defeat.

Soviet propagandists helped develop the mythology surrounding Dynamo Kiev that included the martyrdom of the entire team following a "Death Match" against a German side in 1942. But as Kuznetsov and others looked into the events at Babi Yar, peeling away the myth and circumventing the Soviet regime's own wish to control the story, they found that the former Dynamo players had for a time been in service as prisoners of the Nazi occupiers. Many worked in a bakery and continued playing soccer on a new team, FC Start, created for an ad hoc league the Nazis conceived to help pacify the Kiev population. In its unbeaten run through the short season, Start twice defeated a German-select side.

In August 1942, not long after the second of these victories, many of the players were arrested and taken to Siretz—the concentration camp near Babi Yar—according to Andy Dougan in *Dynamo: Defending the Honour of Kiev* (2001). Three players were ultimately shot, Dougan writes, and their bodies dumped with others in the ravine that Kuznetsov describes as "deep and wide, like a mountain gorge." Here bodies—including that of goalkeeper Nikolai Trusevich, still dressed in a team jersey—were buried and then burned in pyres before Kiev's liberation.

Before a service at Babi Yar in 2006 to remember the thirty-four thousand Jews murdered at the ravine from September 29–30, 1941, Jewish leaders complained that children could still play soccer and families could picnic near the memorial site, which forms part of a park.

This almost incredible story occurred in the summer of 1942, and it was so popular that at one time people referred to the ravine as, "the self-same Babi Yar where they shot the soccer players." In those days it made the rounds in the form of a legend, one so fine and so satisfying that I want to set it down in full. Here it is:

Kiev's Dynamo soccer team had been one of the best in the country before the war. Its fans knew all about the players, especially the famous goalie Trusevich.

Because of the encirclement, the team had been unable to get away from Kiev. At first they sat tight, found work wherever they could and kept in touch. Then, longing for soccer, they began to hold practice in a vacant lot. The boys in the neighborhood discovered this right away, then the adults, and finally the German authorities.

They called in the players and said, "Why use a vacant lot? Look, here is an excellent stadium going begging, so by all means practice there. We have nothing against sports, in fact, the opposite."

The Dynamo team agreed and moved into the stadium. Sometime later the Germans summoned them again and said, "Kiev is returning to normal; the movie theaters and the opera are open, and it's about time we opened the stadium too. Let everyone see that peaceful restoration is in full swing. We offer you a match against the all-stars of the armed forces of Germany."

The Dynamo men asked for time to think it over. Some were against it on the grounds that playing soccer with the fascists would be disgraceful treason. Others felt differently: "On the contrary, we'll whip them, humiliate them in front of all the people and raise the morale of the Kievans." This side won. The team began to train in earnest under its new name, "Start."

Bright posters appeared on the streets of Kiev: SOCCER. GERMANY'S ARMED FORCES ALL-STARS VS. CITY OF KIEV ALL-STARS.

The stadium was filled; half of the stands were occupied by the Germans and all their important leaders, including the commandant himself. They were in fine spirits and expected a happy outcome. The poorer seats were occupied by the hungry, ragged populace of Kiev.

The game began. The Dynamo men were emaciated and weak. The well-fed German team played a rough game, openly tripping their opponents; but the referee noticed nothing. The Germans in the stands roared with glee when the first goal was scored against the Kiev team. The other half of the stadium kept gloomily silent: now they were spitting on us in soccer.

Then suddenly the Dynamo men seemed to rally. They were seized with fury. They drew strength from unknown sources. They outplayed the Germans and, with a desperate surge, drove home the tying goal. Now the German rooting section subsided into a disappointed silence, and the rest of the crowd screamed and embraced.

The Dynamo team recovered its prewar finesse and, with some brilliant teamwork, scored its second goal. The ragged crowds shouted, "Hurrah!" and "They're licking the Germans!"

This "licking the Germans" remark overstepped the bounds of sportsmanship. Germans swept through the stands shouting, "Stop that!" and firing in the air. The first half ended and the teams left the field for a rest.

An officer from the commandant's box visited the Dynamo locker room during the intermission and very politely told them, "Well done, you've played good soccer and we appreciate it. You have upheld your athletic honor sufficiently. But now in the second half, take it easy; because as you yourselves must realize, you have to lose. You must. The German army team has never lost before, especially not in occupied territory. This is an order. If you don't lose, you'll be shot."

The Dynamo men listened in silence and then went out to the field. The referee blew his whistle and the second half began. The Kiev team played well and scored a third goal. Half of the stadium was roaring, and many wept for joy; the German half was grumbling with indignation. Dynamo kicked in another goal. The Germans in the stands leaped to their feet and fingered their pistols. Guards ran out along the sidelines and cordoned off the field.

It was a game to the death, but the people in our section did not know it and so they kept up their joyful shouting. The German players were utterly crushed and dispirited. The Dynamos scored again. The commandant and all the officers left the stands.

The referee cut the game short with his whistle. The guards, not even waiting for the teams to reach the lockers, grabbed the Dynamo players right there on the field, loaded them into a closed truck and took them off to Babi Yar.

Nothing of this kind had ever happened in the history of soccer. In this game, however, athletics was purely political from start to finish. Because the Dynamo players had no other weapons, they turned soccer itself into a weapon and accomplished a truly deathless exploit. They had known victory meant death, but they had won anyway, in order to remind the people of their dignity.

In actuality, the story was not quite so tidy. The ending was the same, but like all things in life, the events were more complicated. Not one game, but several, took place, and the fury of the Germans mounted from match to match.

The Dynamo players wound up in occupied territory not because they had been unable to get away but because they had been in the Red Army and were captured. Because a large part of the team went to work as loaders at Bakery No. 1, in time they were enlisted on the bakery team.

There was a German stadium in Kiev, but Kievans were not admitted. But posters really did go up on July 12, 1942:

OPENING OF UKRAINIAN STADIUM
The Ukrainian Stadium will open at 4 p.m. today.
(Bolshaya Vasilkovskaya, 51, entrance from Prozorovskaya.
Opening programme: gymnastics, boxing, light athletics
and—as the main item—a football match. (At 1730 hours.)

The team of some German army unit really was defeated in that game, and the Germans didn't like it; but no arrests occurred. The

Germans, annoyed, simply signed up the stronger PSG army team to play the next game, on July 17. Start routed, literally routed, this team, 6–0.

The newspaper report of that game was priceless:

> . . . But this victory can hardly be called an achievement on the part of the Start men. The German team was made up of fairly strong individual players, but was not a team in the full sense. This is not surprising, for the team consisted of players who were in the unit for which they were playing by chance. Another factor was the Germans' lack of practice, without which even the strongest team could accomplish nothing. The Start team, as everyone well knows, consists mainly of former players for the select Dynamo team, so one would expect them to make a far better showing than they actually made in this match.

The ill-concealed irritation and the note of apology that permeated every line of this commentary were only the beginning of the tragedy.

On Sunday, July 19, Start played against a Hungarian team, MSG Wal, and won 5–1. This is from the report on that match:

> Despite the final score, the two teams can be considered almost equally strong.

The Hungarians proposed a return match, which was held on July 26. The final score: 3–2, in favor of Start. Now it looked as though the team was ready to be beaten, and the Germans would have their gratification.

A new match was announced for August 6 between Start and the "most powerful," "mightiest," "undefeated" German Flakelf team. The newspaper went simply wild in its advance coverage of the Flakelf team, citing its fabulous record of goals scored and prevented and other such statistics. This was the match described in the legend, that culminated in that German defeat. The newspaper carried no report of it. However, the soccer players were not arrested yet. On August 9, a small notice appeared in *Novoye Ukrainskoye slovo*:

> A friendly match between the best football teams of the city, Flakelef and Start (from Bakery No. 1), will be held at Zenith Stadium at five o'clock this evening.

Start was getting another chance. But it defeated the Germans in this game, too; and on August 16 it beat the Ukrainian nationalist Rukh team by a score of 8–0. After this game the Dynamo soccer players were finally sent to Babi Yar.

This was at the time when there was heavy fighting on the Don and the Germans had reached the approaches to Stalingrad.

39. Boycotting the World Cup

Hebe de Bonafini and Matilde Sánchez
Translated from the Spanish by Sandra Kingery

On March 26, 2006, before another contentious derby match with Buenos Aires rivals Boca Juniors, players from River Plate unfurled a white banner reading "Nunca Más" (Never Again). Following the lead of President Néstor Kirchner, the players lent their support to sacralizing March 24, the date of the 1976 coup that began seven years of military dictatorship in Argentina. Up to thirty thousand died during this period, when opponents of the regime were abducted, tortured, executed, and "disappeared." The latter term retained the most resonance, such that victims were referred to as *los desaparecidos*.

Seeing their hosting of the 1978 World Cup finals as a mark of legitimacy, military rulers sought to direct all attention to the sporting festival's "wild party," which concluded with Argentina's 3–1 victory over Holland and the country's first World Cup trophy. The ruling generals were subverted, however, by leaders of the women's group Asociación Madres de Plaza de Mayo. The women turned the media presence during the World Cup to their advantage, walking in protest through the city's political center, the site commemorating the May Revolution against Spain in 1810. Hebe de Bonafini was one of the founders of the group, which began its demonstrations in 1977—the year her oldest son, Jorge, disappeared. Matilde Sánchez helped assemble de Bonafini's 1985 autobiography, *Historias de vida* (Life Stories), from which the following excerpt is drawn.

Some thirty years later, members of the organization continue to demonstrate weekly for other social causes. Mindful of the burdens faced during dictatorship, when the government banned public gatherings of more than two people, they still walk around the plaza in pairs.

We knew it was going to be a hard year. The frenzy surrounding the World Cup had already begun. A treasonous report obtained in the worthless office of some high and mighty priest established that "they plan to wipe the country clean of disturbing elements before the first tourist sets foot in it. Argentina is going to show the world its capacity for recuperation." That meant they would exterminate dissension at all costs.

The World Cup is coming: just as they move shantytowns and put up walls to hide the poverty, they have the same need to cover us, and the children a few of us still have left, because we're a stain, a blemish. With so many people looking at the country—and wasn't that their goal? to be seen and at the same time prove they're capable of hiding the atrocities and be applauded, to convert the lies into reality—they can't afford to let women like us keep making a racket and publishing the names of the disappeared in the papers.

A few days before the World Cup the family the Mothers have formed is dealt a final blow: on the afternoon of May 25 combined military forces abduct a group of women in a bakery in Lomas de Zamora. Among them is María Elena Bugnone, la Negra, who was searching for her husband, her brother-in-law Raúl, her sister, and her sister's husband. Not one of the women in that group ever returned. Subsequent information from released prisoners indicates that María Elena was held in the prison at Ezeiza for two years.

As the new year began, those of us who were the "leaders of the Mothers" continued meeting. Back then the leaders were simply the women who were given the titles of "government," "courts," "secretary," "treasurer," and a few others who, like me, dedicated a lot of time to this task. In my case, I was the contact person for the Mothers from La Plata. We knew the country would be jam-packed with tourists and professional journalists: "It's a question of making all those TV cameras work for us, using them to demand our children and to cause a real scene."

"But we don't know how to talk very well, Hebe. We know how to take care of our homes, and we've learned how to fill out their forms, but what are we going to say if they ask us something in English?"

"It's easy, Clarita," said one of the Mothers who was new to the group and who had a lot of energy. "You look the reporter in the eye and you say: 'We want our children. We want them to tell us where our children are.'"

Our chants and rallying cries began to be born. Later on these slogans would help us break the silence of our processions around the plaza. But during the whole month of May we weren't allowed to occupy the plaza: the police were waiting at exactly three o'clock, and they charged whenever they saw more than three Mothers together. But we fought it out with them as long as we could: they would throw us out on the right side, and we would reappear on the left; they would kick us out on one end, and we would sneak back in from the other, after going around the block. This cat-and-mouse game that exasperated them so much had a nearly symbolic objective for us: to occupy the pyramid, the center of the plaza. People would see us better from there.

And the World Cup began: Argentine flags, confetti thrown out of every office window, indifference from those other Argentines who didn't want to hear anything about death, who wanted to lose themselves in the wild party that the authorities offered them, that the four TV channels crammed down their throats until they were filled to overflowing or were completely brainwashed. We, meanwhile, increased our efforts at spreading the word: we sent hundreds of letters to politicians from other countries, and we offered interviews to television stations from around the world. The journalists listened to us wide-eyed, some of them became indignant, all of them thought we were a good story. We had achieved our goal.

June 1, three o'clock in the afternoon: the opening ceremony of the World Cup. While Argentine stations like ATC were broadcasting the joyous release of hundreds of doves in the stadium, the majority of the journalists were with us, in the Plaza de Mayo, covering the flip side of the Argentine coin. "Boycotting the World Cup." The police, accustomed to attacking us without needing to wait for permission, were halted by a superior officer just when we were expecting their assault. This delighted the Dutch broadcasters, who decided to transmit images of the Mothers instead of the simultaneous shots of the opening ceremonies. We were interviewed by TV stations who recorded our procession around the Plaza. Protected to some extent by the soccer cease-fire, we continued to build bridges to the outside world, making use of the journalists who were there to cover the championship.

As if the World Cup wasn't enough for the government, they had also ensured themselves more successful fanfare with the International Conference on Cancer. We made an appearance; the doctors listened. Three days later two doctors appear at the march. They've come to support us; their credentials hang over their elegant suits, and no one can touch them. The plaza is taken over by the police; we circle city hall. The doctors walk out front, defying the guards. A female voice is heard. Protected by the doctors, she shouts out, "When you took them, they were alive. We want them back alive." She yells it again. It becomes a rallying cry, the rest of us repeat it. "When you took them, they were alive. We want them back alive." Minutes later everyone splits up, we disperse onto Avenida de Mayo. But another chant had just been born. It was nothing and, at the same time, it was everything: it managed to summarize our feelings; it denounced. That shout of ours had shaken us and perhaps, we thought, it had also awakened, from their worker-ant existence, a few sullen passersby, lost in a haze of dollars, soccer goals, and foreign travels.

40. Football in Athens, with Her

Donna J. Gelagotis Lee

While a growing number of women watch football and participate in league play, gender inequalities persist. Media coverage routinely favors the men's game over the women's, reflected both by sheer column space and in subtle word choices. As Liz Crolley points out in "The Representation of Women in Sports Journalism," an article written for the British Council, the UK cultural organization, British sportswriters commonly refer to male players by their last names and to female players by their first names, a practice she calls "asymmetrical gender marking." Other forms of separation by gender are more blatant. Although countries such as the United States have mixed leagues for adults, England does not, following a rule of the English Football Association that stipulates separate leagues for males and females beginning at the age of twelve. Worldwide the professional ranks remain strictly gender-divided, and it seems likely they will remain that way for the present. In 2004, when a second-division club in Mexico tried to sign the women's national-team standout Maribel Domínguez, FIFA intervened, and its ruling went unappealed.

The following poem by Donna J. Gelagotis Lee, a writer and editor in New Jersey, may best be read within this largely pessimistic context. With all its potential to bring the sexes together, football shows an equal capacity to push them apart.

Every Sunday, he left her
to play football, until
she complained, and then he promised
to take her out each week
after the game—compromise
was *their* game, and so she agreed—

not knowing how tired he'd be, barely
awake at dinner and then falling
to sleep the moment they got home
to their rented house in a suburb
along the coast. He'd never give it up—sweaty,
once she went to watch—stayed
on the sidelines—dirt and dust on her lips—he,
covered with dust, his nails
black, blood where he scraped
the earth to get a goal—
the goal, the goal, the meaty
goal—two posts and a net—if only
she could catch the ball and not give it
back—would he give in? His best
friends—changing sides—it didn't matter which
team—and then, on TV, cheering
that was so fierce the country exploded
with the goal—
she lost track of the goal—she lost track
of him running on the field—
his hands outstretched, just as they were
with her.

41. Sierra Leone, Social Learning, and Soccer

Paul Richards

Paul Richards, an anthropologist with the School of Oriental and African Studies at the University of London, compiles what he calls "ethnographic vignettes" from civil war in the west African nation of Sierra Leone. Rather than seeing soccer as a pretext or conduit for violence, Richards views the local, grassroots game as a social resource for reintegrating disaffected soldiers of the Revolutionary United Front (RUF), many of them teenagers, back into society.

Conducting fieldwork among the Mende in the southeastern part of the country in 1994—three years into a civil war that would continue until 2000—Richards recognizes the potential of football as a commonly held cultural resource, along with popular music and street theater. "It is nobody's game," writes Richards in another section of the essay excerpted here, "but everybody's," popular among all social classes, Muslims and Christians, women and men. Soccer, he observes, also functions locally as a form of hospitality. Once when leading a team of students, Richards "was invited to pick and captain a side against the village eleven . . . as a way of 'announcing our presence.'" Richards's group, as outsiders, had to introduce itself in this way to the village populace, again showing soccer's place as social facilitator.

Yet at the time that Richards writes, the damages to society were extreme. Rebel soldiers—awaiting an amnesty that would be delayed for several more years—faced rejection by their families. More than two million people—more than one-third of the population—ultimately were forced from their homes.

Another legacy of the war are the thousands of amputees, mutilated by militias, bullets, or land mines. Some of these war wounded, too, have sought rehabilitation through football. Freetown, the capital, is home to the Single Leg Amputee Sports Club, which since forming in 2001 has competed worldwide in amputee soccer events. Team members play on crutches, without prostheses, but "when I get the ball and play it, it's the same," Mohammed Lappid told the *Los Angeles Times* in 2006. "I cross it to my colleague. He passes and reaches the goal. . . . We hold onto our friends to celebrate."

Referees

It is Saturday afternoon in Mandu, a large Mende village north of Bo. Mandu is the headquarters of Valunia Chiefdom. A feeder road to the railway in Bo was constructed early in the twentieth century, and Lebanese traders ventured to Mandu to buy palm produce. When the British introduced a poll tax, the first of these Lebanese traders paid tax for the entire chiefdom, to be reimbursed in palm produce at the farmer's convenience. The road remains untarred. Mandu is now a Saturday gathering-point for village-based fieldworkers for the main rural development agency in the region—the German-funded Bo-Pujehun Project. Today, the health workers from the area have challenged the agricultural extension workers to a match.

The game is billed as a novelty event—women and men in fancy dress. Arriving at the field (belonging to a local school) we meet twenty-two very fit young men already changed into two sets of distinctive strip. There is no sign of fancy dress or of any women participants. I am asked if I will take charge of the game. Fortunately I am with a colleague who is a qualified referee, and after some discussion he agrees to step in. My friend calls the sides together and points out the obvious—there are no linesmen (indeed no lines). Off-side will be hard to judge. The players will have to abide by whatever he decrees.

The game begins. It is energetic and skilful, despite the dust (rendering some of the action invisible to the crowd at times) and the fact that many of the participants are playing barefoot on gravelly ground. The green side scores a goal. The referee is immediately besieged by the players of the red side, and some of the spectators, protesting off-side. The clamour will not die down. Scuffles break out among players and the referee is jostled. Serious accusations begin to flow—the referee made a mistake, he is incompetent, he is biased—maybe he even took a bribe before the match began.

Unwilling to be insulted further, my friend walks smartly off the pitch, and heads for home. As if by magic the scuffling players are brought under control by their peers, and the crowd retreats to its rightful place. My friend is entreated not to abandon the game. He gives a little speech. He came to the match merely to accompany me. He had no warning he would be asked to take charge of the game. He has no linesmen. There is no way he could make accurate off-side rulings in such circumstances. He told everyone that at the outset. Offended and insulted by their actions, he makes it clear once again that he will blow as he sees fit, like it or leave it.

There is a general murmur of assent. Yes, indeed, a game played at speed and with passion cannot be regulated without a referee. Better to abide by the referee's rulings than for the game to be abandoned. Somebody mutters the proverb "bad osban beta pas empti os" (a bad husband is better than an empty house). Order returns and the game is played out in a friendly spirit, resulting in a 1–1 draw.

Rules

The scene now shifts to the grassy patch in front of a house in Bo town. Bo is the main urban centre of provincial Sierra Leone. Two days previously the town came under attack from a small contingent of a hundred or so rebels of the RUF. The attempted invasion was beaten off by an uprising of citizens. Clearing the town of insurgents, the civil defence later drove off the army as well, and imposed its own curfew, with vigilante patrols extracting summary revenge on looting soldiers and checking the credentials of incoming refugees to identify would-be rebel infiltrators.

Now the army has returned with reinforcements. These reinforcements include new rocket-launchers with a louder than usual explosive bang. They serve little tactical purpose since the rebels are by now well hidden in villages back from the roads, but the noise they make serves to terrify citizen and rebel alike.

It is the school holidays and the small boys from the surrounding compounds have gathered on the grass for an impromptu soccer game with a rag ball. They are all between nine and eleven years old, typical of the age-group the rebels had set out to capture as recruits in their raid on the town.

The game rages for twenty minutes or so, but is interrupted by an enormous racket from the brigade headquarters as the new rocket-launcher is test-fired. Some young women nearby cry out in terror. The soccer players decide to rest from their game for the time being, and begin instead to recapitulate the major incidents of the recently completed 1994 World Cup.

Nearly every game has been seen on video by each of the participants. They are children from low-income households, but there is a good steady electricity supply in Bo, and there are many video parlours showing a mixture of mainly Indian and Kung Fu films, and war movies of the *Rambo* genre. Entrance costs only a few pence. The video parlours also show sporting and news items copied from the satellite connections owned by wealthier members of the Bo community. Most young people in Bo are familiar with media events such as CNN coverage of the Gulf War or the video made by Prince Johnson's people of the torture and killing of Liberian dictator Samuel Doe. It was through video shows that these young soccer players had gained intimate knowledge of nearly all the main matches in the World Cup.

As we sheltered from the sun under a dusty ornamental palm, the topic turned to the use of the red card. It seemed that the young participants had almost complete recall of red-card incidents in the World Cup competition. Each was now subjected to elaborate examination. Fairness was weighed in the balance. The objectivity and eyesight of each referee passed under scrutiny. Older boys struggled to remember the origins of each of the match referees, coaching the younger boys as to where the countries in question might (or might not) be found. The argument then swept up and around the question of the national bias of match officials. A global social order was constructed before my eyes—shaky in details but recognizable in larger outline. The games and results themselves seemed but mere incidentals. And then, as if reminded by the engines of war in the background, their attention swung back to the social purposes of the referee. Without an official there cannot be a game. Beggars cannot be choosers. Referees and their red cards are a necessary evil. "Bad osban beta pas empti os."

Something I had recently been told came to mind. Apparently there was a brave human-rights lawyer working for one of the agencies in Monrovia whose job it was to motor out to the road-block checkpoints and teach the Geneva Convention to militia fighters. These under-age warriors were at first baffled, but later intrigued (I had been told), to find that war had rules. It crossed my mind that the lawyer might have been more readily understood had he started with the rules of soccer.

Trust and Co-operation

In the midst of war we were interviewing young people in Bo about their likes and dislikes in video entertainment. Many placed sports videos high on their list. Soccer was mentioned often.

What was it that was so attractive about the game? One young man said that watching soccer made him understand a great deal about human nature. Was it the glory of victory or the tragedy of defeat that attracted his interest? No, he said, he paid less attention to the competitive aspects of the game than to what was happening to players on the same side. Studying the game closely made one understand team effort. Some players were too selfish. Others combined and co-operated well. In life, it was the people on your own side you had to watch and understand, more than your opponents even.

42. Parity

William Heyen

In the following selection from American poet William Heyen, the author alludes to a passage from *The Drowned and the Saved* (1986) by Primo Levi, an
Italian chemist and author who would base many of his works on the eleven
months he spent at Auschwitz-Birkenau from 1944 to 1945. Levi quotes a
survivor, a Jewish doctor named Miklos Nyiszli, who briefly recounts a soccer game in the crematorium courtyard—a surreal spectacle in which the
meaning of sport is subverted as members of the German security force play
soccer against the Sonderkommando, prisoners conscripted to help operate
the killing machines. As Heyen suggests, the game creates a mock parity, with
executioner and victim momentarily set on par.

Summarizing Nyiszli's account, Levi writes that other members of the
Nazi ss "take sides, applaud, urge the players on as if, rather than at the
gates of hell, the game were taking place on the village green." The scene
also figures in the story collection by survivor Tadeusz Borowski, *This Way
for the Gas, Ladies and Gentlemen*, published originally in Poland in 1946.
As the narrator, Tadeusz reflects on the field bordered by lawns and flowers
yet notices that recent arrivals from a train have disappeared: "Between two
throw-ins in a soccer game, right behind my back, three thousand people
had been put to death."

After reading of the soccer match in Levi's book, Heyen was "pretty much
speechless, thinking of the situation of the Sonderkommando, especially,"
the author says in personal correspondence. "[It] sounds to me that a kind
of disgust permeates the poem, a sardonic disgust. The mind just disin-
tegrates thinking of sport in this context." A soccer player himself in high
school and college, Heyen was born in Brooklyn in 1940. His father, however,
had grown up in Germany playing soccer as a boy; two of Heyen's uncles
died fighting for the Nazis. He describes his upbringing in Long Island,
New York, as anti-Semitic, a "dark undersong" that later helped push him

toward reading and writing about the Holocaust. In addition to *Shoah Train* (2003), from which this poem is drawn, Heyen published *Erika: Poems of the Holocaust* in 1984.

It is, apparently, a fact,
that in Auschwitz in its season
occurred at least one soccer match
between ss who ran the camp,
& sk, the *Sonderkommando*,
the Special Squad, mainly Jews
whose daily survival depended
on beating order into arrivals,
on shorning, sorting clothes,
keeping the ovens operating,
pulling corpses from the gas,
removing gold teeth, slashing
orifices for coins & gems,
disposing of ashes.

In *The Drowned and the Saved*,
Primo Levi says that the ss
could not have played against other
than these "crematorium ravens"
of their own creation. Forced
to help kill their own people,
embraced & corrupted
by the Satanic Aryan engine—
with these existed parity,
a logical opposition &
the conjoining of spirit
for mutual health & benefit:
Come, said the ss, *today*
we must play.

43. Penalty Phase

Gay Talese

July 10, 1999, produced the most famous team victory in the history of American women's sports. More than forty million television viewers in the United States and over ninety thousand at the Rose Bowl in Pasadena, California, watched the women's soccer teams of China and the United States compete to a 0–0 draw in the final of the third Women's World Cup. In the penalty-kick phase, after 120 minutes of regulation play and overtime, Brandi Chastain became an iconic figure for women's achievement in sport by converting the decisive penalty kick with her left foot, ripping off her jersey, and initiating a mad celebration. Naturally, however, the defeated Chinese players had to cope with disappointment, in particular Liu Ying. The player wearing number 13 had her penalty kick saved by U.S. goalkeeper Briana Scurry; the miss gave the United States the opening it needed.

Watching the game in New York, writer Gay Talese saw potential in Liu's story. In an interview with the *New York Times*, Talese said that Liu's "moment of humiliation reached me in ways that were very personal" and suggested that his own depression created a connection with Liu's heartbreak. Several months later Talese arrived in Beijing and, after negotiations with Chinese soccer authorities, he ultimately met Liu; Liu's mother, Sun Zhixian, whom Talese refers to as Madam Sun; and Liu's family. Talese's pursuit of Liu's story occupies most of the final pages of his 2006 memoir, *A Writer's Life*, from which this selection is taken.

As our taxi proceeded slowly through the traffic of Chang'an Boulevard in the direction of the Oriental Plaza and the Forbidden City, Madam Sun pointed to a large white modern building on the north side of the boulevard; it was the Jianguo Garden Hotel and she said that this was where she had come to watch the televised broadcast of the

World Cup match in California. "I would have preferred to watch the match at home," she said, "but the sports association had invited all the players' mothers to be guests of the hotel and attend the Mother's Hope Dinner on the evening before the game. The dinner was held in a private room in the hotel and everybody was very enthusiastic and friendly. The mothers were from different parts of China, and had been brought to Beijing on planes, buses, and trains. The coach's wife was there and also some Chinese reporters. Most of us were meeting for the first time, but we suddenly felt very close because of our daughters being bonded to one another and to all of us, as well. A child leaves home and the mother's heart must follow.

"After dinner we went to our rooms, but I don't think anybody slept much that night. At three AM we were awakened and met for breakfast in a hall where a large television screen was set up, and soon we saw our daughters wearing their red uniforms, representing China, playing soccer, and running up and down the field. There was no score; they started taking penalty kicks. The tension was terrible, and when Liu Ying's kick was blocked, I began to feel tears in my eyes. Everybody was now crying, each for our own reasons. I cried for my daughter's pain and my pain. Everyone tried to console me, but I just wanted to go to my hotel room. I did not want the others to see more of how I felt."

Our taxi had turned off the boulevard and we were now passing through an alleyway that was crowded with pedestrians and bicyclists and was lined on both sides by gray stone walls that were about seven feet high and were cracked and crumbling in many places. Within a matter of moments we had moved from a city of modern hotels and office towers to what my guidebook described as a classically antiquated Chinese neighborhood in which millions of walled-in residents occupied centuries-old single-story homes with lattice-arched entranceways opening out to an ancient alleyway called a *hutong*. . . .

Although Liu Ying no longer lived at home—she shared an apartment with another soccer player near the women's stadium in southern Beijing when not traveling with the team—she regularly returned home for overnight visits, and whenever she did, she slept on the cot that Madam Sun pointed to in the far corner of the room. Next to the cot was a cedar chest, and near it was a plastic compartmentalized container holding loafers, sneakers, and cleated soccer shoes. Hanging on the wall above the cot was a four-by-three-foot poster featuring a broadly smiling Michael Jordan.

"My daughter is now in Guam, competing in the Asia Cup," Madam Sun told us. "She telephoned last night. She telephones a few times a week no matter where she is. All the team members have cell phones, given to them by one of their sponsors, the Ericsson company. Now that she has a cell phone, I talk to her more than when she used to live here. But she was barely a teenager when she went off to room and board at the soccer academy, returning home only on weekends." Madam Sun recalled that during the weekend of the Tiananmen Square trouble in 1989, as the bloodshed began on Saturday night, June 3, and continued through the following morning, Liu Ying was staying at the family home. She was then fifteen. "My son was out walking on Saturday night and saw a lady get hit with a stray bullet," Madam Sun recalled. "I myself could hear the gun noises and lots of people screaming and shouting. The noise carried throughout our neighborhood. It didn't disturb Liu Ying, however. She lay on that cot all night, sleeping peacefully through all that noise and commotion. She was not aware of anything until we told her about it the next morning, and then she said, 'Oh, Mom, why didn't you wake me?' Later on Sunday, the two of us took a walk around the neighborhood and we saw vehicles turned upside down, and lots of rubble everywhere. Most of the people were very fearful and confused. . . ."

As we sat listening to Madam Sun, we were joined by an elderly but agile gray-haired woman who came in carrying a pot of steaming tea and three cups on a tray. As she smiled, the many wrinkles on her broad face deepened. She was wearing a gray worsted Mao-style jacket and a long sweater vest knitted in a pattern of beige and gray concentric squares. After she had poured the tea and handed a cup to each of us, she sat down on the bed next to Madam Sun, who, with seeming pride, introduced her as her mother. Her name was Zhang Shou Yi. She had turned seventy-five a few years earlier and had worked until then. . . .

Madam Zhang told me that, in addition to herself, there were now twenty-six people lodged within her property—eleven family members and fifteen neighbors. She had a two-room suite on the northern side of the courtyard, which was the side customarily reserved for elders. Her bedroom was slightly more spacious than any other, and, of the five television sets hooked up on the property—two within the quarters of her neighbors—her newly purchased twenty-five-inch-screen Peacock model was the most reliable and emitted the most clearly delineated images in color.

It was this set that she had been watching as Liu Ying competed in the China-USA World Cup final. Madam Zhang and four members of her family—two of her sons and their wives—had gathered around the set in the early-morning hours, joining together in calling out words of encouragement toward a tiny red-shirted figure of a girl who wore number 13 and was shown running up and down the field, amid her teammates and opponents, focusing her attention upon a soccer ball on the other side of the world.

On that morning, Liu Ying's twin sister and her brother were watching the game in the latter's bedroom, while their nearby neighbors were doing so in their courtyard dwelling. On the other side of the wall, within the rows of homes that lined the *hutong*, there were hundreds and perhaps thousands of other television viewers. Lights could be seen glowing in countless windows during the predawn darkness as the game began, and throughout the four-hour telecast the quiescence that usually accommodated late sleepers on Sundays, at least along the back streets of the city, was now penetrated by the lively commentary of a play-by-play announcer in California and by the soaring and syncopated sounds of people in China venting their responses through the raised windows of their homes—cheering, jeering, clapping, sighing, and finally voicing their displeasure and disappointment when the game was over and the Chinese team had been defeated by the Americans. As I have mentioned, more than 100 million people in China reportedly viewed the telecast. Nowhere was the final score more silently and sadly accepted than within the household at number 74 Wuding Hutong.

After turning off her television set and veiling it with a black cotton dustcover, Madam Zhang tried to comfort and reassure her kinsmen, who sat around her, most of whom seemed to be stunned. "It is a part of life," she said. When a few of her neighbors came in from the courtyard, she repeated, "It is a part of life." Throughout the morning, everyone remained within the walls of the compound. And then the telephone in Madam Zhang's anteroom began to ring, and her younger brother got up to answer it.

"Please let me speak to my mother," said the sobbing voice of Liu Ying. She was calling from Los Angeles.

"I'm sorry, she is not here," her uncle said, explaining that her mother had gone off to watch the game with the coach's wife and other women at a hotel, but he did not know the name of the hotel.

"Then let me speak to my brother," she said. As soon as her brother picked up the receiver, she began to cry: "Oh, it's all my fault, it's all my fault. . . ."

A day later, after the team had gotten off the plane in Beijing, Liu Ying's mother, along with the mothers of other players, stood waiting in the marble-floored lobby of a reception hall near the airport while the arriving group of young women wearing red warm-up suits ascended from ground level via an escalator. After tossing their carrier bags to the floor, the young women ran with their arms outstretched and tears in their eyes to be embraced by their mothers. As they greeted one another, a chorus of sibilant sounds was heard through the lobby—*Mei shi, mei shi, ni mei shi ba: Ni ye mei shi ba?*—words not easily translated, my interpreter explained to me, but words meant to comfort, to express concern and regret while at the same time stressing positiveness and reassurance.

Still, as Madam Sun told us during our interview, the players and their families were not sheltered from the fact that millions of people in China had been let down by the outcome of the World Cup match. When Liu Ying's twin sister, Liu Yun, returned to her job in the department store on the day after the telecast, she was approached by many customers and coworkers who asked, "What happened to Liu Ying? How could she have messed up when it was so important?"

"Oh, I'm so sorry," the sister replied, saying repeatedly, "please accept my apologies."

But such criticism subsided on the following day after there were stories in Chinese newspapers and on television claiming that the United States team had won the game unfairly, blaming the American goalkeeper for moving improperly in front of the net *before* Liu Ying had begun her penalty kick. Some of these reports were accompanied by photographs purporting to show Briana Scurry in the act of committing an infraction. Liu Ying's brother, Liu Tong, saw the photos and stories while surfing on the Internet, and, after printing them out, he distributed them to members of his family and several people he knew in the neighborhood.

Later in the week, the Chinese soccer players and the coaching staff were invited to the Great Hall to be greeted by President Jiang Zemin and receive medallions identifying them as honored citizens of the People's Republic. The women were uniformly attired in gray skirts and jackets, white blouses, and black pumps. As President Jiang walked toward Liu Ying and placed a ribboned medallion on her shoulders, he smiled and told her, "Don't worry, there will be another day, and you will have another opportunity."

44. Platko (Santander, May 20, 1928)

Rafael Alberti
Translated from the Spanish by Kirk Anderson

Coaxed on by a friend to attend the Spanish King's Cup final between Barcelona and Real Sociedad on May 20, 1928, Rafael Alberti studied the play of Barcelona's Hungarian goalkeeper and later penned one of the most enduring poems in football literature. Perhaps the fact that Alberti was not a fan contributed to the strength of "Platko," a work that demonstrates deep human sympathy and eschews more simplistic supporter enthusiasms. What Alberti finds in the play of Barcelona's Hungarian goalkeeper is a heroism that transcends the game and might, therefore, stand for other forms of noble resistance. In fact, as novelist Ronald Reng points out in "The Goalkeeper Is the Poet's Darling" (published in *Anstoß*, a limited-issue German magazine produced for the 2006 World Cup), Alberti may have had in mind the contemporary struggle for democracy, very much a part of Spain in 1928, then under military rule. Seen in this light Alberti's poem typifies his work as one of Spain's greatest poets, whose concern for his country's turmoil drove his art and directed his life.

The ostensible subject of the poem, Franz Platko, played for only three more seasons, retiring in 1931. He then began a coaching career that lasted until 1953 and included stints with Barcelona, Chilean club Colo-Colo, and Argentine clubs River Plate and Boca Juniors. Although Alberti never records another encounter with Platko, the two both lived in Argentina for some of the same years—when Platko coached and Alberti, in the wake of Franco's victory in the Spanish Civil War, fled to South America in exile. Platko later immigrated to Chile and died in Santiago in 1982. Alberti died seventeen years later at the age of ninety-seven.

To José Samitier, captain

> Nobody forgets, Platko,
> no, nobody, nobody, nobody,
> you blond bear from Hungary.

Not the sea
that jumped before you, unable to defend you.
Not the rain. Not even the prevailing wind.

Not the sea or the wind, Platko,
bloody, blond Platko,
keeper in the dust,
lightning rod.

No, nobody, nobody, nobody.

Blue and white jerseys, in the air,
royal jerseys,
rivals, against you, flying and dragging you along,
Platko, distant Platko,
broken, blond Platko,
burning tiger on another country's pitch. You're a key,
Platko, you, a broken key,
a golden key dropped before the golden gate!

No, nobody, nobody, nobody,
nobody forgets, Platko.

The sky turned its back.
Blue and crimson jerseys fluttered,
subdued, without wind.

The sea, eyes turned away,
laid down and said nothing.
Bleeding in the buttonholes,
bleeding for you, Platko,
for your Hungarian blood;
without your blood, your instinct, your stops, your leaps,
the insignias were frightened.

No, nobody, Platko, nobody,
nobody, nobody forgets.

It was the return of the sea.
There were
ten speeding banners
blazing, unstoppable.
It was the return of the wind.
The return of hope to the heart.
It was your return.

Heroic blue and crimson,
surged through air into the veins.
Wings, azure and white wings, broken,
embattled wings, whitewashed the pitch, plucked featherless.

And the air had legs,
a body, arms, a head.

And all because of you, Platko,
blond, Hungarian Platko!

And in your honor, for your return,
because your steady hand came back to the fight,
the wind opened a gap in the opponent's goal.

Nobody, nobody forgets.

The sky, the sea, the rain, they remember.
The insignias.

The golden insignias, flowers in buttonholes,
closed, were opened by you.

No, nobody, nobody, nobody,
nobody forgets, Platko.

Not the end: your departure,
blond bear of blood,
limp banner borne across the field on shoulders.

Oh Platko, Platko, Platko,
so far from Hungary!

What sea could be left with dry eyes?

Nobody, nobody forgets,
no, nobody, nobody, nobody.

Part 5. Belief

I don't know about this
game. You don't stop! Ever!
How about stopping? How
come they keep running?
— TAKIA THOMAS, age 10,
Washington DC

Introduction

Soccer commentators and managers speak of belief as a vital intangible. Football teams, according to the pundits, demonstrate either a presence or lack of belief at the crucial moments: when down three goals at halftime, facing a penalty shootout, or suddenly reduced to ten players after a red-card offense. The quality of belief is ingrained, the experts would have us think. Teams and players believe in themselves, or they do not. "I was amazed that the sportscaster could say the word *believe* with more intensity than a preacher or religion class teacher," writes Friedrich Christian Delius in "The Sunday I Became World Champion" of listening to the 1954 World Cup final on radio.

In a sport where failure and loss assume outsized roles—as seen in the previous section—belief must survive in some fashion, or the player stops running, the manager stops managing, the fan stops watching. Writers in this concluding section employ ecclesiastical language at times to express a secular faith in their team, as in Edilberto Coutinho's "The Lord's Prayer, Recast," or to urge a fallen hero to recovery in Hernán Casciari's "Living to Tell a Tale (Letter to Diego)." Other authors pick up on additional points of contact between football and organized religion. In one of Elísabet Jökulsdóttir's prose poems the faithful gather at a football match and participate in a ritual, looking for meaning that comes from the "scoreboard that told . . . god's answer to humanity: 2–1."

In daily life football may be viewed as spiritual salve, offering a "much more pleasant and appealing world than the one left outside," according to Mario Vargas Llosa. Or the game may achieve the miraculous, as in Delius's novella, leading to change in both an individual and a country. Football can also serve as a medium for self-renewal, writes Lawrence Cann of his team of homeless and formerly homeless players. Crispin Thomas conceives of football as pure joy in "Football Is," and Philippe Dubath imagines a spiritual communion of sorts—mediated by the ball itself—between the adult and inner child in "Zidane and Me."

Perhaps the most numinous vision within these entries lies in Mark Nuttall's report from among the Inuit of Greenland. In the shimmering, swooping, and leaping of the northern lights—called *arsarnerit* (the football players) in the Inuit language—spectators watch their ancestors engage in a cosmic kickabout. The Inuit believe that "the souls of the dead players will ultimately be reborn."

45. The Lord's Prayer, Recast

Edilberto Coutinho
Translated from the Portuguese by Wilson Loria

Journalist and writer Edilberto Coutinho was born in the northeastern Brazilian state of Paraíba in 1933. In his collection of short stories *Maracanã, adeus*, which was translated into English as *Bye, Bye Soccer* (1994), Coutinho explores his country's national game, finding many parallels to contemporaneous social and political struggles. The volume was published originally in 1980, as Brazil approached a third decade under military dictatorship. According to Elzbieta Szoka in her introduction to the English translation, Coutinho intended the collection as a protest and envisioned *futebol*, given its strong roots in Brazilian popular culture, as a form of resistance. Players in Coutinho's stories, through no fault of their own, seem to be caught in a tangle of commercialization, politics, and race that has stripped soccer of its nobler ideals.

At least one of Brazil's most prominent players found his consciousness shaped by those times—Sócrates was ten years old when the military seized power in 1964. He tells Alex Bellos, in *Futebol: The Brazilian Way of Life* (2002), that as "the child of a dictatorial system" he later felt inspired to organize his club team, Corinthians of São Paulo, into a utopian socialist cell. They called the group Corinthians Democracy and advocated for political causes while fighting for control of their destinies as players.

Below, in a cleverly altered version of The Lord's Prayer that begins his story collection, Coutinho mixes religion with the devoted fervor of a football fan. The poem is addressed to a higher power, but the speaker's earthbound referents include this petitioner's wife, who is losing faith in the capacities that soccer and her husband's related obsessive wagering have to bring happiness.

Lord Supreme Mathematician,
Thy power of infallible and perfect calculus come
Give us each day our daily news

about lots of goals
beautiful goals by my suffering little Bangu Soccer Team.
Forgive my wife for being a pain in the ass
as we forgive ourselves for our stupidity when perforating
the tiny holes on the
Soccer Lotto ticket mistakenly.
Lead us not into temptation to root for another team.
Deliver us from the goals of our opponents
and bestow cramps upon the shins
of their forwards.
Amen.
What now woman?

46. Communicate, Lads

Elísabet Jökulsdóttir
Translated from the Icelandic by Baldur Ingi Guðbjörnsson and
Katherine Connor Martin

Elísabet Jökulsdóttir, raised in Reykjavík, Iceland, has worked in construction and as a deckhand on fishing boats. She also has a well-established literary reputation on the volcanic island of some three hundred thousand as a poetess, novelist, and playwright, who has had several of her plays produced both at home and abroad. In her first poetry collection, *Dans í lokuðu herbergi* (Dance in a Closed Room), published in 1989, and then again in her one-woman play from 2004, *The Secret Face*, she explores loneliness, love, and the dream world. "I am writing to make something out of the heritage I have been given, the language and the literature and my vision of the country and the people, myself," she writes in a 2003 online self-assessment. Jökulsdóttir is also known as an environmental activist, and in 2003 she made headlines for grabbing a microphone during a domestic flight and speaking passionately against the construction of a dam, needed to power an aluminum smelter, in one of Iceland's last remaining pristine areas.

As a source of inspiration for her 2001 novel *Fótboltasögur (tala saman strákar)*, translated in 2002 as *Football Stories (Communicate Lads)*, Jökulsdóttir drew from her own family life: two of her sons played for Knattspyrnufélag Reykjavíkur of the Icelandic league. Jökulsdóttir dedicates the book to her sons—Kristjón, Garpur, and Jökull—with the "wish that one of these days it will rain footballs."

The following selections emerge from this collection of prose poems, which critic Soffía Bjarnadóttir calls "micro stories," written from the perspective of a club physical therapist. Writes Julian D'Arcy, professor of English literature at the University of Iceland, "The players, all men, can only seem to express themselves through talking football, a wonderful metaphor for men's general inarticulateness when expressing their feelings." Yet despite connections drawn between missed chances on the pitch and in Icelandic life more broadly, a positive spirit survives. As one junior coach concludes, "You never know what these guys will amount to."

The Superstition

I don't know how I should begin, he said sadly when he had positioned himself on the bench, and when I bent his shooting leg something snapped in his knee so I told him that we would start by cooling it down and he would have to try cooling himself down but then he raised himself on his elbows and asked how was he supposed to do that, he had been offside at the only scoring opportunity of the match and the sight of the linesman's flag had grieved him at the same moment that the cheers of the spectators suffocated like when a mass grave is covered over and the earth had disappeared beneath his feet, he who had done everything right today, put his underwear on backwards, said good-night at the breakfast table, started his car with the house key, rung a wrong number and washed his hair with aftershave, because he had the custom of doing everything wrong on a match-day so he would do everything right during the match, but he was wondering if he had forgotten something on his list, the one thing that made all the difference, and then he gave the well-practised speech that superstition wasn't merely superstition rather a matter of connections, connecting your mind to actions and tightening a grid of events until there wasn't any room for error but when I asked if maybe it wasn't a good idea to connect yourself to god and yourself he said frustrated that he could never hear god over the coach's yells and the cheering of the crowd and for all he cared he had started this custom himself, otherwise he would lose the ground beneath his feet. At the end of the session I patted him on the knee and said that this didn't look bad and his knee would soon feel better and after all, he could always pray and then something snapped, he dug his face in his hands and said that he had forgotten the lord's prayer then mumbled something in the air as if to settle down but the words carried him away like balloons and the last thing I thought I heard him say was that he didn't know how this was supposed to end.

The Sermon

Things weren't exactly heavenly this season and the coach came to the bench, looking suspicious even though he regarded me with beseeching eyes like I was his saviour and claimed that he would resign if giving the guys a sermon, a hell of a sermon, wasn't enough for them, as he intended, but it was like I always had this urge to be humorous in my relations with the coach and I told him that even though people have been given sermons for over two thousand years the churches remain empty but then he looked at me like his last hope had vanished and said that someway or somehow he would manage to get out of this hellhole. I told him that I had never heard that resignation was enough to get out of that evil place and that to my best of my knowledge you at least had to do a few press-ups.

The Left Back

He sometimes claimed to have been born a left back because his left foot came out first or at least that was what his mother told him, it came up at every family gathering and roberto carlos was rubbed in his face and it was repeatedly said that *he* went forward but no one knew that he had long ago turned roberto carlos off because he himself was the back who didn't go forward, on the contrary he liked backing, because he wanted to back up as far as possible and he felt most comfortable when he could back up all the way to the goal, where his strength was tested and no one figured out that he was always being backed at, his mother backed him into corners, as did his father, brothers, sisters, that was the way he learned how to back and that was it, this was his position in the family, perhaps it was all predetermined, it was just amazing that he had gotten so far with his family on his back and it showed that his talent was innate and perhaps had even matured as a result of them backing him into corners, that is how he had learned to cope with it and when he couldn't back down any further and had everything down his throat, and even further down various paths of his body then he began defending, in his heart, in his heart yes, and he had never let anyone know about it but he could tell me, he knew that it wouldn't go any further, that he passed from his heart up to his head, and got some ideas that way, yes ideas that developed in the head about defending the heart, if I knew what he meant, but in taking me as a confidant he was on the verge of figuring out various things that had been sitting stuck, and felt like he could take a step forward, and a spark of the notion that perhaps his mother had failed to see right, we will never know, what does a woman see in the euphoria of giving birth, maybe he should check the doctor's report, but then I suddenly felt his voice was up against a wall, he grabbed his heart and said that he would back up now, back up yes, he was well on his way to back out of the position now, at the very least he was completely a back.

The Opportunities

All these opportunities, he moaned and when I asked him to look east and then west in order to loosen his neck, he said that he had lost contact with the opportunities, there was no shortage of opportunities in the match it was like some kind of a joke and nothing had been gained from them and then I asked him to move his neck but he seemed to be trying to see something in the air so I grabbed his lower jaw and pretended I was examining him in the hopes that it would stop the muttering about us Icelanders, which would follow, about how through the ages we had let all the opportunities pass by, the herring lay in stacks on our coast, mountain grass grew on our moor, seaweed curled around our feet, the eggs rotted in the cliff face and all that water warm and cold sprayed from the ground or fell through the air, and the only opportunity that we took advantage of was the language, all because of those sagas, we could talk (and we talked constantly), but no one knew if anything had ever come out of that talk but he was sure that we had talked about this, sat in our dirt houses and said: there is seaweed on our coast, the sea has thrown herring our way, the mountain grass is touching the sky, the eggs are rolling from the nests and so forth, but because we never did anything about it our language developed through the years so that it struggled through and became muttering, people were muttering in every corner and we probably muttered about our opportunities without comprehending the matter and finally we saw the opportunity to develop the mutter into a murmur; yes a murmur.

A Match That Was Not Postponed

Fountains, splashes and puddles, pouring rain and they didn't know where they were, there was nothing, absolutely nothing that indicated that this was a football pitch, nothing, absolutely nothing that indicated that they were playing football even though they were kicking something, and even though they heard a distant bawling it could just as well be bulls and not spectators, and the chirp from the whistle could just as well come from a broken-winged bird, yes, there was nothing that indicated anything about what this was except that it lasted ninety minutes, and there was a scoreboard that told the meaning of life or god's answer to humanity: 2–1

The Junior Squad Coach

I tell them that life is Saturday morning practise at nine o'clock, that they should be there with their bags, uniforms, pads, boots, towels, I announce the drills, watch them run three kilometres, do a hundred and fifty press-ups, head the ball, dribble the ball, inside, outside, heel kick, knee it, divide into two teams and play, I watch how they do it, who fights, who surrenders, who gets angry, I watch how they play, who plays for the team, who plays for the ego, I stand on the sidelines, watch, practise after practise, pass to pass, motivate them, guide them, give them pointers, yell at them, tell them to move back, go for the wings, into the centre, and back on defence, pass forward and cross to the sides, pass in front of the goal and on into the net and the 'keeper came close to catching it, back to the pitch with the ball. And then you never know what these guys will amount to.

47. Five Poems for the Game of Soccer

Umberto Saba

Translated from the Italian by Geoffrey Brock

Umberto Saba is the pen name of Umberto Poli, the Italian poet born in Trieste in 1883. According to Italian commentaries, four of the poems in "Cinque poesie per il gioco del calcio" ("Five Poems for the Game of Soccer") were composed following a match in October 1933: a 0–0 draw between Saba's hometown Triestina and rival Ambrosiana—the name assigned to Internazionale of Milan under Fascist rule. Of the first poem, "Small-Town Team," Saba himself comments that he sees Triestina, known as *rosso alabardati* (Trieste red) in the local idiom, as guardians of a city in need of a protector. The players, "living for [their] mother"—that is, Trieste itself—move with the wind to "her defense."

The best-known poem of the series is the last, "Goal," written in 1934. The poem's composition coincides with the World Cup, held that year in Fascist Italy, and may contain not-so-subtle political commentary. According to Tim Parks, author of *A Season with Verona* (2002), the phrase "unita ebbrezza" in the first line of the second stanza—referring to a crowd as "collectively drunk" as translated by Geoffrey Brock below or as "one with frenzy" in Parks's version—"would have immediately reminded readers of the dangerous crowd phenomenon that was Fascism."

To Parks, however, the critical allusion is to "those consumed by hate and love" in the same stanza, an implication that the spectacle of Italian football in 1934 was both negative and positive. "A little sad . . . don't you think, for a poem called 'Goal'?" asks a Hellas Verona marketing executive in Parks's book. The man is able to quote Saba's work by heart, but adds: "Please don't write a sad book about football. It's a joyous thing."

1

Small-Town Team

I too among the many greet you who wear
the Trieste red,

exuded
by your native land, by a whole populace
beloved.

Nervous, I watch your match.
Oblivious,
you give expression through it to ancient things,
astounding things,
on that green carpet, in the air, beneath
bright suns of winter.

The worries
that in an instant turn the hair to white
are so remote from you! Glory lends you
a fleeting smile: the best
that it can manage. Embraces
run among you, and joyous gestures.

You're young, and living for your mother;
the wind carries you to her defense. The poet
loves you for this, too; loves you differently
than others do—but is equally moved.

2

Three Moments

Having run out onto the field, you first
wave to your fans. And then,
what happens then,
when you turn toward the other side, the one
crowded with black, is not a thing to speak of,
is nothing with a name.

The keeper paces back and forth, a sentry.
Danger is distant still.
But when it, cloudlike, comes, as it will,
a young wild beast
will crouch there, waiting
to spring.

The very air is festive, the streets ring.
So what if it never lasts?
No offensive gained the goal, the cries
criss-crossing the air were rocket-blasts.
The glory that belongs to you eleven boys
like a river of love ornaments Trieste.

3

Thirteenth Match

Up in the stands the meager company
made its own warmth.

And when the sun—immense corona—snuffed
its glare behind a house, the field made clear
the augury of night.

Back and forth
they ran, red jerseys, white ones, in a light
that was a strange and shifting glass. The wind
altered the course of the ball, and Fortune
tied the blindfold back around her eyes.

And it felt good
to be so few together,
numb in the chill,
like the last men remaining on a hill
who watch from there the final competition.

4

Boys in the Stadium

Cock-like
the voices of boys; sharply they engrave
capricious loves, and woes.

At the field's edge a solitary banner
fluttering lonely over a low wall.
Climbing atop that wall, the boys would vie
by launching, in the lulls, beloved names,
one at a time, like arrows. And it lives
in me, that happy image; and it marries,
at dusk, a memory from my beardless days.

So haughty they were odious, the players
passed there beneath that wall.
Except for those unripe boys, they saw it all.

5

Goal

The keeper, fallen in his vain
attempt at a save, presses his face
to the grass, to blot the bitter light.
A teammate, come to ease his plight,
urges him up with words and hands,
revealing eyes that are full of tears.

The crowd—collectively drunk—spills
onto the pitch. The scorer's brethren
embrace him wildly, shout and shove.
To those consumed by hate and love
few visions beautiful as this
are ever, under heaven, granted.

Downfield, beside his unbreached net,
the other keeper stands alone.
Yet his soul tastes what his body misses.
His joy does flips as he blows kisses
down the length of the pitch. *I, too,*
he thinks, *am part of the celebration.*

48. Living to Tell a Tale (Letter to Diego)

Hernán Casciari
Translated from the Spanish

In April 2004, Diego Armando Maradona lay in intensive care at Suizo-Argentina clinic in Buenos Aires for treatment of heart and lung ailments believed to be related to obesity and past drug use. Newspapers started preparing obituaries, while fans of the soccer player some columnists call the "male Eva Perón" kept vigil outside the clinic.

The return to health of the stout playmaker for Boca Juniors, Barcelona, and ssc Napoli reaffirmed his special status in Argentine culture. After the illness and subsequent gastric bypass surgery, Maradona hosted one of the country's most popular television chat shows. He remains the object of academic study and of a faith, centered at the Church of Maradona in Rosario, Argentina, where supplicants re-create the so-called Hand of God goal that Maradona scored against England in a 1986 World Cup quarterfinal. His second goal in that game (alluded to in Casciari's text below), a mesmerizing, weaving run through the English midfield that ultimately beat goalkeeper Peter Shilton, demonstrated the skill that complemented the cheekiness shown earlier when he had scored—deliberately, he later admitted—with his fist. According to Argentina teammate and author Jorge Valdano, he embodies what Argentines call *gambeta*: an idealized combination of technical ability and deceit.

The following is a fictional letter written to Maradona during his illness, part of the "blognovel" *Más respecto, que soy tu madre* (A Little Respect, I'm Your Mother) that Argentine writer Hernán Casciari posted online over eleven months, beginning in September 2003. The entry of April 21, 2004, "Vivir para contarlo (carta a Diego)," translated below, is narrated by Mirta Bertotti, married to Zacarías and mother to daughter Sofi and sons Nacho and Caio. Nonno is Mirta's Italian-born father-in-law.

The letter demonstrates Maradona's elevated place in Argentina, even within the consciousness of non–football fans. With his exploits in 1986, guiding Argentina to a second World Cup trophy, he helped revive national belief during a time of economic crisis under President Raúl Alfonsín. "In Argentina we are addicted to discussing Maradona," a psychologist tells Marcela Mora y Araujo, translator of *El Diego: The Autobiography of the World's Greatest Footballer* (2004), in the *Observer* (London). "He is our drug. It is not him who is ill, it is us."

I only ever saw Zacarías cry three times: when they told him his newborn baby Nacho was a boy, when you scored the second goal against the English, and when you were thrown out of the 1994 World Cup. So you should know, Diego, that thanks to you, I discovered my husband has emotions after all. That's why when he prays for you, I pray too. I don't mind if I have to pray for you. In this house, when my husband says we have to light a couple of candles for you, then we light a couple of candles—end of story.

But you're no saint; I've told you that many times before. There's no devotion from me. I never liked you because you're vulgar and big-headed. Zacarías always tells me that if I understood football I wouldn't feel that way. He said that there were no words to describe you and how you were out of this world, that in your heyday you could do things that defied the laws of physics, blah blah blah. But I'm not interested in that side of things. I am a woman. I don't understand, nor do I want to, this fascination with men in shorts chasing footballs.

On the other hand, there are things that I do understand, and it's because of these that I'm praying these nights. But don't think it's because of you. Do you really want to know why I'm praying? Well, because there were times when we had nothing, and I mean not even food on the table, and in those moments you brought some cheer and some joy into our house.

Alfonsín was driving us mad at the time, and then, like manna from heaven, along comes that World Cup where you won all the games for us. For me that was the worst winter I can remember. All we had for breakfast were chard fritters, and all we had for dinner were chard fritters. But when I ask Nacho or Zacarías what they remember about that winter, they don't mention the hunger, all they talk about is you. They have no idea we almost starved.

Outside the clinic, where they have you breathing on that machine, there are hordes of foreign journalists sending pictures around the world. They show people lighting candles and saying the rosary as they hold vigil through the night. Sometimes I feel ashamed that the rest of the world sees us like that, and I worry that they'll take us all for a bunch of simpletons. Then I feel like telling the world that we're not praying for the loudmouth or the foulmouth either. I feel like telling the world what this country is really like, how little we've had to cheer about over the last twenty years, and how of the little joy we've had, you've been at the heart of it.

I'd like to tell them how hard it is for us to agree on anything, to laugh or cry or shout for a common cause. How hard it is for us to sing "Argentina, Argentina" and let our chests swell with pride. How hard it is for us to get anything done, to better ourselves, or even express our anger. On the day you tested positive for ephedrine, I went out in the street, and I swear on the life of my kids that it was the first time I saw grown men cry. All around there was a deathly silence but for the sound of sniffling and the dragging of feet. The whole country was just speechless and deflated. What strange creatures we are, I thought, but at the same time I felt proud of our emotion, of my emotion, as I too cried that day. From where it came I don't even know.

Even Caio, who never saw you lift the World Cup, has a poster of you on his wall and talks about you like he knew you. What about Nonno, even he saw fit to forgive you when you told all of Italy "to go to hell" on live television. Even Nacho, who knows nothing about football, defends you. He knows that you are much more than that. So I ask you, how could I not pray that you get better?

Many years from now, Sofi's children's children will live in a country that's much better than it is today. Of that I'm sure. And nobody will remember then that you had a foul mouth and a big head. The history books will only say what was important: a poor boy was born here, a boy who went on to become the greatest player of all time. They will say that you were able to take a country racked with pain and hardship and make it almost insanely happy, even in its darkest hour. In the hope that this gift you have will never die, I pray.

I also pray that you may be cured, that you find respite from the strain of being "el Diego," and that you have time to enjoy being just an ordinary person. I pray that you live to see your grandchildren, to hold them and tell them who you were. How beautiful it would be to grow old and look into the eyes of one's grandchild and say: "Do you know who I am? I am Diego Maradona." And I lived to tell the tale.

49. The Empty Pleasure

Mario Vargas Llosa
Translated from the Spanish by John King

Mario Vargas Llosa treats football as a utopian vision and a lay religion in one of his series of reports commissioned by Madrid daily newspaper *El País* during the 1982 World Cup finals, hosted in Spain. The novelist and politician—who in 1990 lost to Alberto Fujimori in a runoff for the presidency of his native Peru—considers the World Cup, in particular, an empty vessel into which one can pour infinite meaning but that appeals in part because it is fleeting, "an experience where the effect disappears at the same time as the cause." Later reflecting on the player Diego Maradona in a newspaper column, which also appeared in the 1997 essay collection, *Making Waves*, he elaborates that "to admire a footballer is to admire something very close to pure poetry or abstract painting. It is to admire form for form's sake, without any rationally identifiable content."

Still, some persist in reading the outcomes in soccer matches, especially in international football, as if they were tea leaves or gnomic texts that only need proper interpretation. Some commentators make much, for instance, of Argentina's surrender in the Falkland Islands (Las Islas Malvinas) the day after a shocking 0–1 loss to Belgium in the 1982 World Cup, which they see as a natural consequence to Argentina's humiliation on the field. Pablo Alabarces, an Argentine sociologist and author in 2002 of *Fútbol y patria* (Football and the Motherland), refers to such dubious connections as "the never proven, but often accepted, premise that links soccer and politics in a relationship of cause and effect." Still, ever the contrarian, Maradona would refer to an Argentine victory over England in the subsequent World Cup, in 1986, as "recovering a little bit of the Malvinas."

A couple of years ago, I heard the Brazilian anthropologist Roberto da Matta give a brilliant lecture in which he explained that the popularity of football—which is as strong today as ever—expresses people's innate desire for legality, equality and freedom.

His argument was clever and amusing. According to him, the public sees football as a representation of a model society, governed by clear and simple laws which everyone understands and observes and which, if violated, brings immediate punishment to the guilty party. Apart from being a just arena, a football field is an egalitarian space which excludes all favouritism and privilege. Here, on this grass marked out by white lines, every person is valued for what he is, for his skill, dedication, inventiveness and effectiveness. Names, money and influence count for nothing when it comes to scoring goals and earning the applause or the whistles from the stands. The football player, furthermore, exercises the only form of freedom that society can allow its members if it is not to come apart: to do whatever they please as long as it is not explicitly prohibited by rules that everyone accepts.

This is what, in the end, stirs the passions of the crowds that, the world over, pour into the grounds, follow games on television with rapt attention and fight over their football idols: the secret envy, the unconscious nostalgia for a world that, unlike the one they live in which is full of injustice, inequality and corruption, gripped by lawlessness and violence, offers instead a world of harmony, law and equality.

Could this beautiful theory be true? Would that it were, for there is no doubt that it is seductive and that nothing could be more positive for the future of humanity than to have these civilized feelings nestling in the instinctive depths of the crowds. But what is probable is that, as always, reality overtakes theory, showing it to be incomplete. Because theories are always rational, logical, intellectual—even those that propose irrationality and madness—and in society and in individual behaviour, unreason, the unconscious and pure spontaneity will always play a part. They are both inevitable and immeasurable.

I'm scribbling these lines in a seat in Nou Camp, a few minutes before the Argentina-Belgium game that is kicking off this World Cup. The signs are favourable: a radiant sun, a clear sky, an impressive multi-coloured crowd full of waving Spanish, Catalan, Argentine and a few Belgian flags, noisy fireworks, a festive, exuberant atmosphere and applause for the regional dancing and gymnastic displays which are a warm-up to the game (and which are of a much higher standard than is normal on these occasions).

Of course this is a much more pleasant and appealing world than the one left outside, behind the Nou Camp stands and behind the people applauding the dances and the patterns made by dozens of young people on the pitch. This is a world without wars, like those in the South Atlantic and Lebanon, which the World Cup has relegated to second place in the minds of millions of fans throughout the world who, in the next two hours, will be thinking, like those of us here in the stands, of nothing else except the passes and the shots of the twenty-two Argentine and Belgian players who are opening the tournament.

Perhaps the explanation for this extraordinary contemporary phenomenon, the passion for football—a sport raised to the status of a lay religion, with the greatest following of all—is in fact a lot less complicated than sociologists and psychologists would have us suppose, and is simply that football offers people something that they can scarcely ever have: an opportunity to have fun, to enjoy themselves, to get excited, worked up, to feel certain intense emotions that daily routine rarely offers them.

To want to have fun, to enjoy oneself, to have a good time, is a most legitimate aspiration, a right as valid as the desire to eat and work. For many, doubtless complex, reasons, football has taken on this role in the world today with more widespread success than any other sport.

Those of us who like, and get pleasure from, football are not in any way surprised at its great popularity as a collective entertainment. But there are many who do not understand this fact and, furthermore, deplore and criticize it. They see the phenomenon as deplorable because, they say, football alienates and impoverishes the masses, distracting them from important issues. Those who think like this forget that it is important to have fun. They also forget that what characterizes an entertainment, however intense and absorbing, and a good game of football is enormously intense and absorbing, is that it is ephemeral, non-transcendent, innocuous. An experience where the effect disappears at the same time as the cause. Sport, for those who enjoy it, is the love of form, a spectacle which does not transcend the physical, the sensory, the instant emotion; which, unlike, for example, a book or a play, scarcely leaves a trace in the memory and does not enrich or impoverish knowledge. And this is its appeal: that it is exciting and empty. For that reason, intelligent and unintelligent, cultured and uncultured people can equally enjoy football. That's enough for now. The King has arrived. The teams have come out. The World Cup has been officially opened. The game is beginning. That's enough writing. Let's enjoy ourselves a bit.

50. Match

Sarah Wardle

Born in London in 1969, Sarah Wardle supports English Premier League team Tottenham Hotspur. For a period beginning in 2004 she served as the club's official poet in residence, marking another significant crossover between literary and football circles. In the same year Britain's poet laureate, Andrew Motion, chaired a judging panel that selected the nation's laureate for football chants. A self-employed lawyer composed a winning entry about Aston Villa striker Juan Pablo Angel ("An Alice band keeps up his hair, / Juan Pablo from Col-om-bi-air") and went on to earn ten thousand pounds writing chants for the 2004–5 Premiership season.

Wardle taught writing at Middlesex University in London and over a season wrote twenty poems about the north London club that generations of her mother's family had also supported. Her work was published in match programs at Tottenham's home ground, White Hart Lane. Using her access behind the scenes, Wardle composed verses about the treatment room ("Savlon wound wash, pre-injection swabs, / insect repellent, Nivea after sun, / reclining beds that could hold poolside gods") and specific games. Of a 1–0 victory over Blackburn, Wardle writes: "The final score has a pleasing sound / the Proustian rush of childhood weekends, / the storytime lilt of that voice on *Grandstand*, / a piano scale that climbs, then descends." Some of her football poems also appeared in the 2005 collection *Score!*, which was dedicated to Spurs. Other English clubs also boast poets in residence, including Barnsley (Ian McMillan) and Brighton and Hove Albion (Attila the Stockbroker, the pseudonym of John Baine).

> Imagine you and I are playing the field.
> I make a pass to you. Your first touch
> stops the game's momentum in its tracks.

For a split-second you think how to proceed.
Now I'm the one afraid to run ahead
and risk offence by being thought offside.
You kick it on and at the right time
I give you possession. You chip it in the net.
Forget the other players and who's watching,
the referee and who decides the rules,
but see the last two strikers in the world,
the Eden of a stadium revolving
round us, as we practise for the final,
over again like kids against a wall.

51. Zidane and Me

Philippe Dubath
Translated from the French by Anna Kushner

Trying to communicate across a gulf of perceived gender difference, Swiss author Philippe Dubath, in the form of a man writing a long letter to his wife, Nanon, explains how childhood football fantasies play themselves out in adulthood. The writer treats soccer as a path to self-knowledge, albeit a knowledge, in his view, that is peculiar to the male. Soccer, as shared in his fraternity, implies a range of associations and relationships, forced jokes in the shower, and obtuse, soccer-specific vocabulary for humiliating opponents: *le petit pont* ("the little bridge," passing the ball through a defender's legs); *le grand pont* ("the big bridge," passing the ball around an opponent to oneself); *l'aile de pigeon* ("the pigeon's wing," sideways-flicking the ball with the leg raised behind, in a winglike motion); *la bicyclette* ("the bicycle," executing an overhead kick); *la lucarne* ("the skylight," shooting the ball into one of the goal's upper corners); and *le râteau* ("the rake," placing one's foot on the ball and dragging it out of an opponent's reach).

From the letter's peroration, the selection translated below, we learn that the intermediaries helping to provide the narrator's self-revelations are footballers and sportsmen of superhuman skill—principally Zinédine Zidane, the tonsured midfielder of Algerian Berber descent who helped lead France to a World Cup championship in 1998 and to the final in 2006. Earlier sporting icons such as Michel Platini, another French midfielder, and Philippe Pottier, a Swiss player that Dubath remembers from his childhood, are also mentioned. In the scattering of Zidane's passes from midfield to teammates Raúl González and Luis Figo of Real Madrid and David Trézéguet and Thierry Henry of France, the writer pieces together a belief system, a sense of his life. The ball as an object of veneration gives meaning to one man's existence and facilitates communion with his fellow humans, both past and future.

Football offers to its followers the pleasure of a series of brief lives in the guise of matches. Whether you win or lose, you move on, charging into the next match with the same uncertainty, the same risks, but also with the feeling that you're living life just like anyone else, bound by the same rights and duties. Another of football's gifts: you follow it for a long time and notice, in your own game, in your own ideas, in your way of seeing things, improvements that are all the more appreciable at the matches in question or not appreciable at all—improvements very small in and of themselves. It's the happiness of feeling, at last, beneath your graying locks, your eye sharpen and spot the angle that might allow for a pass or an interesting shot. In football intelligence increases with age and takes care of the crippled, groaning body.

You know how old people, in these times of frantic youth, aren't treated or listened to as they should be anymore. In football it's the opposite. The players of ages past are bowed to, respected. I know an old guy who kept on playing, who would play, he said, as long as his small muscled legs would sustain him. I spy him in our matches and watch the care with which he still and always gives us tight, precise passes that show his esteem for us, as if he were playing with the greatest players in the world. He does that for everyone, for the ones who are younger or older than him, for the few gifted ones, for those who haven't enjoyed any glory except for that of pure pleasure. His passes show us, teach us, love us, and respect us. We watch him, and we discover how one can learn here and everywhere from these future ancestors, from these old friends that the world wants to isolate and forget so that they don't challenge it.

I was speaking to you about gentleness . . . all in good time. I don't think that men are less gentle than women. I simply think that they don't know how to show their altruistic sweetness because their fathers, not having learned it from their fathers, and on and on, didn't teach them anything about the matter. In football one doesn't play at being sentimental. The stakes are too high. What stakes? I don't know. But they're too high. Nonetheless, I'll repeat it: we ask the ball to speak for us. And so it is that our feet dictate a path that looks like a pretty phrase.

Look at Zidane, Nanon, look at Zidane, look at the ball he's making glide toward Raul, toward Figo, toward Trézéguet, toward Henry, toward everyone who is with him, look at that ball that rolls as if it had the pleasure of giving itself to wherever it's going. They're millionaires, but they pass the ball to each other just like the naked children of Africa's bare fields. They all, we all, belong to Zidane, some part of us, because, even if our own ball doesn't always purr happily, it often rolls on charged with good intentions. We love to receive it like that, we do, all ready for us, all adapted to our speed, to our slowness, to our thoughts.

We're not loved by everyone, we footballers. We're scolded for the embraces that follow a goal, as if such a collective and ephemeral achievement for which different but complementary souls have blended and come together, as if such an achievement that leaves nothing more than a recollection of the very moment in which it was born, didn't deserve that carnal greeting, puerile and childish, yes, why not. I've been known to plant a spontaneous kiss on a friend's sweaty cheek, grateful for an ideal pass, and have not in any way been disgusted nor otherwise excited by the saltiness left on my lips.

Some tease us gladly with this shocking suggestion: "Let's give everyone his own ball, so they don't have to fight each other for control of just one!" They are mistaken: we don't want the ball just for the sake of it, we want it because of the desire to do something, to the extent that we can, all together. Herein lies the happiness of a one-two pass, herein the ceremonial greeting of the goal kick, herein the solidarity that can breed friendship. Each one his own ball, that's guaranteed boredom.

We're cornered when big competitions come around, like the World Cup or the European Cup. We're described as wallowing TV-watchers in our armchairs, plied with beers and sandwiches by wives who've suddenly become nothing more than good little girls. We men are coarse, macho, vulgar, and lazy. Women are our slaves. Rednecks don't need football to become and remain oxes, or to transform their wives into servants.

Speaking of women, because that's what we're talking about, could one conceive of a realm of expression for them comparable to football, in which they could, with collective enthusiasm, exchange moods instead of words, view matters body-to-body instead of eye-to-eye, pool their strengths? And meet up with that on this Earth? Aren't their lives lacking that rendezvous with the purest game that cultivates bitterness and childishness but also the sincerity and charm of fun for the sake of fun? If one day such a game should become known to the feminine world, I am sure that we footballers would be the first to rise to the occasion to kindly and gracefully serve our wives sustenance during the great televised transmissions of their passion.

I have often thought, Nanon, that football is disparaged and inspires envy as it does because it is universally popular. And that people don't want to see beyond the abundance of its movements, forgetting what it brings to the world and to childhood, yes, childhood, to which it provides another family, a complementary family, a family that is both patient and impatient, fair and unfair, accessible and demanding, sweet and rough, generous and merciless. A family that is like life itself. But a family that lasts, that renews itself, remains present, makes its own rules, will still welcome you tomorrow. As long as the ball is round.

Let's imagine that some intellectuals who deem football to be violent and repulsive walk onto the field. Let's imagine that they see three nude men juggling a small leather ball with their feet, which they pass back and forth in the air without ever letting it fall. The astonished witnesses would without a doubt see in that game the outward expression of a fascinating culture, of an admirable tradition, which they would assume has always allowed for the organization among tribes by juggling matches instead of bloody battles. They would analyze the structures, the reach, the roots and social repercussions of it, only to bring this information to conferences they would give around the whole world, boasting of the example we'd all do best to follow, we civilized people, rather than playing at real wars.

I am fifty years old. I am speaking to you, I am speaking to you. I would have liked to have explained to you the meanings of the names that are chanted in football. *Le petit pont, le grand pont, l'aile de pigeon, la bicyclette, la lucarne, le râteau,* but I have preferred to speak to you about myself. About us. About them. About the footballers. All similar and all different. But a little bit of all of them in each one.

For example, the other day, you remember, I was worried about my right testicle. My right nut. When I was in the shower, back from the operation, my friends pretended they were modest (always John Wayne, messing around, messing around, but your nuts, they're the most sacred thing). Discreet looks at my shaved pubis. How's it going? It's great! That's it. Under the water, it was like normal, we went over the match and analyzed it, but most importantly, we used thousands of ploys, both feint and cunning, to turn the water cold on the one who was in the middle of washing himself with his eyes closed. That made me laugh more than any comic spectacle. I thought about it and I laughed, as if I were six years old. As we were coming out of the dressing room, one of the guys came up to me.

"How is it, your nut?"

"It's okay."

"You see, I've also had something since forever that I don't talk about. My penis makes a right angle. But you can't tell unless I have a hard-on. For a long time I was annoyed. But I don't give a damn now. I've talked about it with the women I'm with, with the one I'm with now. She could give a damn either. She finds it hilarious. See you Thursday, my friend."

One day I'll die. I'll die a little bit the first time I can't play anymore, can't pick up a ball and bounce it. The day on which I won't be able to say anymore, "Maybe tomorrow I'll go play football."

Football has slowly revealed to me who I am: a child who loves to play and an adult who loves to feel that child within himself.

One day I will die, but I'll come back.

I'll be a great player, you'll be my wife, and our children will be our children.

I'll be a great player, and I'll sign autographs for hours for the kids waiting for me outside the stadium.

I'll sign, I'll talk to them. I'll tell them that in the old days there was a player named Zidane, another named Pottier, a Pelé, a Platini, and that they were my friends even though they didn't know me.

I'll tell them that in those days the ball, and the men surrounding it, already existed. I'll tell them that if on some days the ball seems heavy to them, and won't let itself be led, they should keep playing, and they'll notice a new lightness. Something between it and themselves.

I'll write a book about my life. No, I'll write a book about their lives as children who play, who hide their secrets or reveal their happiness in their dribbles and their shots, in their passes and their hugs.

I'll tell you how one day they'll find themselves grown up and feel comforted, because they are never alone in the world.

But that's enough for today, Nanon. Thanks for having read this. I have to go out now. It's not yet nighttime.

In the garden, a child is sitting on the lilacs.

He has slipped his hands into his gardener's gloves.

There's a ball on his lap.

He's waiting for me to play.

52. The Sunday I Became World Champion

Friedrich Christian Delius
Translated from the German by Scott Williams

The following narrative is told from the perspective of a pastor's son in rural Germany on July 4, 1954—the afternoon of the World Cup final between Hungary and underdog West Germany. The boy describes a typical Sunday consisting of rising, church service, a family meal, but then turns to the irruption of the radio broadcast from Bern, Switzerland. "The Sunday I became world champion began like every Sunday," the 1994 novella, published as *Der Sonntag, an dem ich Weltmeister wurde*, begins, but by the end a person, village, and country have been transformed. In *Tor! The Story of German Football* (2002), Ulrich Hesse-Lichtenberger explains how the voice of broadcaster Herbert Zimmermann transfixed the country during the final. Hesse-Lichtenberger insists that "every true football fan beyond school age can still recite the words as if they were a poem," referring to Zimmermann's call of Helmut Rahn's match-winner—*Rahn schiesst . . . Tor! Tor! Tor! Tor!* (Rahn shoots . . . goal!)—that gave West Germany a 3–2 come-from-behind victory. Hesse-Lichtenberger notes that the broadcast became a recording that "sold in astounding quantities."

European Member of Parliament Daniel Cohn-Bendit calls the victory a turning point in postwar West Germany. "After 1945, the German identity was broken and there were two things that rebuilt it," Cohn-Bendit told the *New York Times*. "One was economic growth and the other was the 1954 football championship." West Germany's triumph was memorialized in the popular 2003 film *Das Wunder von Bern* (The Miracle of Bern). The memory helped cultivate a growing patriotism, which found fuller expression in the unified nation's hosting of the 2006 World Cup finals.

I had never heard a soccer game announced on the radio before. Words kept coming up that had nothing to do with soccer . . . *miracle!* . . . *thank God!* . . . *This is what we all hoped and prayed for!* . . . and I was amazed that the sportscaster could say the word *believe* with more intensity than a preacher or religion class teacher. Almost a goal for Hungary again, almost one for Germany, and Toni Turek again stops an *unbelievable* shot at the goal, again a threat, the ball, in the goal, no, no it's not . . . *Turek, you're a devil of a fellow, you're a Soccer God!*

I was shocked by these words, while at the same time I was overjoyed that Turek had stopped the shot, but the shock ran deeper. As the echoes of jubilation faded away I began to suspect in the most timid of ways just what kind of shouts those were: A new form of worship, a blasphemous, scandalous ritual, a pagan communion in which one person was addressed as devil and God simultaneously. Even if it was not meant literally, just jubilant phrases, I turned the volume down a little because I would have been embarrassed if someone had caught me listening to words like *Soccer God.* I resisted this blasphemy and mustered up all the arguments against it that I had been taught: *Thou shalt have no other gods before me. Thou shalt not take the name of the Lord thy God in vain.* And yet still entranced by the echo of the three syllables, *Soccer God.* I was pleased that this god was very human, that gods stood there in the goalie box or shot goals, instead of hanging bloodily on the cross. I was pleased that they struggled in the pouring rain and fought like *Liebrich, Liebrich, and it's Liebrich again,* and I slowly began to realize why my parents did not care for my timid enthusiasm for this sport, that here they feared the possible competition of other gods who were more alive.

The excitement of the game eased my intractable feelings of guilt about violating the First Commandment by just listening. From minute to minute I liked it better and better, having a secret god, a *Soccer God* alongside the Lord God. The Commandments man hung directly behind me on the wall. I looked back at him, at the postcard-sized, gold-framed picture of the dark, bearded Moses with quill in hand jotting down the Ten Commandments. But he was looking to the side, at the Lord, was busy writing with his goose quill and not paying any attention to the blasphemy of the sportscaster and my momentary complicity.

I was alone, but surrounded by pictures and objects that are part of what makes up a pastor's office, a place where sermons are written, devotionals recited, instructions given to engaged couples and godparents, where books were stored in the shadows behind glass, awaiting their resurrection, where the sternness of two crucifixes characterized the walls, and the family coat of arms, the triple rose, was a decoration. We had to come here every day at eleven in the morning for a short prayer; here my father interpreted the miracle of Jesus of the Holy Land for the farmers of Wehrda, Rhina, Schletzenrod, and Wetzlos; here he radically changed the word of God and came up with new ideas, citations, important points; here he did not want to be disturbed and here he played all the well-known church songs on the piano; here is where he administered punishment and doled out presents: If there was anywhere in the world where the Ten Commandments ruled, then in this room. The shouts of the sportscaster: *A miracle! . . . prayed for . . . Soccer God!* rang in my ears and defied everything I saw in this room. But the crucifixes had not dropped from the walls, and glaring out from below the Cross was the halfway understandable Latin: VENI SANCTE SPIRITUS / PASCE PASTOREM / DUC DUCEM / APERI APERTURO / DA DATURO, meant as encouragement for the shepherd of souls, each word written with an exaggerated flair, but the Holy Ghost had not intervened, the thick Holy Scripture lay like a child's black gravestone on green felt upon the desk, and when the sportscaster spoke of our *guardian angel*, the music angels above the piano remained as motionless as the angel Messenger of God on the opposing wall, stiffly raising a hand in blessing before the kneeling Mary. This blasphemy was looking better all the time, and in those minutes I moved away from that triadic occupation force of God, Jesus, and the Holy Ghost, and began to believe in a *Soccer God* and an *Underdog God*, and not just one, for if Turek was a *Soccer God*, then the other ten had to be gods, too.

In Bern the game went undecided . . . *it hit the goal post, the goal post! Turek surely would have missed it* . . . changing with astonishing rapidity from one penalty area to the other as I hung on every name the sportscaster uttered, *Kohlmeyer, Posipal, Otmar Walter,* who were running with the ball, shooting the ball, heading it, intercepting it, stopping it. I breathed easier when the good names were mentioned, *Eckel the greyhound, May with the incomparable warrior's heart, Rahn from Essen, Fritz is everywhere,* while I flinched at the mention of the Hungarian names, expecting the worst from the likes of *Puschkasch, Hidegkuti, Lorant, Butschanski, Zakarias,* each of these hissing, tricky names stabbed into me . . . *here come the Hungarians again . . . the Hungarians are pressing towards the goal . . . the Hungarians in full force.*

I leaned back in my chair, turned towards the desk with the telephone, ink well, pen holder, pencils, red markers, and letters . . . *a frantic pace* . . . unconsciously picked up the letter opener, held the ivory handle, looked for my opponent, whirled around to every side, saw crucifixes and angels and Jesus and Moses and the large photograph of the portal of the cathedral in Chartres . . . *the Germans with another miraculous passing combination* . . . and laid the letter opener back down. I was so excited that I wanted to pace through the room, past the bookcase, to the sofa in the corner, or around that fortress of a desk, but I stayed where I was, right there in the seat of patriarchal power from which my father ruled the parishes of four villages. I could not tear myself away from the radio, the source of my Good News. The voice had drawn me back close to the loud speaker. Beneath the radio were the *Stuttgart Biblical Reference Book,* the *Evangelical Church Lexicon,* sermon books, commentaries, files, tools of my father's trade. My father, who was asleep, or maybe was not sleeping anymore—I had lost track of the time, only the minutes left on the game clock mattered . . . *six minutes to go, two to two, that's more than our wildest expectations.*

Above the radio the triumphal arch, a copperplate print from Rome with a scene from the edge of the Forum . . . *a day like no other in our soccer history . . . and Germany has the ball again* . . . I did not want to think about Rome now, but in the growing excitement I had to fix my gaze on something. Rome was much farther away than Bern. The picture did not move. *Veduta dell'Arco di Settimio* was written beneath it, in the foreground a partially sunken triumphal arch and endless stairs in the background, a few tiny people, a donkey, no color, gloomy and empty despite delicate lines dominated by tall buildings with dark walls, dark doorways, a world of stone . . .

53. Art Works Football Club

Lawrence Cann

Affiliated with the city's Urban Ministry Center, Street Soccer 945 of Charlotte, North Carolina, originally came together as the Art Works Football Club (AWFC) under the oversight of former Davidson College player Lawrence Cann, who also directs the ministry center's arts program, Art Works 945. Soccer proves ideal, Cann says, for teaching responsibility, teamwork, and healthy lifestyles to homeless and formerly homeless women and men, a realization that first took hold in 2001 among organizers of the International Network of Street Papers. The Homeless World Cup has been held each year since 2003 and by 2006 had grown to include forty-eight countries for the event in Cape Town, South Africa. Ataka Jansen, captain of Namibia, told the Inter Press Service of Johannesburg that football rescued him from a life of crime and alcohol abuse in Swakopmund: "I really wanted to uplift my life. I didn't want to be the same Ataka anymore."

The Charlotte team started from scratch in September 2004 and went until July 2006—forty-five games—without a match victory. Despite only one win (by forfeit) to its credit, the team was selected as the American representative to the 2005 Homeless World Cup in Edinburgh. The following year the Urban Ministry Center organized the first Homeless USA Cup to select a U.S. team for Cape Town.

Through Cann's diaries leading up to and including the team's trip to Edinburgh, one can glean the struggles behind team formation as well as the potential for soccer, and sport, in facilitating personal transformation.

March 10, 2005

Dear Fans of Art Works FC,

The dynamics are getting interesting. The whole team piled into the van together after the game (that's ten people plus the dog

Takota); Casey Williams sat in the front. Casey is young, tall, and athletic. His parents, not his biological parents, never let him play sports. He's soft-spoken, intelligent, a charmer. I watched him get a hot cup of soup tossed in his face when he was mistaken for someone else. He reacted calmly, said nothing, walked away. Casey's been on the street, on his own for almost two years, working here or there, moving from place to place. Our job counselor got him an interview in the fall for a janitorial job. Casey never went to the interview. Casey found his own job two weeks ago at Burger King. He'll hear about another at Bojangles this week.

Casey said to me as we rode home, "You know we started this soccer thing, and it was for fun, and it was good to actually play a sport with a real coach, and you know, be a part of team, but you heard the other team tonight right?"

I hadn't, I said.

"Yeah you did," retorted Casey.

"No," I insisted.

"Yeah, talking all that trash, saying how fat Andrea and Connie were, and how we were out of shape and no good. They can say what they want, and I know we're getting better, but it really bothered me, I mean I want to show them how good we can be. I think I can quit smoking and get in better shape."

Casey recently moved out of the shelter and into the house of his girlfriend; it's precarious, but at least it's a place for now. "At the house they have this new puppy, and I can run with it in the mornings, you know." When I dropped Casey off, he asked for one of the balls from our bag and I gave it to him, because we have several extra right now.

Casey's attitude is indicative of the team in general. We have begun setting our three-, six-, and twelve-month personal goals. Getting a job, getting a better job, "turning my own key" are on the list, but specific things have made it, too. One person wants to lose twenty-five pounds in three months, fifty by August. Several want to quit smoking, and one wants to complete his forty-two-day sobriety program. "Being able to see my kids more regularly," "scoring five goals in the World Cup," "getting twenty-five juggles," "tracking down my biological family," and "getting into the child-care profession" are other goals. Another wants to be a street-paper vendor. The list goes on, gets personal, but is overwhelmingly positive.

The game itself was a 12–2 loss, but it was a step forward. The team played completely by themselves with no coaches in the game. We were missing Ray Isaac and Abdul Wright, who have been regulars since last season—one is visiting his brother, and the other changed medication and fainted during lunch at the soup kitchen. Still, we had ten participants who showed great improvement. The real standouts were our two ponytailed men: Oscar Duran, who did a cartwheel and handspring flip after he scored our team's first goal, and Michael Simpson, who recently joined the team. Michael played the whole game. In the last game he was so timid he hardly knew what to do. Yesterday he opened up and even smiled.

April 29, 2005

Dear Fans of Art Works FC,

Our soccer program serves a lot of our clients directly with the activity, diversion, and motivation they need to break free from their present situation. Oscar Duran is not one of those players. Oscar, twenty-two years old, is from Chiapas, Mexico. The sides of his head are shaved and he has a long ponytail running down his back. Every time our team scores a goal, Oscar does a handspring and a flip. He came to the United States to escape poverty, he says. He went through a period of anger and frustration with the world, but he left that behind when his mother became ill. Very much in Mexican character, he says, "My love for my mother is greater than any love I have in the world, and I changed because of that." Oscar worked and paid for his mother and brothers to come to the United States. He wants to make an honest living, not selling drugs, but that has been hard.

The family lives now in Greenville with Oscar's American wife. Oscar came to Charlotte three months ago to look for work, as he could find no honest work in Greenville. He moved into the shelter here, where he pays a small fee, because with what he had left after working day labor and sending money home, he had no other options. Last week, Oscar began roofing, his specialty, and the boss likes his work. He's putting Oscar in an apartment on Monday. Oscar says he won't be able to come to practice anymore on account of work, but that he wants to play with us whenever he can. He said, "How come you don't play on Sundays?"

Oscar has papers and is eligible for Scotland, but he says, "No, send the other people, I need to stay here and make more money." Oscar never needed the Art Works FC, but we have needed him. Young and engaging, an aggressive player—not only sharing solidarity with our homeless team, but also possessing an understanding of soccer as someone who grew up with the game—Oscar has helped push his teammates forward. Last night Art Works FC went out fighting in the first round of the playoffs. We suited up fourteen players for the game and everyone made an appearance.

Clearly last night's game was the best game we ever played. Our opponents did not ease up on us in the least, which is not something we have yet been able to say about our other games. Despite our 0–8 loss on the scoreboard, the team left feeling excited. The game was exciting. We had many chances and the game was played on both ends of the field. Our entire bench cheered and encouraged one another. Besides that we played in position, pursued our strategy, and connected passes consistently throughout the game. Defensively we were solid, but our lack of offense was notable.

Leo Johnson played an outstanding game. Leo recollected after the game, "You all remember the first practices out there in Freedom Park, and Lawrence was trying to make us learn how to control the ball and we couldn't do it at all? I've got to say that I really have improved. I've come a long way, for real."

May 21, 2005

Dear Fans of Art Works FC,

Art Works FC lost its second game of the outdoor season last week by the score of 7–2. Quite a good result when you consider some of the following details. Goal-scorer number one was Andre. He scored a good hustle goal following up a misdirected shot by Leo Johnson. Andre is in his early twenties and not an official team member. He has come to a few practices and expressed much enthusiasm about the team. He was unusually recalcitrant on Monday night, but we convinced him to come anyway. In the van ride to the game he revealed that he had just learned that his younger cousin had been shot to death.

The rest of the team was in high spirits, and two women on the team were vocal in telling Andre not to bring everyone's spirit down before the game, that this soccer team was positive, and that they didn't need any negative energy. Andre, already emotional, felt wronged. In short, the situation was volatile. After getting out of the van Andre and others kept at one another until we were able to get Andre back in the van and drive around the block a few times in order to have a heart-to-heart. Andre and I talked about composure, having your own goals, and allowing others to say and act as they please as long as you stay focused on your goals. . . . Fortunately, team leader Stephanie Johnson apologized to Andre when we got back from our little drive. Still, why had the girls acted so negatively to Andre's unfortunate condition? Well, it might have to do with Marguerite's new job. She works nights at the University of North Carolina–Charlotte in the laundry; but, having nowhere to stay during the day, she gets little sleep, less than three hours, making her understandably cranky. Stephanie, on the other hand, is stable right now, but she has clearly become a team leader, starting nine games in a row and second only to Tony Kelly in practice attendance. Leadership responsibilities are not always the easiest thing to handle when you are just getting your own life in order. I was proud that Stephanie reconsidered her position and put team unity ahead of ego after the initial altercation.

Consider also goal-scorer number two, Tony Kelly. Our single most consistent player on the team, Tony is a young man, twenty-five, completely on his own. He never knew his dad, and his mother died shortly before he graduated from high school in Dallas, Texas. He then moved to Charlotte to live with his sister, who herself was struggling to make ends meet. Then Tony earned his nickname, "Statyk," after being struck by lightning. As a result, Tony has a variety of health issues, some real, some psychosomatic, others a complete farce. Tony has many admirable characteristics. He is helpful at the soup kitchen, he stands up for and supports his friends, and he held down a great job at Jillian's last fall before going to Iowa to look after his dying aunt. Or perhaps he followed a girl there? On the other hand, Tony is woefully immature and pulls any number of stunts from hilarious impersonations, silent treatments, loud cursing, denying his own racial heritage, and so on to get attention. Last week he simulated a diabetic seizure for which we suspended him from practice and limited his playing time on Monday, making him fully aware that any other such activity would mean he could not compete again with us. Tony scored on an outlet pass from our goalie, Clayton. He outran a defender and slipped a one-on-one past the goalie with his weaker right foot. Seeing the joy on Tony's face, like seeing the relief on Andre's, launched the whole Art Works team and fans into celebration. Teammates' and coaches' frustrations were forgotten in a moment of camaraderie.

Another reason a 7–2 loss was a good result was because two of our strongest, more consistent players, Abdul Wright and Michael Schell, who played in six and seven games respectively of our last seven-game season, checked themselves into drug treatment last week after relapsing. Each is now twelve days into a twenty-eight-day program at the McCloud Center on Remount. Each had spoken frankly about their drug addictions with the

coaching staff, but had not exhibited any symptoms of relapsing. Completely of their own volition they matriculated in these
programs. We were proud not to have them last week.

May 30, 2005

Dear Fans of Art Works FC,

If you missed the first five minutes of last week's game you
missed the greatest five minutes in AWFC history. The game
started with an AWFC kickoff from rising star Leo Johnson. Leo
struck a cheeky back-heel to Stephanie in the midfield. This
casual, relaxed moment shows that the team has advanced light
years over the past months. It was only nine games ago in the
first game of our indoor season that Teresa Ledford stood in silence at midfield, completely intimidated and baffled as to how
to start the game. She put her foot on top of the ball and tried to
roll it to her teammate. She missed the ball and nearly fell over
backward. Then Stephanie tried to pass the ball for a kickoff, but
the pass didn't make it to her teammate Abdul. Both teams kind
of looked at the ball rolling to a stop between Stephanie and Abdul and wondered what to do until the referee yelled, "Play! Go
ahead, ball's live!"

If the cheeky back-heel was a fun start, a quick outlet from
goalie Oscar Duran moments later, leading to a breakaway goal
by Tony Kelly, was incredible. Before we could finish cheering,
Oscar again made a quick toss to Tony, who duplicated his first
goal only two minutes later. We were winning two–nothing!
What was amazing was to see how our team focused even
harder after grabbing the lead. Ray Isaac and Randy Saxon cut
down angles and guarded their men with more attention than
ever, and Margaret Lindsay, who barely knew the rules two
weeks ago, was playing, cheering, and coaching her teammates
all at the same time. At one point AWFC strung together six consecutive passes, a major breakthrough for our team.

By the half we had lost the lead. We added a goal in the

second half against three by our opponent to bring the final tally to a 3–6 loss. Tasting the lead was sweet, however. The Urban Ministry Center director, Dale Mullennix, made a keen observation after attending that game nine games ago when the AWFC depended on coaches entering the game to help direct things (now we are just players). Dale said that watching the team on the soccer field was a good metaphor for understanding homelessness. Typically you encounter people who are homeless at the soup kitchen, where they are congregated in number, where they know the rules and are comfortable with the game. On the soccer field, however, you could see how they are when they are on their own, interacting with the rest of the world: They are timid, quiet, unsure of how to act, or what exactly the rules are; they are easily discouraged and seem lost. Truly our team has shown their capacity to adapt and learn over the course of the season. We played a genuinely good game last Monday.

We all wore our uniforms, we all hustled, and we showed we weren't afraid to try. When as organizers we use the phrase "social integration through sports," I guess this is what we mean.

Of course, our integration isn't limited to soccer. This week we want to recognize Teresa Ledford, who shortly after joining our team moved off the street and into the women's shelter. Now she has moved out of the shelter and into the home of a friend, where she helps out with rent. She helps out with rent because she is now working six days a week from 1–9 p.m. with the Police Benevolence Association. Getting a job and getting out of the shelter were both three-month goals of Teresa's. She also set as a goal to move from ten cigarettes a day to two. Currently she says she is smoking around five, but some days she doesn't smoke at all because they don't like it at work and she doesn't really have the money for it anyway.

Teresa has not accomplished her goals of being able to run the whole game without getting tired or improving her left foot, but we forgive her. She plans to come to soccer games and practices on her days off.

June 25, 2005

Dear Fans of Art Works FC,

Friday night I walked toward the intersection of Trade and Tryon
up the hill from College Street (those of you who don't know
Charlotte, this is the very center of the city surrounded by sky-
scrapers) to meet friends and head down to the McColl Center
for Visual Arts where there was an opening. Coming down toward me were two AWFC players, Myrah and Andrey, each with
small backpacks on and their heads down. They weren't sad or
downtrodden, despite our 11–5 loss last week and despite the
frustration of living in a tent in the woods. Incidentally, Myrah
almost couldn't make our Washington, DC, trip because of a se-
vere spider bite she suffered while camping out. Actually, their
heads were down because they were doing what anyone else
would be doing on a Friday night a month before they were leaving to represent the United States in a world soccer championship. They were passing the soccer ball.

"What's up coach?" They looked up and greeted me. I asked
them to join me for the art exhibit, and we walked through
uptown to meet my friends. No sooner had we met them than
Stephanie Johnson rolled in on her bike. The bike she was riding was given to her by her teammate Ray Isaac. Stephanie
needed the bike because presently she doesn't stay on the bus
line, and it's too long of a walk to get to work and Ray figured he
could help out. Stephanie mentioned that "Prince" (who scored
four of our five goals on Monday) was only a couple more blocks
away. I started to think we were going to have an impromptu
scrimmage. As it ended up, Myrah, Andrey, and I walked about
ten blocks down to the art exhibit, passing the ball or playing
keep-away the entire time.

The exhibit was nice. Andrey recalled living with his mom in
New York and how she would take him to "art places and things
like that" before she left him to be raised by his uncle when she
moved back down South. Andrey was about nine years old. He

mentioned he had spoken with his mom last week for the first time in several years and that she was really happy he had gotten back into sports.

This week, we also want to say a goodbye to Oscar Duran. Oscar is sad to be leaving the team after playing in ten consecutive matches and making the majority of our practices over the last three months. He's been a real leader, and his upbeat attitude has made a positive impact on his peers. Still, we're happy to see him move on, and he's more thrilled than anyone to move out of Charlotte to the Belmont area, where he is living with a crew of construction workers. They have jobs out there this month, and next month he'll travel with them to Georgia. In a month he says he'll have a car. Before he goes to Georgia or after, he'll drive back for our games when he can, he promises.

At 1 a.m., after our game and before our overnight trip to Washington, we went by the house off North Tryon where Oscar had been staying since he was discharged from the shelter for not signing back in one night. Oscar wanted to get his things, because after DC he wasn't going back to that house. The house was locked and no one came to the door. Oscar said the house was horrible. If rent was late, or even if it wasn't, the owner would knock at the door late at night looking for favors. At least it was indoors, and some nights were quiet. After DC, we went by the house again. Oscar went to the door. I was surprised to see a shirtless man in dreadlocks come out screaming at Oscar in the most bullying manner. "The old man doesn't want to give me my clothes until I pay him more money. Forget it! I am out of this hell." We drove off. Oscar laughed, leaned his head back and against the headrest, and looked out the window.

July 8, 2005

Dear Fans of Art Works FC,

Being the coach of a homeless soccer team is like driving around with a dead man in your car. No, actually being the coach of a homeless soccer team is driving around with a dead

man in your car, or at least the remains of dead man, which is
to say the remains of some remains. Whatever the phrasing, I
ended up with a heavy box containing a tin of ashes in the back-
seat of my car for about a week because one of our players had
respected his dying mother's wishes to take care of her husband,
his stepfather, in her absence. That vow left our player with the
ashes in a small tin (cheaper than a coffin), no family to contact,
and a lot of uncertainty as to how to respectfully scatter, bury,
say goodbye to the last strong connection he had to his mother,
whom he loved dearly for protecting him against an abusive father. Leaving the ashes in my car was a way for him to postpone
that last farewell to his mom.

"So what's in that box anyway?" I asked over the phone.

"That's G—" was the response.

"Excuse me?"

And so the tragi-comic dialogue continued. "Thanks, coach,"
the dialogue ended, and I passed a week with a faithful companion in my car until emotions were collected and G— was properly laid to rest.

I begin this week's note this way to emphasize the theme of
family that has come to the forefront for our homeless soccer
team. Ray Isaac called me Monday morning to suggest that we
get together as team for the Fourth of July, because, in Ray's
words, "Our team is a family, and that's what families do, get
together on the holidays and kinda come together-like." Ray was
with Andrey and Myrah, and he said he could get in touch with
Abdul. So I swung through uptown and collected whom I could
find while my brother, Rob, who is interning with Art Works FC
this summer, picked up Ray and his crowd. We met at Carla's
house for bit of street soccer and a cookout.

Carla, in case you wondered, is doing an internship with me
for her major at Belmont Abbey College. She came to the program through one of our players, Randy, who used to be her
boss a few years ago at the Home Economist before he ended
up on the street. Carla herself is a remarkable story. Almost ten

years ago she was a teen on the street eating at the Urban Ministry Center, then in its second year of existence. While raising her children Carla finished her GED and earned herself a full ride at Belmont Abbey. Recently she has given Randy a place to stay as he completes his process of getting back on his feet. Carla has been a tremendous aid with all kinds of details for the program, and she and her roommate were great hosts last Monday. Carla also purchased her own plane ticket to accompany the team in Scotland this summer.

So at our family get-together we watched video footage of the previous Homeless World Cup, listened to Crystal, Carla's roommate, play the guitar, ate hamburgers and hot dogs, and played soccer with the neighborhood kids. It was small group: me, Rob, Carla and her household, Ray's crowd, and Prince from Ghana, but the rest of the team was glad to hear we had gotten together. Myrah was the big news at the cookout. She had been sick, unable to keep anything down, and had been like that the past three days. Given her symptoms—despite her protests that it couldn't be—when she said she was nearly a month late, we all concluded that a new family member was on the way. In the end, it was a stomach virus, but the support from team members for what would have been an unfortunate situation was impressive.

When Thursday's practice rolled around, Rob had already passed a day feeling ill, Ray was unable to come to practice because he was throwing up, Abdul sat out with an upset stomach, and Tony nearly missed our team photo because he was in the bathroom vomiting. All this queasiness was a negative consequence of the otherwise positive fact that our team has become very close. Of current practicing members of the team, Clayton, Stephanie, Ray, and Fred have found their way off the street. That leaves another large group still staying with friends or sleeping outdoors. The makeshift solution has been for them to share a camp in the woods or to stay over at Ray's place.

Besides a stomach virus, the other thing that has come out from among the team is the idea of having a house together, a transitional soccer home. It seems our team independently has conceived of a "housing-first" model of recuperation for themselves, which of course mimics the current in-vogue idea in Washington for treating the growing homeless epidemic. So we hereby put that idea out in the open for starters, and perhaps someday something will come of it. For now we are focused on the World Cup.

August 1, 2005

Dear Fans of Art Works FC,

It was a dream. It was a dream a year ago when we started things, to go to the World Cup. So we dreamed. And our team was the dream team, reaching down to trap the ball with our hands in a moment of forgetfulness, booting in a goal from thirty yards out in steel-toed work boots, answering a pre-paid cell phone while playing goalie in sunglasses, wearing soccer shorts on top of blue jeans. So many months later the dream got stranger. We weren't in Charlotte anymore. There was a six-foot-five Slovak with a mohawk and no teeth chasing us around and chanting "USA, USA." It was me, my coworkers, and nine of our homeless soccer players wandering down a maze of cobblestone streets, dressed in sharp soccer uniforms looking professional with shin guards and socks pulled up. There was an enormous castle on a rock where the seat of destiny was housed, statues of William Wallace and Robert the Bruce. Down below were myriad spires, gray stones, and beyond that undulating mounds of green that carried on into the clouds on the horizon.

We kept having to ask people to repeat themselves because everyone spoke a wee bit faster than we were used to. We ended up in a narrow valley full of flowers among people lounging on blankets having picnics. The castle leaned over the cliff above us as we marched to the end of the valley where there was a stadium. Flashes of warmth and coolness fell upon us several times within a minute as a fast sky full of clouds blew magically overhead. In the stadium everyone sang national songs. We danced together with motley Norwegian fisherman, shale-blue-eyed Irishmen, a team of bald Poles, jovial Argentines, introspective Chinamen, fit and dignified South Africans. We ran in circles waving the American flag. It was a strange and beautiful dream, and when it was over, you really had to question which reality was more of a dream. Our players fit in so well, adapted so naturally, enjoyed themselves so thoroughly. They seemed more at home in Bonnie Scotland than I ever remember seeing them anywhere else. The only choice is to believe in both realities and let them converge into one as we go forward.

To begin to report on our participation in the Homeless World Cup, let me tell you that the quality of soccer was fantastic. On a small pitch, given the size of our players and the size of the hearts of our players, we thought we could close the game down and compete well in the tournament. Compete we did, but not competitively. Our players, who had come a long way in several intense months, could not match young, fit players with soccer instinct flowing through their veins. In our first game, we drew the home nation Scotland and were efficiently dispatched with a bevy of goals. We had been training and working hard for months for that moment, and to be beaten so handily was tough to handle. We reacted poorly, argued, blamed one another. The performance elicited a dramatic five-minute-long vituperative lambasting by the coach, which our players have never heard from me before. "I don't care if you lose one hundred to nothing, you keep your head up and your chest out, you congratulate the other team, and you earn their respect; you represent your country!"

In our second match, we faced Slovakia and were up by two goals in the second half. Perhaps a coaching error led to our defeat as we broke up a good rhythm with substitutions. In the waning minutes, we gave up the ball in the back four times in succession and lost our lead. Led by Tony Kelley and Stephanie Johnson, the USA team brought tears to my eyes, celebrating as if they had won, hugging the Slovaks, and cheering with them after the game. We gave them small American flags, which they all had us autograph. The Australians had been watching and joined in on the fun. Our three teams formed an alliance and cheered each other in all our games.

When the tournament finished, Australia beat out China and the Czech Republic for best new team. Our Slovak friend Miro won the best-goalkeeper award, and we, the USA, won the Fair Play Award for best embodying the spirit of the Homeless World Cup. Besides the World Cup, which was won by Italy, these were the only awards given out.

Gavin White is the head immigration officer in Glasgow. As some of you may know, five African nations were denied visas to enter the UK for the Homeless World Cup. Despite letters from the mayors of Graz, Göteburg, and Edinburgh, the United Nations, and the European Union, our team was also denied a special category of visa before entering the country. Still, as Americans we had the chance to enter as tourists. Gavin appreciated that we went out of our way to be honest and forthright, applying for visas that we did not need, entering the country in our soccer uniforms, and being honest with him about our criminal records. To our relief he reversed the decision made by the UK office in New York and gave us entry into the country. Gavin wrote us the following note by e-mail after seeing us off to the States in Glasgow:

> I'm glad you got the chance to participate in the tournament and I hope that the experience will help the team in the future as they continue to face the challenges before them. You are a remarkable group and you demonstrated all that is best in the human spirit and I think the crowds clearly saw that in Edinburgh. I'm glad I met you.

Given the chance, this is what our team has proven to the world. Michael Schell, one of our players, wrote the following in an Art Works writing class the day he got back:

The Homeless World Cup 2005 was held in Edinburgh, Scotland, where 32 teams from many countries came to share in the chance to play for the Homeless World Cup. What I learned from this experience is it doesn't matter if you win or lose. It's about your spirit as a team. It's a chance to grow with other team members and to have fun playing the game we all came to play. We live to learn and we learned to live with each other. We were selected to receive the fair play award for our generosity to other teams and great sportsmanship to come and compete with the best of them.

The sites were splendid. There was princess gardens, the castle, the mountains, fine dining, and many extras. Also it was luxurious to stay in Edinburgh dorms while in the tournament. The best part of the whole trip was that the USA was the most trusting and most focused to play hard, and all other teams saw our encouragement and wished us their best, and this is what is important. If you do not have good sportsmanship and a good team ethics, then you can't make it in life.

Michael battles to stay on his medications and completed a drug program before our departure and has remained clean. Given all the forces of chaos in his life, his remarkably lucid account of the Homeless World Cup is a great testimony to his will to change and to the positive power of sports.

I wish everyone who has supported us could have marched with us up the Royal Mile and down to the stadium in the parade of nations. We were in between the Ukraine and Wales. I wish you could have sung "My Country 'Tis of Thee" and "Who Let the Dogs Out?" with us and joined in to support Ukraine's songs and the Welsh cheers. Photographers were everywhere and the crowds were excellent. We played our best game of the tournament against Sweden in front of a crowd of two thousand people. We missed two penalty kicks and lost the game 1–0.

After the game Stephanie came off the field and burst into tears. In an interview shortly thereafter she said, "This is a feeling I'll never forget. It's wonderful. I feel important."

We congratulate Stephanie and her teammates because they are important. The average daily experience inculcates all too harshly the opposite message to people who are homeless. Our players have shown that, despite not knowing the rules when they started, despite mental illnesses, criminal records, being victims of abuse, and so on, despite being scared to death to get on an airplane, that they, given the chance, can adjust to anything and succeed—even a steady diet of haggis.

54. Football Is

Crispin Thomas

Performance poet Crispin Thomas leads writing workshops at schools, libraries, and prisons in the United Kingdom. He also edits the Football Poets Web site (www.footballpoets.org), which features more than eight thousand football poems. Noted for his improvisational skills, Thomas has appeared on BBC radio and television programs, including *Match of the Day*.

football down the alley way football in the street
football for the whole wide world not just the elite
football under lamp-light football on the beach
football with a rolled up sock football with a peach
football in the job centre football in the gutter
football in the superstore with organic butter
football belly dancing football shiatsu
football when you're half asleep football on the loo

football with your budgie when the goals are small
football with a walnut or up against the wall
football in the school-yard shorts ripped and grubby
football when the goalies had sweaters and were tubby
football when you're little football when you're big
football down at B & Q football at a gig
football in the rain and snow football in the shower
football with oranges or even elderflower

football for the very young football for the old
football in a wheelchair football up a pole
football with traffic wardens football with police
football in the Shetlands and the Middle East

football out in Africa football down in China
football off the MI5 and down in Carolina
football in some dingy pub football in Tibet
football on the telly football on the net
football on the radio football on the dole
football with a satchel and jacket for a goal
football on your duvet football under cover
football with a veggie burger football with your brother

football up the mountainside football on a log
football played with girls and boys football with your dog
football with a siamese cat lovely silky moves
football with a dj with all those techno grooves
football with a poet i hate it when they rhyme
but don't you just love football every single time

55. *Arsarnerit:* Inuit and the Heavenly Game of Football

Mark Nuttall

The genesis for this original essay lies in a footnote from a collection of academic articles about soccer published as *Entering the Field: New Perspectives on World Football* (1997), edited by sociologists Gary Armstrong and Richard Giulianotti. The editors mention ongoing research by Mark Nuttall—a social anthropologist at the University of Alberta, Canada, with expertise in the cultures and ecology of the Arctic—into the "centrality of football to the everyday cosmology of the Inuit in Greenland." Recalling his travels to Greenland—known as Kalaallit Nunaat in the Inuit language—Nuttall for the first time fleshes out the ethnographic evidence for a unique football culture in a land traditionally considered too frigid to sustain a grass pitch.

The game, as Nuttall describes, has nevertheless taken hold in the belief system of Inuit culture. In the cosmic spectacle of the aurora borealis, the Inuit in Greenland see the souls of the dead playing football with a walrus skull—a long-standing mythology with variants among the Arctic region's indigenous peoples. For the Inuit the northern lights are known, through this spiritual tale, as *arsarnerit* (the football players). The accounts below testify to football as a global game that reaches into the heavens and into myths helping to make sense of the universe—a universe, incidentally, that astronomers in 2003 hypothesized as being bounded, with a shape bearing a rough resemblance to a soccer ball.

According to the Danish Greenlandic explorer and ethnographer Knud Rasmussen, playing ball is "the Eskimos' favourite game." Rasmussen was writing in his 1929 study *Intellectual Culture of the Iglulik Eskimos.* Yet Rasmussen was not the first to observe this passion for a game that for centuries seems to have been played by Inuit on ice, snow, and tundra at the northern edges of the world. Football games were described in West Greenland by Hans Egede, the first missionary to reach Greenland's coasts in 1721, and his wonderful 1741 account of Greenland and the life of Greenlanders contains perhaps the earliest illustrations of Inuit playing both football and handball. In *The Central Eskimo* Franz Boas described ball games (and recorded songs about ball games, including football) played by the Inuit of southern Baffin Island in the eastern Canadian Arctic during the 1880s:

> The ball is most frequently used in summer. It is made of sealskin stuffed with moss and neatly trimmed with skin straps. One man throws the ball among the players, whose object it is to keep it always in motion without allowing it to touch the ground.

Writing in *The Eskimo about Bering Strait* in 1899, Edward Nelson noted that football was an important game for the widespread Inuit communities along the coasts and river deltas of western Alaska, with the ball made of leather and stuffed with deer hair or moss, and being played by young men and children at the end of winter or during spring. Nelson described how two participants act as leaders, each choosing a player alternatively from among those assembled until they are divided equally:

> At a given distance, two conspicuous marks are made on the snow or ground which serve as goals, the players stand each by their goal and the ball is tossed upon the ground midway between them; a rush is then made, each side striving to drive the ball across its adversaries' line.

Nelson also described variations on the theme:

> Another football game is begun by the men standing in two close, parallel lines midway between the goals, their legs and bodies forming two walls. The ball is then thrown between them and driven back and forth by kicks and blows until it passes through one of the lines; as soon as this occurs all rush to drive it to one or the other of the goals.

He also noted that women played their own game of football during fall and winter using a considerably larger ball than used in the men's game. Women's football games usually involved four players, although there were occasions when there were as few as two players.

Writing in 1928, Christian Schultz-Lorentzen said that for Greenlanders the "game of ball has everywhere been a favourite sport," explaining that it had been played in different ways, either as football or handball. Anthropologists have generally recorded that games are important for Inuit for three main reasons, all necessary for physical and cultural survival: first, games were played to help people develop strength, endurance, and resistance to pain; second, games were ways of acquiring knowledge about how to survive in extreme environments and for learning skills for hunting and fishing; third, games celebrated social life and culture. In Greenlandic stories, being able to play football with the entire skin of a large seal, stuffed with grass, was one of the attributes assigned to the ideal legendary hero as well as to great hunters who provided for entire communities. Strength in playing football, it seems, was an indication of skill, dexterity, success as a hunter, and the ability to perform heroic deeds.

Early observers noted how football was a sport, a game, something played for leisure, yet one that was competitive nonetheless. This competitive element of Inuit football was not confined to people playing from the same community or locality. In Greenland, Schultz-Lorentzen recorded that football was the game "for which combatants assembled from far and near" to win prizes. Possibly games between different groups along Greenland's west coast were played during *aasiviit*, traditional summer hunting camps where families from different areas gathered annually to hunt, fish, and trade. *Aasiviit* were vital social and economic gatherings — social ties between families and groups from different areas were strengthened, news was exchanged, disputes were settled, knowledge about hunting was shared, myths, stories, and legends were told, and games were played.

In Canada's Mackenzie Delta region, Knud Rasmussen recorded a tense football game between different Arctic peoples in the early 1920s:

Every summer, the Eskimos used to come up to Fort McPherson and camp on a great plain near the hill where the Indians had their tents. They played football on the plain, but on one occasion, trouble arose owing to the rough and unsportsmanlike behaviour of the Eskimos; the Indians retired from the game and the Eskimos struck camp and went off in anger. Next year they came again in great numbers, ready for battle, but the Indians, not wishing to give any occasion for bloodshed, moved into the bush with their tents and loosed their dogs.

Violence was thus avoided, but Rasmussen's account speaks to the often difficult relations that existed between the Inuit and some First Nations in northern Canada.

During my travels in the North, especially in Greenland, and in my readings of the classic ethnographic literature on the Inuit, another type of football captured my attention. This is a heavenly version of the terrestrial game early observers of Inuit life described. Throughout the circumpolar North, brilliant displays of the aurora borealis (or northern lights) can often be seen on clear nights during the long, dark polar winter. Science explains auroral displays as the result of electrical discharges in the earth's ionosphere. Solar particles, mainly protons and electrons, bombard and interact with the gases of the earth's upper atmosphere. The aurora borealis has long fascinated travelers, who have been at pains to describe their feelings of awe, dread, and mystery when confronted with it for the first time. Its luminous glow of greenish white, red, or crimson light is more often described as a manifestation of the numinous in the writings of whalers, explorers, traders, and other visitors.

The aurora borealis occupies a prominent place in the mythology, cosmology, and spiritual beliefs of the Arctic's indigenous peoples. For the Chuvan of Siberia, the northern lights bring relief to a woman in childbirth, while the Saami of Finland have a story that relates how the aurora borealis offers protection from sorcery and evil. A traditional Labrador Inuit story tells how at the end of the world there is a great abyss, with a dangerous pathway leading through a hole in the sky and on to the land of the dead. The souls of those who have crossed this path light torches to guide the new souls. In his 1916 classic, *The Labrador Eskimo*, Ernest Hawkes explained that only the spirits of those people who had died a voluntary or violent death had crossed this pathway. The notion of a voluntary death refers to an old practice of the old or infirm walking away from a village or camp in winter, or at times of starvation, so as to ease pressure on the group.

When I first went to live among Inuit seal-hunting families in northern Greenland in the late 1980s, I heard people tell many stories of how, when people die, their souls ascend to the heavens to form part of the northern lights. On journeys I make in Greenland today I continue to hear these stories. In Greenlandic belief, the person (*inuk*) is seen as consisting of body (*timi*), soul (*tarneq*), and name or name-soul (*ateq*). The name is both a social and spiritual component of a person. Upon death a person's name-soul leaves the body and is said to be "homeless" until it is recalled to reside in the body of a newborn child. A person who is named after a dead person is called an *atsiaq* (pl. *atsiat*). As this includes all people, then Greenlandic Inuit communities are made up entirely of *atsiat*. A dead person can have more than one *atsiaq*, but the first child to be born after the death of another person is called that person's *ateqqaataa*. It is during the period following the end of life, and before the naming of a newborn child, that a person's soul becomes an *arsartoq*, a football player.

In traditional Greenlandic belief, the land of the dead is a land of plenty. The souls of the dead feast and play football with a walrus skull as the ball (*arsaq*), and it is this football game that appears as the aurora. Indeed the Inuit call these shimmering curtains of light *arsarnerit*, "the football players." In this way not only are the northern lights comprised entirely of human souls waiting to be reborn on earth; for the Inuit the word *arsarnerit* is devoid of any reference to light or solar activity. By playing ball in the night sky, the souls of the deceased remind the living that they are never too far away and are waiting to return home. The dead do not wish to remain apart from the living, so the *arsarnerit* communicate with them by whistling. A living person who hears this must reply with a soft whistle of their own, and the ball players will come closer to earth. The *arsarnerit* are to be marveled at, yet one must be fearful of the *arsarnerit* and not be too tempted to see how close they can come to earth. Without warning, children are told, the *arsarnerit* can swoop down and grab a living person. Even worse, they can lop off a person's head. If the *arsarnerit* appear too close to the earth for comfort, they can be sent away by clapping one's hands together loudly and firmly.

Similar Inuit traditions and accounts of the aurora borealis as football players are found across the Arctic from the Bering Strait coasts of Siberia and Alaska, to northern Canada, and all the way to East Greenland. In Alaska and the Canadian Arctic, they are known as *arsarniit* or *aqsarniit*, while in East Greenland they are *arsarneq* or *alusukat*. In West Greenland, Moravian missionary David Crantz in 1767 described the aurora borealis as "the souls of the dead striking at a dance or a foot-ball." According to Hinrich Rink, in his 1875 *Tales and Traditions of the Eskimo*, after death the souls of West Greenlanders either traveled to an underworld of abundance or to an upper world where there was only starvation and cold:

> Those who go to the upper world will suffer from cold and famine, and these are called *arssartut* or ball-players, on account of their playing at ball with a walrus head, which gives rise to the aurora borealis, or Northern Lights.

For the Inuit of western Alaska, Edward Nelson wrote in 1899 that the

> aurora is believed to be a group of boys playing football, sometimes using a walrus skull as the ball. The swaying movement of the lights back and forth represents the struggles of the players. When the light fades away the Eskimo utter a low whistle, which they say will call the boys back.

In *Across Arctic America*, his popular account of his epic three-year-long expedition by dog team, from northern Greenland across northern

Canada to Nome in western Alaska, to study the cultural, material, and intellectual life of Inuit groups in Arctic North America, Knud Rasmussen recorded his encounter with the Inuit of the eastern Canadian Arctic. He described the belief in the land of the dead as

> the land of glad and happy souls. It is a great country, with many caribou, and the people who live there live only for pleasure. They play ball most of the time, playing at football with the skull of a walrus, and laughing and singing as they play. It is this game of the souls playing at ball that we can see as the northern lights.

In *Intellectual Culture of the Iglulik Eskimos*, Rasmussen elaborated on the nature of the game:

> The object is to kick the skull in such a manner that it always falls with the tusks downwards, and thus sticks fast in the ground. It is this ball game of the departed souls that appears as the aurora borealis, and is heard as a whistling, rustling, cracking sound.

For the Inuit of East Greenland at the end of the nineteenth century, Gustav Holm wrote that the aurora borealis represents the souls of deceased children playing football with their own placentas, with games being played between teams of children who have died violently or were stillborn and those who were orphaned. And in an interesting inversion of human-animal relationships, one Alaskan story relates how the *arsarnerit* are actually the souls of walruses playing football with a human skull.

Whatever its variations across the Arctic, this heavenly game of football is spectacular to watch. *Arsarnerit* appear almost nightly during the northern winter, and in northern Greenland I have stood and marveled with people as these astonishing games take place. People are not only spectators of this football game, they are living relatives of the *arsarnerit*. As the *arsarnerit* shimmer, swoop, and leap, people watch and discuss the game. They listen out for the souls of the deceased making a crackling sound as they run, chasing and kicking the football across the frost-hardened snow of the heavens. The souls of the dead players will ultimately be reborn. Names have power, and some of the personal qualities of the deceased are inherited by the receiver of their name. As a*rsarnerit*, the souls of the deceased are "in training" for eventual rebirth. Because of the extreme physical conditions and climate, the Arctic environment is a dangerous and uncertain one. It is this game of football that is an important starting point for the acquisition of the strength and skill needed to survive back on earth. Indeed, when terrestrial football matches are played within and between villages, exceptional and gifted players are said to have honed their skills as *arsarnerit*.

In Greenland the appearance of the *arsarnerit* is said to be an indica-tor of the type of weather to come. The sky, both during day and night, is an important indicator of changes being observed by both scientists and Inuit. An elderly hunter once explained to me that the North is his *ulloriarsiorfik*, his observatory. People throughout Greenland have told me about their concerns with the changing nature of *sila*—the Greenlandic word for weather, as well as a fundamental principle un-derlying the natural world—with the changes they have observed in the characteristics of the sun over the last fifteen years or so, and with the dimming and changes in the appearance of the aurora borealis. "The *arsarnerit* have not disappeared," an elderly woman once told me, "they are simply moving elsewhere." Scientists stress the importance of understanding how climate change in the Arctic is correlated with solar activity in both the lower and upper atmospheres. The appearance of the aurora borealis and the increase in major auroral disturbances (known as magnetic storms) are both linked to this, yet the precise mechanism relating solar activity to weather and climate change re-mains unknown.

The *angakkut*, shamans of old, would have their own accounts for the dimming or absence of the *arsarnerit*. Souls would often go astray, or evil hunters, sorcerers, and malevolent *angakkut* would often travel to the sky and the land of the dead to steal food. The souls of the dead would become famished and starve (*perlerneq*). Unable to play football, the *arsarnerit* would soon appear pale and feeble, mere shadows of themselves, affecting the movement of the sky and the appearance of the aurora borealis. The soul of the *angakkoq*, often assisted by a helping spirit in the form of an animal such as a polar bear, would have to travel to the land of the dead to retrieve the lost souls and restore the food for the *arsarnerit* that were hungry, reviving them, giving them strength. As the *angakkut* often warned the living, the movement away of the *arsarnerit* meant that the football players were taking their game elsewhere as a result of some calamity or dreadful event.

56. On the Origin of Football

Miroslav Holub
Translated from the Czech by Ewald Osers

Czech poet Miroslav Holub (1923–1998), an immunologist with more than 120 scientific monographs to his credit, in his writing drew upon his background in medicine and biological research. Critics remark on an unadorned free verse described as "semantically exact" and well-suited to translation, while friends recall poetry readings staged in a historic Prague operating theater amid surgical instruments from the nineteenth century.

"I prefer to write for people untouched by poetry," Holub says in an essay published in *Vacerní Praha* (The Evening Prague) in 1963. "I would like them to read poems in such a matter-of-fact manner as when they are reading the newspaper or go to football matches. I would like people not to regard poetry as something more difficult, more effeminate, or more praiseworthy." Referents from the natural world appear in the poem below, as Holub suggests that passion for football might be primordial, extending even to the trilobite—the marine invertebrate from some five hundred million years ago.

The poem refers, too, to the way in which the game merits comparison to belief systems. Holub mentions the splitting of the curtain in the Jerusalem Temple as Jesus breathes his last (Matthew 27:51 and parallels). Such is the gravity of football given a daily experience of repression. And Holub's range of association, given a lifetime of sparring with censors and Communist Party functionaries in the former Czechoslovakia, extends clearly to politics. Holub once described himself within the authoritarian system as "a nonperson of the third order." He had to publish anonymously at times, and his books and works were destroyed and cribbed by other poets. From this context comes the power of "an electrified wire / barbedly garrisoning" a possible football ground—the spirit of freedom and the everyday arrayed against a stalwart barrier.

A small pebble embedded in concrete:
a statue to the genius of earthworms,
not budging at all.

A small milestone of history,
such a tiny little
triumphal arch
where nothing has ever happened:
not budging at all.

A small rheumatic post
from which someone has stolen the notice
forbidding the stealing of notices:
not budging at all.

An electrified wire
barbedly garrisoning
the dreams of shin ulcers:
not budging at all.

And so, when one day someone encounters
something that's rolling
he kicks it.

And his heavens reverberate,
the temple curtain is rent,
the unrinsed mouths of thousands open wide
in a stifling explosion of silence

like trilobites
yelling *Goal.*

Source Acknowledgments

The editors and publisher have made every reasonable effort to contact all copyright holders. Any errors that have occurred are inadvertent and anyone who for any reason has not been contacted is invited to write to the publisher so that a full acknowledgment may be made in subsequent editions of this work.

Part 1. Space

"The Orb" by Klaus Rifbjerg. Originally published in Danish as "Kuglen," in *Fodbold: Forfattere om faenomnet fodbold*, ed. Peter Christensen and Frederik Stjernfelt (Copenhagen: Gyldendal, 2002), 309–10. Translation copyright © 2006 Thom Satterlee. Used by permission.

"The Origins" by Eduardo Galeano. Originally published in *El futbol a sol y sombra* (Montevideo, Uruguay: Ediciones Del Chanchito, 1995). Reprinted from *Soccer in Sun and Shadow*, trans. Mark Fried, rev. ed. (London: Verso, 2003), 22–24. Used by permission.

"Hem and Football" by Nalinaksha Bhattacharya. Reprinted from *Hem and Football*, published by Secker & Warburg, by permission of The Random House Group Ltd.

"The Daily Life of Cameroonian Football" by Bea Vidacs. Reprinted from "Visions of a Better Life: Football in the Cameroonian Social Imagination" (PhD diss., City University of New York, 2002), 73–77. Copyright © 2002 Beata Vidacs. Used by permission.

"The Soccer Moms—1996" by David Starkey. Reprinted from *The Malahat Review* 126 (Spring 1999): 69–70. Used by permission.

"Atiguibas" by Julio Ramón Ribeyro. Originally published in Spanish in *Cuentos completos* (Madrid: Alfaguera, 1994). Translation copyright © 2006 John Penuel. Used by permission.

"Why Eleven, of All Numbers? Football between Carnival and Freemasonry" by Erik Eggers. Reprinted from *Anstoß* (Die Zeitschrift des Kunst und

Kulturprogramms der Bundesregierung zur FIFA WM 2006™), no. 2 (May 2005): 76–77. Copyright © 2005 FIFA World Cup Artistic and Cultural Programme™. Used by permission.

"Klapzuba's Eleven" by Eduard Bass. Originally published in 1922 in Czech as *Klapzubova jedenáctka* (Klapzuba's Eleven). Reprinted from *The Chattertooth Eleven: A Tale of a Czech Football Team for Boys Old and Young*, trans. Ruby Hobling (London: "The Czechoslovak," 1943), 5–9.

"Holland, a Country of Clubs" by Simon Kuper. The essay appears here for the first time in this form. Some portions originally appeared in a slightly different form in *The Financial Times* (London) and *The Observer* (London). Copyright © 2004 Simon Kuper. Used by permission.

"Readymade" by Álvaro Enrigue. Originally published as "Objectos encontrados" in *Medio tiempo* (Summer 2006). Published in *Words Without Borders* (www.wordswithoutborders.org), June 2006. By permission of *Words Without Borders*, an online magazine for international literature hosted by Bard College and supported by the National Endowment for the Arts. Translation © 2006 Anna Kushner.

"Soccer Fields, Fort Missoula" by Bridget Carson. Copyright © 2006 Bridget Carson. Used by permission.

"'Get Him a Body Bag!' (A Brief, Enthusiastic Account)" by María Graciela Rodríguez. Copyright © 1996 María Graciela Rodríguez. Translation copyright © 2006 Miranda Stramel. Used by permission.

Part 2. Improvisation

Epigraph from Reed Johnson, "A Smaller World with Cup Blogs," *Los Angeles Times*, June 27, 2006.

"Young Shoots" by Lady Murasaki. Excerpt from *The Tale of Genji*, trans. Arthur Waley, vol. 1 (Boston: Houghton Mifflin, 1929), 640–42. © copyright by permission of The Arthur Waley Estate.

"A Boy Juggling a Soccer Ball" by Christopher Merrill. Reprinted from *Motion: American Sports Poems*, ed. Noah Blaustein (Iowa City: University of Iowa Press, 2001), 175–76. Copyright © 2001 Christopher Merrill. Used by permission.

"Fallen from the Sky" by Javier Marías. Originally published in Spanish as "Caído del cielo" in *El País* (Madrid), May 20, 2002. Translation copyright © 2006 Miranda Stramel. Used by permission.

"Combing over History" by Stanley Matthews. Reprinted from *The Way It Was: My Autobiography* (London: Headline, 2000), 217–21. Copyright © 2000 Stanley Matthews. Used by permission.

"Encomiastic Arts of Our National Gamesmen" by Antonio Skármeta. Reprinted from *I Dreamt the Snow Was Burning*, trans. Malcolm Coad (London: Readers International, 1985), 168–76. Copyright © 1985 Readers International, Inc. Used by permission.

"The Longest Penalty Ever" by Osvaldo Soriano. Originally published in Spanish as "El penal más largo del mundo," in *Memorias del Míster Peregrino Fernández y otros relatos de fútbol*, ed. Paolo Collo (Bogotá, Colombia: Editorial Norma, 1998), 193–200. Copyright © Osvaldo Soriano and Herederos de Osvaldo Soriano. Translation copyright © 2006 Miranda Stramel. Used by permission.

"Fretting while the Scarlet Tide Make History" by Elvis Costello. Reprinted from *The Times* (London), May 30, 2005. Copyright © Elvis Costello. Used by permission.

"Streaker Disrupts Iceland versus Albania" by Einar Már Guðmundsson. Originally published in Icelandic as "Um raunsæi" (About Realism) in *Kannski er pósturinn svangur* (Perhaps the Postman Is Hungry) (Reykjavík: Mál og menning, 2001). Reprinted from *Transcript: The European Internet Review of Books and Writing* 2, http://www.transcript-review.org. Copyright © University of Wales, Aberystwyth. Used by permission.

"Football at Slack" by Ted Hughes. "Football at Slack" from *Collected Poems* by Ted Hughes. Copyright © 2003 by The Estate of Ted Hughes. Reprinted by permission of Farrar, Straus and Giroux, LLC. "Football at Slack" from *Remains of Elmet* by Ted Hughes. Reprinted by permission of Faber and Faber Ltd.

"Dead Radio" by Charles Simic. Copyright © 2006 Charles Simic. Used by permission.

"Fahrenheit 1976" by Rogelio Ramos Signes. Originally published in Spanish at Ficticia, http://www.ficticia.com. Copyright © 2004 Rogelio Ramos Signes. Translation copyright © 2006 Toshiya Kamei. Used by permission.

Part 3. Challenge

Epigraph from Tim Parks, "Soccer: A Matter of Love and Hate," *The New York Review of Books*, July 18, 2002.

"Dreaming of Sunday Afternoons" by Giovanna Pollarolo. Originally published in Spanish as "El sueño del domingo (por la tarde)," in *Entre mujeres solas* (Lima: Comillo Blanco, 1991). Translation copyright © 2006 Toshiya Kamei. Used by permission.

Part 4. Loss

Epigraph from Alex Bellos, *Futebol: The Brazilian Way of Life* (London: Blooms-bury, 2002), 334.

"On a Painting of Playing Football" by Ch'ao Yueh-chih. Reprinted from *Poems of the Masters: China's Classic Anthology of T'ang and Sung Dynasty Verse*, trans. Red Pine (Port Townsend WA: Copper Canyon Press, 2003), 199. Used by permission.

"Beauty Is Nothing but the Beginning of a Terror We Can Hardly Bear" by Uroš Zupan. Originally published in Slovenian in *Pedestrian* (Ljubljana, Slovenia: Beletrina, 2003). Translation copyright © 2006 Erica Johnson Debeljak. Used by permission.

"Playing Football in Secret" by Driton Latifi. A slightly different version of this speech was delivered at "Play the Game: World Conference of Sports Media" in Copenhagen, November 12–16, 2000. Copyright © 2000 Driton Latifi. Used by permission.

"Why Does My Wife Love Peter Crouch?" by Thom Satterlee. Copyright © 2006 Thom Satterlee. Used by permission.

"The Dynamo Team: Legend and Fact" by Anatoly Kuznetsov. Reprinted from *Babi Yar* by Anatoli Kuznetsov, trans. Jacob Guralsky, copyright © 1967 by Dial Press, a division of Bantam Doubleday Dell Publishing Group, Inc. Used by permission of Doubleday, a division of Random House, Inc. Also from *Babi Yar* by Kuznetsov Anatoli, published by Jonathan Cape. Reprinted by permission of The Random House Group Ltd.

"Boycotting the World Cup" by Hebe de Bonafini and Matilde Sánchez. Origi-nally published in Spanish in *Historias de vida* (Buenos Aires: Fraterna, 1985), 157–60. Translation copyright © 2007 Sandra Kingery. Used by permission.

"Football in Athens, with Her" by Donna J. Gelagotis Lee. Copyright © 2006 Donna J. Gelagotis Lee. Used by permission.

"Sierra Leone, Social Learning, and Soccer" by Paul Richards. Paul Richards, "Soccer and Violence in War-Torn Africa: Soccer and Social Rehabilitation in Sierra Leone" in Armstrong, Gary and Giulianotti, Richard (eds.) *Entering the Field: New Perspectives on World Football* pp. 150–154 (Oxford: Berg Publishers, Copyright 1997). Reprinted by permission of the publisher. All rights reserved.

"Parity" by William Heyen. Reprinted from *Shoah Train* (Wilkes-Barre PA: Etruscan Press, 2003). Used by permission.

"Penalty Phase" by Gay Talese. From *A Writer's Life* by Gay Talese, copyright © 2006 by Gay Talese. Used by permission of Alfred A. Knopf, a division of Random House, Inc. From *A Writer's Life* by Gay Talese, published by Arrow. Reprinted by permission of The Random House Group Ltd.

"Platko (Santander, May 20, 1928)" by Rafael Alberti. Published in Spanish in *Antología comentada (poesía)*, comp. María Asunción Mateo (Madrid: Ediciones de la Torre, 1990) 45–47. Translation copyright © 2007 Kirk Anderson. Used by permission.

Part 5. Belief

Epigraph from Petula Dvorak, "DC United Clinic Puts Stadium Hopes into Play," *The Washington Post*, November 10, 2005.

"The Lord's Prayer, Recast" by Edilberto Coutinho. Originally published in Portuguese in *Maracanã, adeus: Onze histórias de futebol* (Rio de Janeiro: Civilização Brasileira, 1980). Reprinted from "Opening Act," in *Bye, Bye Soccer*, trans. Wilson Loria, ed. Joe Bratcher III (Austin TX: Host, 1994), 1. Copyright © 1994 Host Publications. Used by permission.

"Communicate, Lads" by Elísabet Jökulsdóttir. Originally published in Icelandic as *Fótboltasögur (tala saman strákar)* (Reykjavík: Mál og menning, 2001). Reprinted from *Football Stories (Communicate Lads)*, trans. Baldur Ingi Guðbjörnsson and Katherine Connor Martin (Reykjavík: KSÍ, 2002), 20–21, 28, 34–35, 46–47, 73, 74. Used by permission.

"Five Poems for the Game of Soccer" by Umberto Saba. Copyright © 1934 Umberto Saba. Used by permission of Giulio Einaudi Editore, Turin, Italy. Translation copyright © 2007 Geoffrey Brock.

"Living to Tell a Tale (Letter to Diego)" by Hernán Casciari. Published originally in Spanish as "Vivir para contarlo (carta a Diego)," on the blog *Más respecto, que soy tu madre*, April 21, 2004, http://mujergorda.bitacoras.com/1/eng/trad.htm. Copyright © 2004 Hernán Casciari. Used by permission.

"The Empty Pleasure" by Mario Vargas Llosa. "The Empty Pleasure" from *Making Waves* by Mario Vargas Llosa. Copyright © 1994 by Mario Vargas Llosa. Selection, translation, and foreword copyright © 1996 by John King. Reprinted by permission of Farrar, Straus and Giroux, LLC. Reprinted by permission of Faber and Faber Ltd.

"Match" by Sarah Wardle. Copyright © Sarah Wardle. Used by permission.

"Zidane and Me" by Philippe Dubath. Originally published in French in *Zidane et moi: Lettre d'un footballeur à sa femme* (Lausanne: L'Aire, 2002), 64–74. Translation copyright © 2007 Anna Kushner. Used by permission.

"The Sunday I Became World Champion" by Friedrich Christian Delius. Originally published as *Der Sonntag, an dem ich Weltmeister wurde* (Hamburg: Rowohlt, 1994). Reprinted from *The Sunday I Became World Champion*, trans. Scott Williams, in *German Library*, vol. 88, *Three Contemporary German Novellas*, ed. A. Leslie Willson (New York: Continuum, 2001), 216–19. Reprinted with permission of the publisher, The Continuum International Publishing Group.

"Art Works Football Club" by Lawrence Cann. Reprinted from the Art Works Football Club newsletters. Copyright © 2005 Lawrence Cann. Used by permission.

"Football Is" by Crispin Thomas. Reprinted from Football Poets, http://www.footballpoets.org. Copyright © 2002 Crispin Thomas. Used by permission.

"*Arsarnerit*: Inuit and the Heavenly Game of Football" by Mark Nuttall. Copyright © 2006 Mark Nuttall. Used by permission.

"On the Origin of Football" by Miroslav Holub. Miroslav Holub: *Poems Before & After* (Newcastle upon Tyne, England: Bloodaxe Books, 2006) www.bloodaxebooks.com. Used by permission.

Further Reading

For more information on the authors, players, teams, themes, and soccer cultures mentioned in this volume—including an expanded bibliography by region and topic—please visit www.theglobalgame.com.

One would not know it in the United States, but publication of soccer books—academic and journalistic studies with a sociological bent, as well as the ever-present player biographies, club histories, and "hooligan lit"—is a booming business abroad. Simon Kuper (see chapter 9), a freelance football writer based in Paris, mentions that the phenomenon curiously helped doom a four-volume series of football-themed literature, Perfect Pitch, published in the late 1990s. "Two of the issues appeared in 1998," says Kuper, editor of the series, "and that year there were several hundred books published in England on football if I'm not mistaken. So they just drowned in a flooded market." The series included issues titled "Home Ground," "Foreign Field," "Men and Women," and "Dirt," with contributions from a primarily European roster of literary talent. The series is still available through Internet book traders.

Inspiration for Perfect Pitch came from the Dutch literary football magazine *Hard gras* (www.hardgras.nl) launched in 1994. Other examples of magazines in Europe that approach the game from a cultural perspective, or from the point of view of the long-suffering supporter, are *11 Freunde* (www.11freunde .de) from Germany, *So Foot* (www.sofoot.com) in France, and the English *When Saturday Comes* (www.wsc.co.uk). The latter is something of a pioneer, originating, in 1986, during the wake of the Heysel Stadium disaster in Brussels. The deaths of thirty-nine Italian and Belgian fans under threat from Liverpool supporters at the 1985 European Cup final helped make English fans pariahs abroad, with *When Saturday Comes* stepping into the void as a hand-distributed, mimeographed newsletter in order to "provide a voice for intelligent football fans." To some degree the publication anticipated the fan-centered view on football and life well captured by Nick Hornby in *Fever Pitch* (1992).

In the United States, *Aethlon: The Journal of Sports Literature*, a production of the Sports Literature Association, occasionally includes essays, poetry, and fiction about soccer. The journal *Soccer and Society*, since its founding in 2000, has published academic studies two or three times per year.

A trove of football literature in English is contained in Peter J. Seddon's massive bibliographical reference, *A Football Compendium: An Expert Guide to the Books, Films, and Music of Association Football*. The resource claims to list "all books and serials published in the United Kingdom or the Republic of Ireland" up to the time of the bibliography's publication. The second edition, published in 1999, is 831 pages long, with much of the material that Seddon cites available in the British Library in London. To help fill the gap between Seddon's book and the present day, the British Council published a series of essays on sports literature, primarily football, as part of its online magazine *Literature Matters* (www.britishcouncil.org/arts-literature-literature matters-2006.htm).

The attraction of football as a subject for serious literature became clear during the elaborate cultural program that led up to and coincided with the 2006 World Cup finals in Germany. Organizers staged a symposium in Berlin, "Kopfballspieler" (Headers), with twelve writers who have incorporated the sport to various degrees in their work: Calixthe Beyala (Cameroon), Hwang Chi-Woo (South Korea), Per Olov Enquist (Sweden), Péter Esterházy (Hungary), Franzobel (Austria), Thomas Hürlimann (Switzerland), Henning Mankell (Sweden), Javier Marías (Spain), Tim Parks (England), Ugo Riccarelli (Italy), Burkhard Spinnen (Germany), and Victor Yerofeyev (Russia). Furthering the availability of literature on football, the cultural program also published five issues of a magazine, *Anstoß* (Kickoff), between November 2004 and June 2006. Essays, poetry, interviews, reviews of art installations, and transcripts of cultural events appear in English and German. Berlin-based grassroots organization streetfootballworld (www.streetfootballworld.org), a network of community-development groups organized around football, has published magazines containing essays, interviews, and reports from grassroots soccer leagues, rendered in English, German, Spanish, and French. In 2005 the same group produced *Abenteuer Fußball* (Football Adventure), journalistic accounts, written in German, of street soccer around the world, featuring cloistered monks in Nepal, the Vatican City league, and soccer atop Tokyo high-rises.

Football literature in German has its own bibliography, *Auswärtsspiel: Bücher aus Deutschland über die Welt des Fussballs* (Away Game: Books from Germany on the World of Football), a companion to a related exhibition at the 2005 Frankfurt Book Fair. As a vehicle for first-person narratives from the thirty-two countries participating in the 2006 World Cup, travel publisher CaféDiverso of Barcelona (www.cafediverso.com) produced *Everyone Has a Good Football Story* (also published as *Todos tenemos una buena historia de futbol*). On a similar idea, although novel for a publisher in the United States, editors Matt Weiland and Sean Wilsey commissioned thirty-two literary essays for *The Thinking Fan's Guide to the World Cup* (2006).

Writing in Spanish constitutes another major segment of football literature. Jorge Omar Pérez of *Mundo Deportivo* in Spain has compiled *Los Nobel del fútbol* (2006), a survey of twenty who would, in the author's imagination, merit a "Nobel Prize in football writing": Rafael Alberti, Mario Benedetti, Albert Camus, Camilo José Cela, Gabriel Celaya, Miguel Delibes, Umberto Eco, Eduardo Galeano, Gabriel García Márquez, Günter Grass, Miguel Hernández, Naguib Mahfouz, Manuel Vázquez Montalbán, Vladimir Nabokov, Kenzaburo Oe, Augusto Roa Bastos, Ernesto Sábato, Osvaldo Soriano, Mario Vargas Llosa, and Juan Villoro. (Five of these writers are represented in this volume.)

Football anthologies are prevalent in Latin America, with the Uruguayan Eduardo Galeano, in *Su majestad, el futbol: Selección y prólogo* (Your Majesty, Football: Literary Selections and Introduction) from 1968, and Jorge Valdano of Argentina, in 1995's *Cuentos de fútbol* (Football Stories), having edited notable collections. Of special mention regarding the cultural fusion between football and cinema is the comprehensive volume compiled by Carlos Marañón, *Fútbol y cine: El balompié en la gran pantalla* (Football and Film: The Soccer Ball on the Big Screen). Published in Madrid in 2006, the book references close to five hundred films in which soccer plays primary and incidental roles.

To learn more about regions skirted in the present anthology, numerous surveys of the world game as well as publications dedicated to specific regions are readily available. In preparing this volume we have used *The First World Atlas of Football* (2002) by Radovan Jelínek and Jiří Tomeš, published in the Czech Republic but available in English, and David Goldblatt's *World Soccer Yearbook: The Complete Guide to the Game* (published as *Football Yearbook* in the UK), which appeared through 2004–5. Also helpful has been Goldblatt's *The Ball Is Round: A Global History of Football* (2006). The soccer travelogue is a distinct genre as developed by poet Christopher Merrill (see chapter 14) in *The Grass of Another Country: A Journey through the World of Soccer* (1993), by Simon Kuper in *Football against the Enemy* (1994), and by Franklin Foer in *How Soccer Explains the World: An Unlikely Theory of Globalization* (2004). Tim Parks in *A Season with Verona* (2002) and Alex Bellos in *Futebol: The Brazilian Way of Life* (2002) have contributed excellent regional variants. On DVD the *History of Football: The Beautiful Game* (2001), a fifteen-hour, seven-disc set, is recommended.

The full story of women's football has yet to be written, but beginnings have been made in *Women on the Ball: A Guide to Women's Football* by Sue Lopez (1997); in *A Game for Rough Girls? A History of Women's Football in Britain* (2003) and *A Beautiful Game: International Perspectives on Women's Football* (2007), both by Jean Williams; and in *Soccer, Women, Sexual Liberation: Kicking Off a New Era*, edited by Fan Hong and J. A. Mangan (2004). Several histories exist of the pioneering Dick, Kerr's Ladies team, a club of Lancashire munitions workers that formed in World War I and gained sufficient notoriety to tour Europe, Canada, and the United States. Before the 2006 World Cup the German cultural network literaturhaeuser.net compiled *Aus der Tiefe des Traumes: Elf Frauen erzählen Fußballgeschichten* (From the Depth of Dreams: Eleven Women Tell Football Stories). Published in 2005, the anthology included essays on football from the perspective of contemporary women writers.

As a supplement to the above, the soccer enthusiast—especially the soccer enthusiast in the United States—must seek sustenance from the Internet, from the uncounted blogs and other Web sites that contain musings from far and near on the game and its part in the everyday.

CPSIA information can be obtained
at www.ICGtesting.com
Printed in the USA
LVOW13s1244130218
566412LV00013B/212/P